Thinking God'
The Hermeneutics of Humility

Daniel P. Fuller

By the same author

The Unity of the Bible: Unfolding God's Plan for Humanity
Gospel and Law: Contrast or Continuum
Resurrection Faith: Understanding Luke's History of Jesus
Walking in the Light: Step by Step Through 1 John
Walking by the Spirit: Step by Step Through Galatians
Walking in the Dark: Step by Step Through Job
Walking with Jesus: Step by Step Through the Gospels
I Was Just Thinking …: Essays About Scripture and Life
Give the Winds A Mighty Voice

Thinking God's Thoughts
The Hermeneutics of Humility

Daniel P. Fuller

2020

ISBN: 9798635013175

Praise for *Thinking God's Thoughts*

The publication of *Thinking God's Thoughts: The Hermeneutics of Humility* is for me like piling up stones on the banks of the Jordan to memorialize one the most formative events of my life. It was the fall of 1968 in a class called "Hermeneutics." My Christian faith, and the focus of my life, was re-formed in that class, as this book, still in syllabus form, was embodied by Professor Daniel Fuller. Two focuses coalesced with an explosive power that has never lost its fruitful wonder. On the one hand, there was the meticulous attention to biblical words, phrases, propositions, and arguments. On the other hand, there was the breathtaking majesty and unsearchable riches of God. The grammatical link, "in order that," exploded with cosmic purposes worthy of the Creator. And the highest acclamations of divine grace and wisdom and power were rooted in the lowly prepositional phrase. No text was without greatness. No greatness was without a text. I pray that similar experiences of lifelong, Bible-saturated, God-exalting formation will happen, as others read this book.

John Piper
Founder and Senior Teacher, Desiring God
Chancellor, Bethlehem College and Seminary
Pastor Emeritus, Bethlehem Baptist Church

I praise God that he had me take my father's course on Hermeneutics in seminary. Its relentless focus on the text, rigorous hunt for the author's train of thought, disciplined accounting for every word and proposition, and joy in the resulting display of God's glory captured my heart 40 years ago, and has fueled my Bible study ever since.

Steve Fuller
Lead Pastor, Grace Church, Abu Dhabi
Living by Faith Blog

At last, this treasure is available in print. Dr. Fuller taught us to study the meaning of every verse of the Bible, to discover whether there actually is a unity of the whole. This was life-giving to me. It became apparent that the Bible is completely reliable, though some human systems of theology, unsupported by Scripture, would need to be scrapped. Now, forty years later, my faith in God and His word has been rewarded.

Robert A. Blincoe, PhD
President, Frontiers US

The material from Daniel Fuller's seminary course in Hermeneutics, developed over his long and thoughtful career of teaching and now gathered here for access by a wider audience, represents the most valuable tool for biblical interpretation and understanding that I have encountered in my own three decades of teaching and even in a decade of graduate studies prior to that. Many of the students whom I introduce to this material every other year in my teaching rotation report back from their church and parachurch ministries that nothing has prepared them more helpfully for study of the Bible than what appears in this book.

More than a tool, it is a way of thinking that marshals all the common-sense benefits of grammar, of syntax, of historical language conventions, and of logic to discipline a reader's focus on the message a writer is conveying in a text. Moreover, having grasped how a writer has constructed an argument for a conclusion, the reader is put into the practical position of being well prepared also to teach a text with clarity as well as more defensibly to distinguish well-founded from spurious applications.

Good news for those who have heard well-known preachers and teachers speak admiringly of "arcing" or "bracketing" as their approach to sermon and lecture preparation: Here at last in print is the source and inspiration for their effectiveness.

Don Westblade
Dept of Philosophy & Religion
Hillsdale College

Foreword

Although I was a student at Fuller Seminary from 1978–1980 I never took Daniel Fuller's course on Hermeneutics. I didn't need to. My Bible reading and my life were already revolutionized in 1976 through Dr. Fuller's student, John Piper. Piper's own Bible reading and life were revolutionized when he sat in Fuller's hermeneutics class in 1968.

What was then the hermeneutics class syllabus went through several editions. I bought my first copy of it in the Fuller bookstore when it was still in mimeograph form. When I read through it the first time, I could understand more clearly the profound impact it had on Piper's life, and subsequently on my life as I diagrammed (see chapter 3) and arced (see chapter 4) my way through Romans 9–11, hungering to understand God's purpose in redemptive history and relying on the Holy Spirit to make me humble enough to let the apostle Paul's intended meaning take me wherever the exegesis.

Per Dr. Fuller, Piper taught his students to diagram every word of the passage we were exegeting to make sure we could account for how each word fit together to form a proposition. We also learned how to relate every proposition to the one preceding it and the one following it until we had a clearer grasp of the main point of each paragraph. Eventually Piper challenged us to take the main point of every paragraph and to follow painstakingly how each paragraph led to the main point of Romans 9–11. After a semester of this careful study of the Greek text, the vision of God, and the wonder of his purpose that emerged from the text, so overwhelmed the class that we spontaneously began singing the doxology.

All this happened before I had even read the hermeneutics syllabus. Learning from Dr. Piper how to engage meticulously with the Scriptures, and hearing him refer often to his mentor, Daniel Fuller, irresistibly lead my wife, Julie, and me to move from Bethel College in St. Paul, MN, to Fuller Theological Seminary in Pasadena. I wanted to continue studying at the graduate level what had so deeply changed me during my undergraduate days. I took every course I could from Dr. Fuller. I wasn't disappointed. When I eventually read the hermeneutics class syllabus, I realized how comprehensive it was. It introduced me to the early leading voices in hermeneutics, including the common sense yet radical approach of E. D. Hirsch (chapter 1). I saw the seminal ideas for Christian Hedonism articulated in the chapter "Our Concern with the Bible" (chapter 8). His chapter on the historical argument for the truthfulness of Scripture (chapter 9) continues to this day to help me fight the fight of faith.

He and Dr. Piper gave me tools of exegesis that have served me throughout my four decades as a pastor-teacher at Bethlehem Baptist Church of Minneapolis and for the last two decades as a professor at Bethlehem College & Seminary. Almost every year of my forty years of ministry I have taught sentence diagraming, arcing, and the art of asking good questions and seeking solid answers from the text of Scripture. To my delight, one of my students, Andy Hubert, designed a website called Biblearc.com. It brings Dr. Fuller's powerful exegetical tools of diagraming and arcing into the 21st century along with countless other features to aid in the meticulous study of God's Word. Through this website a world-wide community of students has emerged who are benefitting from the methods and insights Dr. Fuller introduced in *Thinking God's Thoughts*.

I am very grateful that Douglas Knighton is now publishing the syllabus which began all of this. I am eager to assign it to my students and watch with anticipation what God may do as more people have easier access to the book that changed my life.

Tom Steller
Pastor for Leadership Development
Bethlehem Baptist Church
Associate Professor for Biblical Studies
Bethlehem College & Seminary

Contents

Introduction—
Why Hermeneutics Is the Foundation of Theology

Whereas *exegesis* is the practice of discovering an author's intended meaning, *hermeneutics* is usually regarded as the methodology that guides this practice so that the resulting exposition of the text is valid. We all use some method of hermeneutics to construe the language (both oral and written) directed toward us every day. Since most of this language, however, comes to us in our mother tongue from people whose culture and outlook is very much like our own, we never feel any need to articulate the hermeneutical theory by which we construe this language.

But this changes when we engage with language that comes to us from authors who resided in another time and place. They may use a language that is no longer spoken by anyone. These authors also had a culture that differs markedly from ours. There is, as it were, a distance between them and us. So, we need to build a bridge between us and them before we can conceptualize what they were trying to say. We keenly feel this need when we know that those authors were speaking about matters of the greatest importance for our lives and destinies. We respond to this sense of need by developing a method of hermeneutics that will make it possible to receive their messages. We can equate hermeneutics with the technology for the bridge that we need to build between us and writers of another time and place who had some very important ideas to communicate.

More than any other literature, the Bible has created the demand for this bridge. In his essay "The Origin of Hermeneutics," Wilhelm Dilthey (1833–1911) declared that the enterprise of "hermeneutics owes its rise chiefly to biblical interpretation."[1] Likewise Hans Georg Gadamer noted that "the contemporary discussion of the hermeneutical problem is certainly nowhere so lively as in the area of Protestant theology."[2]

We can fulfill the desire for an understanding of the Bible that led to the rise of the study of hermeneutics,[3] by meeting two needs. We need to gain an accurate understanding of the *meanings* intended in what the biblical writers wrote, and we need to grasp the *significance* of their messages which we can then apply to our lives with great profit. "Meaning" and "significance" constitute two of the most crucial terms in the vocabulary of hermeneutics. An oft-repeated thesis of E. D. Hirsch, Jr., in both his *Validity in Interpretation* (1967) and *The Aims of Interpretation* (1976), is that the *meaning* of any message is derived just from the words intended to convey that message (and, of course, any historical information that may cast light on why they were written and the particular meaning any of those words may have had). But the *significance* of an author's message arises when a text's message is related to some other context. Hirsch explains: "… the

---

[1] Wilhelm Dilthey, "Die Entstehung der Hermeneutik," *Gesammelte Schriften*, 4th Ed. (Stuttgart: B. G. Teubner, 1964), V, 324.
[2] H. G. Gadamer, *Warheit und Methode*, 2nd ed. (Tübingen: J. C. B. Mohr, 1965) p. 492.
[3] Excellent histories of hermeneutics: Robert M. Grant, *A Short History of the Interpretation of the Bible*, Rev. ed. (London: Adam and Charles Black, 1965); James M. Robinson, Jr., "Hermeneutic Since Barth," *The New Hermeneutic*, Frontiers in Theology. Vols. 1+

term 'meaning' refers to the whole verbal meaning of the text, and 'significance' to the textual meaning in relation to a larger context, i.e., another mind, another era, a wider subject matter, an alien system of values ... In other words, 'significance' in textual meaning is related to ... any context beyond itself."[4]

Naturally hermeneutics concerns itself greatly with the way interpreters lay claim to having arrived at a valid understanding of the meaning authors intended to convey in the literary units which they composed. Therefore, hermeneutics is deeply involved in all of the exegetical work of biblical studies. It concerns itself not only with developing a valid theory for handling the particular genres of the Bible, but also in relating the message of the Bible in one passage to a message found in another passage. Its task is not completed until it has produced an exposition of the Bible as a whole. As Oscar Cullmann has put it, "... a dogmatics or an ethics of salvation history ... ought to be written someday."[5] Energy should be expended in producing a "unity of the Bible," for we should not conclude too quickly that the Bible is composed of disparate ideas. Alan Richardson argues:

> No one has ever imagined that either the Greek or the English literature is a whole in such a sense that any common purpose runs persistently throughout it. But the Bible, the entire literature of the Hebrew people from Moses to the apostles, is just such a unity, and we are therefore, compelled to attribute its inspiration to the Eternal Spirit of God.[6]

As hermeneutics in the realm of biblical studies undergirds the task of constructing a unity of the Bible, it challenges us to reflect upon the question of whether or not there is a "rule of faith" in the Bible, a canon within a canon,[7] by which all the rest of the Bible should be interpreted. Then, too, hermeneutics drives us to face the question of the validity of the way the New Testament writers interpreted texts found in the Old Testament. This will also require hermeneutical reflection on the validity and limits of typological interpretation whereby later biblical writers see a predictive correspondence between earlier and later events in the Bible. Both the matter of the rule of faith and of typology will stimulate interest in how the Church in earlier times handled these questions; so, hermeneutics will be an integral part of reading church history. We will have to pay attention to Origen's allegorizing, as well as to Luther's sharp distinction between the law and the gospel. Gerhard Ebeling saw questions regarding biblical interpretation playing such a crucial role in interpretation that he wrote a pamphlet that calls church history the history of biblical interpretation.[8]

---

[4] E. D. Hirsch, Jr., *The Aims of Interpretation*. (Chicago: The University of Chicago Press, 1976), pp. 2f.

[5] Oscar Cullmann, *Salvation in History*. S. G. Sowers (tr.). (New York: Harper & Row, 1967), p. 292. Cf. Daniel Fuller, *The Unity of the Bible* (Grand Rapids: Zondervan Publishing House, 1992).

[6] Alan Richardson, *The Bible in the Age of Science*. (London: SCM Press, Ldt., 1961), pp. 71f.

[7] See the appendix "Biblical Theology and the Analogy of Faith."

[8] Gerhard Ebeling, *Kirschengeschiechte als Geschichte der Auslegung der Heiligen Schrift*. Sammlung Gemeinverstaendlicher Cortraege, 189. (Tübingen: J. C. B. Mohr, 1947).

As we apply hermeneutics' methodological procedures in the field of biblical studies, the tangible results of these efforts will be some sort of exposition. In writing up this exposition, interpreters will be greatly concerned to use language that is best suited for communicating to the sort of audience they expect to hear or to read this exposition. Following the distinction set forth by Krister Stendahl, an exposition will not only expound "what the text meant," but also "what it means."[9] There is no reason why an exposition of the meaning of a passage of Scripture must confine itself simply to a description of the author's intended meaning, or, in other words, "what it meant." An adequate hermeneutic insists that we make the ancient Bible available for present-day people, fulfilling in them their desire to know "what the Bible means" by building on an understanding of "what the Bible meant." So, hermeneutics must have more than a mere antiquarian interest about what some ancient individuals happened to think. To use the words of Hirsch, hermeneutics must concern itself with *significance* as well as *meaning*. The hermeneutical method we employ, from finding the meaning of the text to telling of the significance of that meaning, is not completed until we *apply* that meaning to some specific need people have. But in working in this matter of significance, we interpreters must speak of something else besides the meaning of the text. (For example, it would be very difficult to expound "turn the other cheek" [Matthew 5:39] without mentioning some of the circumstances in which this would be obeyed.) This will inevitably involve us in routing our methodological course through areas where systematic theology operates, for one of the ways in which systematic theology distinguishes itself from biblical theology is that it relates what the Bible teaches to all human knowledge.

Of course, the biggest question of significance that we can raise is that of the truth of the intended meaning of a biblical writer. Since interpreters must deal with this question of significance, we cannot avoid the consideration of matters that are generally dealt with in the prolegomena of systematic theology. This question of the truth of the Bible will thus force us to reflect on the validity of Calvin's insistence that while there are many splendid evidences to demonstrate the Bible's truth, in the final analysis only the internal witness of the Holy Spirit can give full certainty to the Bible's truth. In raising the question of the Bible's truth, we must also consider questions regarding the extent of the canon.

Another major concern regarding biblical significance concerns the imperatival affirmations of Scripture, for in these we learn how we ought to conduct our lives. We interpreters cannot merely exegete the Golden Rule (Matthew 7:12), or Paul's instructions regarding women in the church (1 Corinthians 11:2–16); we must also say things about how we should carry out these imperatives in our own particular historical milieu. In other words, the route that hermeneutics follows not only takes it through church history, but also through systematic theology, from prolegomena to ethics.

The hermeneutical method of this book addresses a particular aspect of the question of significance raised by the so-called "new hermeneutic" which emphasizes a text's

---

[9] K. Stendahl, "Contemporary Biblical Theology," *Interpreter's Dictionary of the Bible*, 4 vols. (New York: Abingdon, 1962) Vol I (A-D), pp. 418–432.

significance so much that it has scarcely anything to say about the meaning intended by the text's author. The new hermeneutic finds justification for doing this in the philosophy of Martin Heidegger. Consequently, in carrying on a dialogue with the new hermeneutic, we will examine Heidegger's philosophy, as well as that of his pupil, H. G. Gadamer. In this way we will reply accurately to Gadamer's famous statement that "one understands an author differently only when one achieves any understanding at all."[10] By engaging in this philosophical reflection, we will argue effectively that it is possible to grasp what the author of an ancient text intended to say. Then, once we gain an understanding of "what is meant," then with great relish we can move on to the question of "what it means" for our present-day lives.

This desire of hermeneutics to find much significance in a text means that it is intensely interested in preaching, Christian education, counseling, and the crossing of cultural boundaries that the mission enterprise entails. We have already noted how concerned hermeneutics is to state its understanding of the author's meaning of a text in an exposition whose language is best suited to communicate its meaning and significance to a specific receptor audience. This is essentially an exercise in "translation," even though the exposition may not involve going from one language to another. The great requisite for making a communicable exposition is that we have worked through the words of the original text to reach an understanding of all its author was trying to say, so that we can give a reason for each sentence and word that he used. Only the exegete who has acquired such an understanding of a text is in a position to build a bridge of exposition that will communicate readily with a specific cultural group. This is perhaps the greatest reason why hermeneutics cannot regard its task as ended when it tells "what a text meant." The understanding of a text's meaning, which hermeneutics trains a person to acquire, is an absolute prerequisite for the task of "translating" that meaning in a way that shows its significance for some group with a distinctive cultural profile.

Thus, hermeneutics consists of a method, a pathway to follow, which takes us from the intended meaning of the original biblical writers all the way to an exposition of that meaning (which includes its significance) to some people group in an inner-city ghetto or to some stone-age tribe in New Guinea. As it proceeds along this path, it at least touches base with everything in the theological field of study. Hermeneutics is, in distinction to the rest of the theological curriculum, a *methodological* inquiry. It is concerned with the method by which biblical meanings are attained and validated, and then with how we translate these meanings intelligibly and with significant application to the varied groups in the world today.

Gerhard Ebeling observed that "the question of hermeneutics forms the focal point of the theological problem of today." He then proceeded to show how it is vital for each of the divisions of the theological encyclopedia. With reference to systematic theology he says, "The difficult problem of theology's systematic method can be properly solved only when it is likewise [along with church history] set in the light of the question of hermeneutics." As for practical theology, Ebeling said, "The hermeneutical question

---

[10] *Wahrheit und Methode*, p. 280.

presents the one problem underlying all questions of detail, in so far as the *applicatio* must not stand unrelated and all on its own alongside the *explicatio*." He continued: "More particularly also in the study of missions, with its difficult questions (so highly instructive for theological work as a whole) of translating the biblical message into the languages of totally different civilizations, the hermeneutic problem proves to be of fundamental significance."[11]

---

[11] G. Ebeling, "The Significance of the Critical Historical Method," *Word and Faith* (London: SCM Press, 1962), pp. 27f.

Chapter One—The Scope of Hermeneutics

The term "hermeneutics" refers most often to the reading and interpretation skills involved in the study of the Bible. The German philosopher and literary historian Wilhelm Dilthey (1833–1911), in his essay on "The Origin of Hermeneutics," declared that "hermeneutics owes its rise chiefly to biblical interpretation."[12] Mortimer Adler makes the same point when he says: "The problem of reading the Holy Book—if you have faith that it is the Word of God—is the most difficult problem in the whole field of reading. There have been more books written about how to read Scripture than about all of the other aspects of the art of reading. The Word of God is obviously the most difficult writing men can read. The effort of the faithful has been but proportionate to the difficulty of the task. I think it would be easy to say that, in the European tradition at least, the Bible is *the* book in more senses than one. It has been not only the most widely read but the most carefully."[13] A leader in philosophical, secular hermeneutics at the University of Heidelberg notes that "the contemporary discussion of the hermeneutical problem is certainly nowhere so lively as in the area of Protestant theology."[14]

Before Friedrich Schleiermacher (and sometimes since), a sharp division had always been made between the special ways in which the Bible ought to be interpreted (*hermeneutica sacra*) and the ways for interpreting other kinds of literature (*hermeneutica profana*). As a result, treatises on biblical hermeneutics have often consisted largely (to use Schleiermacher's words) "in only an aggregate of observations"[15] and in rules for interpreting specific passages of Scripture. Schleiermacher insisted that the understanding of linguistic symbols, whether they are in biblical, legal, or literary texts, should be derived from a consideration of how understanding in general takes place. Almost every text has some special interpretational problem, and when hermeneutics books have tried to list the rules for interpreting some large corpus of literature like the Bible, it is no wonder that they have often tended to become virtual commentaries. These principles should then be illustrated from one or two passages in the literature which is of particular concern—which in our case is the Bible. When we have grasped the principles underlying understanding, we are expositors in our own right and do not need to be dependent on the often-contradictory ways commentaries solve interpretational problems—even though commentaries, when used correctly, do play a vital role in interpretation.

We can see the whole scope of what is involved in understanding linguistic symbols by answering the question, What is the primary goal of interpretation? Hermeneutical thinkers have given three answers which we will consider in the remainder of this chapter.

---

[12] W. Dilthey, "Die Entstehung der Hermeneutik," *Gesammelte Schriften* (Stuttgart: B. G. Teubner, 1964), V, 324.

[13] Mortimer J. Adler, *How to Read a Book* (New York: Simon and Schuster, 1940), p. 288.

[14] Hans-Georg Gadamer, *Wahrheit und Methode* (Tübingen: J. C. B. Mohr, 1965), p. 492.

[15] Fr. D. E. Schleiermacher, *Hermeneutik*, Heinz Kimmerle (ed.) (Heidelberg: Carl Winter, Universitätsverlag, 1959), p. 79.

The Schleiermacher–Dilthey–Bultmann Tradition

There is a line of hermeneutical spokesmen who argue that the goal of interpretation is not simply to understand what the author was trying to say, but also to attempt to probe into the depths of his soul, so as to have an encounter with him as an individual. Friedrich Schleiermacher (1768–1834) gave some of the most incisive statements to be found in all of hermeneutical literature about the principles for grasping what an author willed to communicate, but this was not enough for him. He argued that the theme of an author's text (gained by "grammatical" interpretation) is a product of his own unique nature, so the ultimate aim of interpretation is to get through to an author's unique individuality ("psychological interpretation") which led the author to choose this theme and elaborate it as he did. "The common starting point for both grammatical interpretation and psychological," said Schleiermacher, "is the universal point of view which grasps the unity of a work and the chief emphases of a composition. But [in psychological interpretation] the unity of the work, the theme, is viewed as the principle which moves the author, and the basic characteristic of the composition is seen as his unique individuality, revealing itself in everything he does."[16] To get through to an author's individuality, the interpreter must not only study all the residue from his life, and compare it with the lives of his contemporaries; the interpreter must also "divine" an author's unique individuality. "The method of divination is that in which one transforms himself into another and seeks an immediate knowledge of [his] individuality."[17] In this way, then, Schleiermacher insisted that an interpreter's task is to reproduce a communication understood "at first as well as, and then better than, its author."[18]

Wilhelm Dilthey (1833–1911) carried on in Schleiermacher's tradition of making the interpreter's ultimate goal that of "inducing in himself an imitation of a life that is not native to him [eine Nachbildung fremden Lebens in sich herbeizuführen]."[19] To substantiate the validity of such a goal, Dilthey postulated the existence of a "universal human nature" which manifests itself in every human being past and present, so that no radical difference can exist between an author in the past and an interpreter in the present. But despite such a presupposition, Dilthey admitted that an interpreter could never fully grasp an author's personality. His famous dictum was "*individuum est ineffabile*."[20] As another writer has put it, "The fullness of sentiment individually associated with certain words is not communicable. It presupposes a particularly individual life, an irreproducible content of strictly personal experience."[21] For example, the particular flavor that the word "work" carries for each person varies according to what he does: bricklayer, draftsman, rug cleaner, and so on, and each individual bricklayer views his work as a bricklayer from the vantage point of his own individual life.

---

[16] *Ibid.*, p. 107.
[17] *Ibid.*, p. 109.
[18] *Ibid.*, p. 87.
[19] Dilthey, *op.cit.*, p. 330.
[20] *Loc. Cit.*
[21] J. de Zwaan, "Hermeneutical Plus-Value," *Coniectanea Neotestamentica*, XI (1947), p. 247.

But the unattainability of the Schleiermacher-Dilthey goal of interpretation is only one objection against it. A number of hermeneutical theorists have pointed out its danger of tending to understand a text's author in terms of our own point of view and approach to life rather than letting the distinguishing features of that author confront us with their full force. Thus, in interpreting the New Testament as a systematic theologian, Schleiermacher was by no means content to let the concepts of the apostles stand at face value. He was most interested in bypassing the apostles' intentional meaning to hasten on to a "psychological" interpretation of them, an interpretation which conformed to his own philosophical preconceptions, and which would enable "the cultured despisers of Christianity" of his day to regain an appreciation of Christianity. In summarizing Schleiermacher's approach, T. F. Torrance has put it nicely: "It is all the more necessary [in Schleiermacher] that the interpreter should divine the seminal determination in the consciousness of the biblical author in order to reconstruct and reproduce it as a determination in his own consciousness and so to remodel it in his own understanding[!]. This is of course consistent with Schleiermacher's fundamental approach to Christian doctrine in his effort to transpose it into another conceptual form and so to make it understandable in the culture of modern Europe."[22]

Rudolf Bultmann really stands in the Schleiermacher-Dilthey tradition of hermeneutics, even though he has proposed what, at first, seems to be a considerable modification of it. Bultmann has argued that while certain kinds of texts do have much to offer in giving interpreters insight into a life that is not native to them, yet there are many other kinds of texts—such as mathematical books and medical treatises—which are read not so much because of an interest in the personalities of their authors as in the things about which they speak. "Are we to suppose," said Bultmann in arguing against Dilthey, "that the interpretation of a mathematical or medical text arises from the consummation of the psychical processes which have been taking place in the author? Or do we only understand the inscriptions of the Egyptian kings telling of their deeds of war, or the ancient Babylonian and Assyrian historical and chronological texts, or the epitaph of Antiochus of Commagene or the *Res Gestae Divi Augusti*—do we understand them only on the basis of their translation into the inner, creative process in which they arose? No, it would appear!"[23] Bultmann does not, however, want to reject the Schleiermacher-Dilthey tradition completely, for he is convinced that the chief interest in reading many texts, particularly philosophical and historical ones, is to have a personal encounter with their authors. His objection, then, is this tradition's one-sidedness in supposing that grasping the author's individual personality is the only goal in interpreting texts.

The broader goal of interpretation, according to Bultmann, is gaining "the possibilities of human being" as they exist in relation to the concrete historical world. The presupposition which makes such a goal possible is that both "the expositor and the author live as men in the same historical world, in which 'human being' occurs as a 'being' in an

---

[22] T. F. Torrance, "Hermeneutics According to Schleiermacher," *Scottish Journal of Theology*, XXI, 3 (September, 1968), p. 262.
[23] Rudolf Bultmann, "The Problem of Hermeneutics," *Essays Philosophical and Theological*, James Grier (tr.) (London: SCM Press Ltd, 1955), pp. 238f.

environment, in understanding discourse with objects and our fellowmen."[24] It is apparent how understanding the goal of interpretation in such a way would apply just as well to a scientific text as to an autobiography. But while Bultmann's definition does make room for texts whose purpose is to set forth a given subject matter, yet his greater interest is in interpreting texts whose subject matter is the humanities so that he, not unlike Schleiermacher and Dilthey, may encounter "the possibilities of human being." "The object [of interpretation] can be given by the enquiry into 'human being' as one's own 'being.' The texts lying nearest to hand for such investigation are those of philosophy and religion and poetry: but fundamentally all texts (like history itself) can be subjected to it."[25]

But no sooner had Bultmann made the grasping of "the possibilities of human being" the goal of interpretation than he went on to make a statement which involved him, like Schleiermacher and Dilthey before him, in doing nothing more than reading into texts in the humanities what he already knew. He says, "Such an investigation [of the possibilities of human being] is always guided by a prior understanding of 'human being'—by a particular understanding of human existence, which may be very naïve, but from which in general in the first instance the categories develop, which make an investigation possible—for example, the question of 'salvation;' of the 'meaning' of personal life or of the 'meaning' of history; of the ethical norms of action, the order of human community life, and such like. Without such a *prior understanding* and the questions initiated by it, the texts are mute."[26]

As is well known, Bultmann believes that Martin Heidegger has accurately and fully traced out the categories defining the possibilities of human existence in his epochal *Time and Being* (1927). Bultmann demythologizes Jesus and Paul by conforming what they taught to these categories. In so doing Bultmann is not, of course, letting the New Testament texts speak for themselves, nor is he open to the possibilities of human existence that they, rather than Heidegger, set forth. As Wolfhart Pannenberg puts it:

> Although there is no intention [in Bultmann] of dumbing down the particular content of the text, but rather of making it visible precisely for contemporary understanding; nevertheless, that content is narrowed down from the outset: anything other than the possibilities of human existence cannot become relevant for existential interpretation … Now, it is rather doubtful that the text which is to be interpreted, on the basis of such handling, can still say what it has to say on its own: the New Testament texts, for example, are concerned, at least explicitly, with many things other than possibilities of understanding human existence, although everything with which

---

[24] *Ibid.*, p. 243.
[25] *Ibid.*, p. 253.
[26] *Loc. Cit.*

they are concerned will *also* be an element of the understanding of existence of the New Testament author.[27]

E. D. Hirsch, Jr.

An English professor at the University of Virginia, Hirsch pays his respects to the Schlei-ermacher-Dilthey tradition. He feels indebted to Schleiermacher, "whose aphorisms on interpretation," he declares, "are among the most profound contributions to hermeneutics."[28] His basic criticism of Schleiermacher and Dilthey, however, is their "loose identification of mental processes and meanings" (H 248). In other words, Hirsch has no use for their attempt to get through to the inner workings of an author's mind and thus to grasp the essence of his individuality. Rather, he is primarily concerned with what Schleiermacher called "grammatical interpretation," that is, with grasping the meaning an author intended to convey when he wrote. Hirsch argues that it is impossible to get access to the mental processes by which an author produced a work. He observes, "We cannot know all the meanings the author entertained when he wrote down his text, as we infer from two familiar kinds of evidence. Whenever I speak, I am usually attending to ('have in mind') meanings that are outside my subject of discourse. Furthermore, I am always aware that the meanings I can convey through discourse are more limited than the meanings I can entertain. I cannot, for example, adequately convey through words many of my visual perceptions—though these perceptions are meanings, which is to say objects of consciousness. It is altogether likely that no text can ever convey all the meanings an author had in mind as he wrote" (H 17). The interpreter's task, Hirsch argues, is simply to get through to an author's verbal meanings, for "any author knows that written verbal utterances can convey only verbal meanings—that is to say, meanings which can be conveyed to others by the words he uses. The interpretation of texts is concerned exclusively with sharable meanings, and not everything I am thinking when I write can be shared with others by means of words" (H 18).

Since texts consist of language, and since language consists of the symbols for the whole range of experience that two or more people in a society can share in common, it therefore follows that, as Hirsch puts it, the interpretation of texts is concerned *exclusively* with sharable meanings. Just as authors choose language conventions which will also bring to mind in others the things they are thinking, so also, we hearers, while we never can see things just the way communicators see them, can nevertheless fully know what they want to share with us by words.

The reason that language is so efficient in transmitting sharable meanings is that it consists of conventions; that is, of elements which the society using a given language has agreed should stand for all its various aspects of common experience. Indeed, the

---

[27] Wolfhart Pannenberg, "Hermeneutics and Universal History," *History and Hermeneutic*, Robert Funk (ed.) (Tübingen: J. C. B. Mohr, 1967), p. 132.
[28] E. D. Hirsch, Jr., *Validity in Interpretation* (New Haven: Yale University Press, 1967), p. 263. In the remainder of this chapter, quotations from Hirsch will be documented in the body of the text by "H__".

meanings of words change in various contexts, and the range of meanings for single words in the lexicon are the different meanings they can have. But a word's single meaning in any one context is also fixed by convention, so that when authors put a word in that context, they call up the intended meaning in the mind of the reader. Consequently, when we seek to communicate to others, we select words and put them in such relations to other words that our readers will know, by the language convention we share in common, the meaning that we intended. As Hirsch explains, "An author's verbal meaning is limited by linguistic possibilities but is determined by his actualizing and specifying some of those possibilities ... A context is something that has itself been determined ... by an author ... It is not something that is simply there ..." (H47f.). Also, as communicators, we can give a new meaning or nuance to a word whenever we so choose. When we do this, however, we must define the meaning for our readers, that is we must establish a new convention that applies as we communicate. In short, the meaning of a text is controlled wholly by the language conventions which exist between authors and readers.

Communication is successful to the extent that the linguistic possibilities which authors select and specify are the ones which will evoke in the mind of their readers the very concepts which the authors want understood. An author will communicate, says Hirsch,

> only if he is familiar with typical past usages and experiences common to himself and his interpreter. By virtue of these shared past experiences the type of meaning he expects to convey will be the type of meaning his interpreter is also led to expect ... Thus, the speaker knows that his type of meaning must be grounded in a type of usage, since it is only from traits of usage, i.e., vocabulary range, syntactical patterns, formulaic invariants, and so on, that the interpreter can expect the speaker's type of meaning. Consequently, types of meaning are always necessarily wedded to types of usage, and this entire complex system of shared experiences, usage traits, and meaning expectations which the speaker relies on is the generic conception which controls his utterance. Understanding can occur only if the interpreter proceeds under the same system of expectations. (H 80)

How successfully, then, can an interpreter grasp the thought of an author? Hirsch acknowledges that "certain texts might, because of their character or age, represent authorial meanings which are now inaccessible" (H 18f.). The convention expressed by a certain usage in an ancient text may simply not be known to us today, as for example the meaning of ἐπιούσιος, which we uncertainly translate "daily" in "Give us this day our daily bread" (Matthew 6:11). But even where we do not lack knowledge of language conventions, interpreters construe texts differently. This is because of the famous "hermeneutical circle" in which a text's parts are construed by the whole and the whole is known only from its parts. Circles begin this way: as we begin to read a text, some parts stand out in our minds, i.e., some conventions, which seem to us to indicate what the author was getting at. Once we believe we are tracking with what an author wanted to say in a text, our hypothesis about its purpose exercises great power in establishing our choice of which of the several conventions a given set of words could signify and in establishing the relative emphasis the language convention of one set of words should have in relation to others.

Just as we construe meanings of individual words in a sentence by reference to the point of the whole sentence, so in dealing with the text comprising a whole literary unit, we also construe the meaning of its parts by reference to a few conventions in the text which seem to tip us off as to what the author is driving at. The great problem of interpretation is that our initial hypothesis about the meaning of a text tends to be self-confirming, because it makes us view all the data in its light. As Hirsch states it, "The contours of the words in a sentence are determined very substantially by our pre-apprehension of the form and meaning of the sentence … This highly constitutive character of hermeneutical hypotheses explains why they tend to be self-confirming and why it is hard to convince anyone to change his interpretation of a text" (H 261).

Is the hermeneutical circle then a vicious circle which cannot be broken? While being realistic about the difficulty any interpreter has in letting go of an hypothesis about a text's meaning, Hirsch nevertheless points out that interpreters do change their minds about a text's meaning, and this is because they become aware of those aspects in a text which will simply not bow the knee to some false hypothesis regarding an author's meaning. Hirsch describes the "*invariant* aspect of the part as a *trait* which characterizes one aspect of meaning rather than another" (H 77, italics added). Thus, the hermeneutical circle is not a vicious one because the invariant traits of certain parts of a text set up a genuine dialectic between themselves and the interpreter's hypothesis regarding the author's purpose.

Then too, any interpreter's understanding of a text has to submit to the cross examination of other interpreters' understandings of it. Thus, as we read exegetical commentaries on a given portion of Scripture, we are confronted by the expositions of some of the very greatest expository minds in the history of biblical interpretation. These help us become aware of certain invariable traits of a text that we might have overlooked, and thus are of great aid in helping us to achieve a correct understanding of a text. This happens when we read exegetical commentaries, not so much to acquire a commentator's construction of an author's meaning, as to become aware of invariant traits in a text which we've hitherto overlooked. According to Hirsch, then, "the hermeneutic hypothesis is not completely self-confirming since it has to compete with rival hypotheses about the same text and is continuously measured against those components of the text which are least dependent on the hypothesis" (H 261).

Thus, Hirsch is highly optimistic about the possibility of understanding what another person has said: "Our chances of making a correct preliminary guess about the nature of someone's verbal meaning are enormously increased by the limitations imposed on that meaning through cultural norms and conventions. A single linguistic sign can represent an identical meaning for two persons because its possible meanings have been limited by convention" (H 262). Indeed, we can never gain a complete understanding of things or of the people about us. But it is wholly possible to have full knowledge of the verbal meanings of others. To know the language conventions various authors use, therefore, allows us to be able to know fully what they are trying to say. Because of the limitless number of ways language conventions can be selected and arranged, it is even possible for interpreters to understand authors fully when they are articulating something brand new. We can fully grasp these new things because the means used to communicate them can only consist in language conventions the readers already share with the authors.

Hence, we do not, like Schleiermacher, say that we should have a better understanding of an author than he had of himself; we simply affirm that we are to understand *what an author is saying* (his verbal meaning) as well as he understood it. Hirsch argues (H 191ff.) that an interpreter, from other sources, can know an author's subject matter better than the author himself, but this is something wholly different from having better knowledge than the author of what he is trying to say.

This hermeneutical theory which Hirsch has espoused is not in vogue today, as he himself is quite aware. In fact, one of his reasons for writing his book was to refute the prevailing mood in literary circles that the meaning imparted to a text by an authorial will is unattainable and that what we should be after is the meaning that a text itself has come to have with the passage of time. The most revered spokesman for this point of view is Hans-Georg Gadamer, a philosophy professor at Heidelberg, whose book *Wahrheit und Methode* has become the classical statement of this approach for those interested in the interpretation of secular literature[29] as well as for those interested in the interpretation of the Bible. It constitutes the basic statement of the philosophy behind the "new hermeneutic" accepted both in some Protestant[30] and some Catholic circles that seems to see a rapprochement between the new hermeneutics' emphasis on letting a text speak its contemporary message, and the way tradition in the Roman church has gone beyond what the New Testament itself said.[31] This being the case, it is important that we examine some of the basic elements of Gadamer's hermeneutic.

Hans-Georg Gadamer

For Gadamer, the ultimate goal of hermeneutics is not to recreate that moment of life when an author composed a text (Schleiermacher), nor to rethink the meaning an author intended to communicate (Hirsch), but rather to come to a vital knowledge of the *subject matter* which, under certain conditions, emerges from a text's language.[32]

---

[29] E.g., Richard E. Palmer, *Hermeneutics* (Evanston: Northwestern University Press, 1969), a literature professor at MacMurray College, Illinois, who dedicates his book to Gadamer and whose concluding chapter is entitled "A Hermeneutical Manifesto to American Literary Interpretation."

[30] E.g., James M. Robinson, "Hermeneutic Since Barth," *The New Hermeneutic*, vol. II of New Frontiers in Theology, Robinson and Cobb (eds.) (New York: Harper & Row, 1964), pp. 1–77, which climaxes with a summary of Gadamer's book.

[31] E.g., Raymond E. Brown, "Hermeneutics," *The Jerome Biblical Commentary* (Brown *et al*, eds.) (Englewood Cliffs, NJ: Prentice-Hall, Inc., 1968), p. 621.

[32] Page references to Gadamer's *Wahrheit und Methode* in the remainder of this chapter will be "G__", whereas those of Hirsch will be "H__".

What Gadamer means by the subject matter (*die Sache*) is best seen in his analysis of what happens when two people, engaged in a genuine conversation, come to agreement (*Verständigung*). The kind of conversation that brings conversation partners to knowledge of a subject matter is one in which each honors the other's point of view. But this does not mean that each goes so far as to repress his own point of view so as to think only in terms of what the other is saying. Rather, each sets forth his own point of view, but allows these to contend with each other and thus modify one another so that agreement regarding the subject matter comes to expression. "Conversation is a process for achieving agreement. Genuine conversation occurs when each becomes truly involved with the other, honors the other's point of view, and transfers himself into the other not to the extent that he wants to become better acquainted with him as a person but rather to understand what he is saying. The important thing is for each to grasp the material justification for what the other is saying so that they can become one with each other with regard to the subject matter" (G 363).

When agreement is thus achieved, it is expressed in language. Gadamer emphasizes that language is not to be viewed as the means by which agreement is reached, but is rather itself the product of agreement. "In its essence, language is the language of conversation. It fashions itself in its reality through the accomplishment of agreement" (G 422). Since the language formed in this way constitutes agreement between two people regarding a certain subject matter, this language mediates something of what Gadamer calls the "world." By "world" he does not mean all that surrounds us and which we are so prone to view as an object. Rather, the world is the subject which, in the form of language, lays a claim upon us and reveals us as completely subject to it. "In language the world itself presents itself. The linguistic experience of the world is absolute" (G 426). It is this world, or subject matter, which constitutes the goal to be achieved, not only in conversation but also in the interpretation of written texts. (Gadamer freely acknowledges his indebtedness to Martin Heidegger and his emphasis that language is not a barrier to the knowledge of being that must somehow be bypassed but is itself the expression of being.)

But the situation in which an interpreter works with a written text is, at the outset, somewhat different from that of two people engaged in genuine conversation. The language of a conversation must be that in which each partner lives and is wholly conversant, but the language of a text, even if it is the mother tongue of the interpreter, is never such a language for Gadamer. It is a foreign language, and the meaning an author intended by a text can no more be fully grasped by an interpreter than can one translate fully a speaker's meaning from one language into another. Just as translators are painfully conscious of how they cannot pass on all the nuances and implications that are present in the original, so also the interpreters of a text can never recover fully what the author intended. "The case of a foreign language signifies only an extreme case of the basic hermeneutical difficulty, which is to overcome a text's strangeness. Actually, all the tasks which have been the concern of traditional hermeneutics present the interpreter with that which is strange in the same, unambiguously defined way. The translator's task of imitating is not qualitatively but only in degree different from the universal herme-neutical task presented by every text" (G 365).

Thus, while distance between two people holding conversation can be overcome, there is "an unbridgeable difference between the interpreter and the author which is neces-sarily tied up with historical distance" (G 280). Consequently, "each age must under-stand a text that has been handed down to it in its own way ..." (G 280). "The meaning of a text surpasses the meaning of its author, not occasionally but always" (G 280).

This historical distance between a text's author and an interpreter should not be viewed as a disadvantage which keeps interpretation from reaching its goal. "The really im-portant thing," says Gadamer, "is to recognize historical difference as a productive and positive possibility for understanding. This historical difference is not a yawning abyss but is something filled in through the continuity of its origin and tradition, in the light of which everything shines that comes down to us" (G 281). In other words, as soon as a text is completed, it enters the stream of history and becomes a part of what is handed down to later generations. "The one who writes things down and passes them on intends his text to have always its own new contemporaries ... What has been fixed in writing has loosed itself from dependence on its origin and originator and has set itself free for a new reference" (G 373).

Gadamer equates the past not with a pile of facts but with a stream (G 175f.); so, a text's meaning does not remain something fixed in the past. Rather, it changes as it moves onward through ever new historical situations. "Through this continuity that which is passed down becomes a part of our own world and so what is communicated is able to come immediately into language" (G368). Because a text has from its origin been in a stream of tradition which reaches down to the interpreters' own time and comprises part of our own historical situation, interpreters therefore have language in which we live and by which we are able to bring the text to expression.

Thus, a text does not speak in its own terms (as Hirsch would affirm) but, rather, only in and through the terms which are available to the interpreter. Only as interpreters ex-pound a text and so set forth its meaning in our own language do we succeed in under-standing a text. "A text becomes articulate through exposition. But no text speaks unless it speaks the language which reaches the interpreter. Therefore, the task of interpretation is to find the right language if it really wants to make the text articulate" (G 375). Gad-amer is most insistent that "in the final analysis, understanding [*Verstehen*] and exposi-tion [*Auslegung*] are one and the same" (G 366). "Understanding is always exposition, and exposition is ... the explicit form of understanding" (G 291). "Normal concepts like the meaning of the author or the understanding of the original reader represent actually more empty blanks to be filled up by understanding from occasion to occasion" (G 373). "One understands [an author] differently, when one achieves any understanding at all" (G 280).

We should not object that we interpreters then will do nothing more than read our own prejudices into a text. Just as the agreement reached in genuine conversation depends on each partner's setting forth his own particular point of view, so in the interpretation of literary documents, we must permit the text as much power to speak as we have. Our task as interpreters is to have our way of looking at things, that is, our horizons, molded and reshaped by our encounter with the past which a text sets forth.

> In reality the horizon of the present is constantly in a process of being formed, so long as we constantly have to test our prejudices. By no means the least important way to carry out this testing is to encounter the past and the tradition out of which we come. The past then is indispensable for shaping the horizon of the present. A present horizon exists for itself just as little as do the historical horizons which men may seek to grasp. Rather, understanding is always the process of fusing these horizons which presume to exist for themselves alone (G289).

But a past horizon cannot shape an interpreter's present horizon unless he brings his own horizon with him into the interpretation of a text.

> An interpreter's own thoughts are always already brought with him into the reawakening of the meaning of a text. Thus, an interpreter's own horizon does play a role in textual interpretation, but not in the sense that the interpreter holds to it doggedly through thick and thin, but more like an opinion and a possibility which he puts up for stakes and thus helps appropriate for himself what is said in the text. Previously we have described this as a fusion of horizons. Now we recognize in this the sort of thing that is accomplished in conversation, when a subject matter comes to expression, which is not only mine or that of the author but which is ours jointly (G366).

Genuine conversation between an interpreter and a text is possible not only because the horizons which we interpreters bring with us are capable of being altered, but also because the horizon of a text, ever since it was fixed in writing, has been undergoing change. "The horizon of the past, out of which all human life lives and which is there in the form of that which has been handed down, has also [like the interpreter's present horizon] always been in movement" (G 288). "The historical life of tradition consists in being always directed towards new ways of being appropriated and expounded" (G 375). Just as laws after they are enacted keep on receiving new interpretations and applications in the courts so that "they must be understood differently in each moment, that is, in each concrete situation" (G 292), so the constantly new expositions that are made of a text in order to keep them understandable to the ever-changing human situation, constitute nothing less than a point of view, or horizon, which is constantly in motion. Since both the text's horizon and the interpreter's horizon are capable of change, it is possible, therefore, for agreement between them to occur as the interpreter works on a text.

But this new horizon, which interpreters have as a result of the fusion of our old horizons and that of the text, is not something final, any more than the Supreme Court's exposition and application of the Constitution becomes fixed and final. As interpreters, our own involvement in the onward movement of our history will modify our horizons, as will our interpretation of other texts. Also, since a text's own horizon is constantly changing, an interpreter's return to that text a year or so later will result in a different understanding. "The drawing out of the true sense which resides in a text … never comes to a conclusion, but is in reality a never-ending process" (G 282). In Gadamer's understanding, the "world" which unveils itself through language, and especially in interaction between past and present, is a world which we never master but rather is that which is always changing and so laying new claim on us.

> Note: Gadamer's great concern is indeed to emphasize that since the interpreters' way of articulating a text's meaning is dependent on our particular historical situations, therefore our understanding of a text changes with the changes in our situations. This should not, however, be taken to mean that we interpreters need expend no effort to get back to what a text meant for its author. "The task of historical understanding includes the demand to recapture, from time to time, the historical horizon so that that which one wants to understand will present itself in its true proportions. He will misunderstand the significance of the contents of a tradition who fails to transpose himself into the historical situation" (G 286). This statement of Gadamer's is not easy to fit into his whole paradigm. Here, despite many opposite pronouncements, he seems to insist upon the need to regain a text's original historical horizon. Perhaps his meaning is that even though when translating from a foreign language we must improvise as we put what is said into another language, yet we must also work hard to understand what the person we are interpreting is saying, or else the resulting translation will be completely wrong. To carry out Gadamer's analogy between conversation and the interpretation of texts, this would then mean that we as interpreters, even though we will not succeed, should try to get back to a text's original meaning, for if we do not make this effort, all of our exposition will be hopelessly befuddled.

A Critique of Gadamer

What takes place in conversation is Gadamer's model for describing what happens in the interpretation of a text. Gadamer makes the transition from conversation to textual interpretation by way of an analysis of how a conversation is carried on from one language to another by way of a translator. An interpreter gains understanding of a text in the way that one partner in a conversation gains understanding of what the other is saying through a translator. As this one conversation partner gains understanding of the other through a translation, which amounts to an exposition, of what the other is saying, so interpreters of a text gain an understanding of a text in terms of an exposition, that is, in language conventions in which the interpreter themselves live. Gadamer is insistent that "a man understands a language in that he lives in it" (G 362), but since an interpreter does not live in the historical milieu of the text's author, he cannot understand it in its own terms and "understands differently, when he understands at all" (G 280). What Gadamer here calls "understanding" is not recognizing the meaning an author intended, in which we determine the meaning a text's language conventions had for its author. Rather, understanding occurs when we interpreters get something from the text supposedly made meaningful for us in terms of the language conventions of our own immediate historical situation. Thus, what is "understood differently" is exposition, and for

Gadamer understanding a text is always in terms of such an exposition, never in terms of what the author himself meant.

However, while in textual interpretation a translation takes place so that interpreters understand in the sense of having an exposition, this translation is *not* like the work of a translator who makes it possible for two people speaking in different languages to converse with one another. While the language into which one partner's words are translated is an exposition, yet the translator does this only as understanding of what the partner was saying in his own language conventions occurs first. By virtue of his being a *translator* he not only knows this person's language conventions well enough to grasp the meaning he is representing by their use, but he also knows the language in which the other partner lives, so that he can make an exposition of what is being said in terms which this partner will understand. In order to make the translation or exposition, he *first* understands. But in Gadamer's system interpreters are not like translators, because they are somehow able to make an exposition of a text without first having understood it.

What is it, then, that interpreters make an exposition of, if it cannot be an author's intended meaning? Gadamer tries to extricate himself from this difficulty by saying that as soon as a text is fixed in writing, it enters the stream of ongoing history, in which the meanings of its words change with the changing historical situation, and thus are only able to yield to any interpreters in a given historical situation a meaning made up of terms current for the time in which they live. But how can interpreters determine the meaning a text has when most texts do not have, like the Constitution, a Supreme Court to tell us what their present meaning is? However, granting, for the sake of argument, that there is a determinate contemporary meaning for each text, if this meaning is already so much a part of the interpreters' historical situation, how then can it be different enough from their own horizon to fuse with it and so make a third and new horizon? If a text's horizon, despite the changes it has undergone during its journey down the stream of history, really confronts interpreters with a *different* horizon, then would it not be speaking a language different from that in which the interpreters live? If this were so, then it would be no less difficult for any interpreters to understand this different horizon than to understand the author's original intended meaning.

More importantly, in Gadamer's thinking, interpreters must understand an alien horizon before they can fuse it with their own to form a third, which amounts to exposition. Gadamer, however, denies that understanding can ever be anything but exposition. But is not this grasping of an alien horizon, which is then to be fused with our own, an instance, in his system, where understanding is not exposition but simply construing an alien horizon *in its own terms*?

Gadamer is convinced that the difference separating present from past is "unbridgeable." Thus, things out of the past can only be known as exposition, that is, in terms of the present. But we should ask, How much time has to elapse before a meaning uttered at one time can no longer be reproduced at another time, but must, instead, be expounded? Gadamer does talk vaguely about an age for understanding a text in its own way (G 280), as though there were, say fifty years, within which texts would continue to have the same meaning. But then again, he says, "In every moment, that is, in every concrete situation, a text must be understood newly and differently" (G 292). Since our concrete historical situation is changing every second, it would therefore follow, on Gadamer's premises, that it would be impossible even to reach agreement in a conversation, because we could not even rethink what we or the other person had thought a moment before. Experience, however, shows that we can reproduce our thoughts of many years ago, despite the great historical changes we have since undergone. Are we not, in many instances, as far removed from the time when we thought those thoughts as interpreters are from the author of a text? If so, then it is altogether possible to have understanding of a text that is not exposition.

It is also significant that historical differences are not merely a function of time but also of environment, so that a person with whom we speak at a given moment may, despite the same language, be as far removed from us as if he lived back in the Elizabethan era. As Hirsch puts it, "To say that men of different eras cannot understand each other is really to say that men who exist in significantly different situations and have different perspectives on life cannot understand each other" (H 257). Experience shows, however, that people from different perspectives do understand each other because they react to what is said in ways that confirm that they have understood. Again, then, it seems that experience denies that understanding is just exposition.

Thus, we conclude that Gadamer's paradigm is not accurate because it counters experience and is inherently contradictory. Although he must equate understanding and exposition to be true to his radical historicism (which asserts that what is said at another time will be understood only in the terms of an interpreter's own historicality), yet his insistence on the alien horizon of a text—which must nevertheless be understood in its own terms so it can be fused with the terms of an author's own horizon—demands that there be an understanding prior to the exposition that takes place in the fusion.

Then too, experience gives abundant evidence that language does function as a bridge between our distinctive individualities and historicalities, so that before reacting to what another person says we are able to reproduce, in our own thinking, the sharable meaning that person willed to communicate. Experience also shows that even though our ever-changing historicality modifies our perception of things from moment to moment, yet language forms a bridge whereby what remains the same in all this change is singled out and represented. For example, every time we look at a tree in front of the house our perception of it differs somewhat. Yet despite noting this difference, we are also conscious of an unchanging identity in our experience of this tree, which we represent to ourselves by "the tree in front of the house." These words are a convention which, somewhere along the road of learning a language, signified what remained the same in our experience of that tree from day to day. These words signified what remained the same in others' experience of it as well as in ours, so that in using these words we knew we could engender the same thought in their minds as in ours. Thus, despite the uniqueness of individuals, and the great differences in the life histories even of those who live in the same general time and place, yet language is the bridge that joins what they share in common.

Language not only bridges the differences in time and culture of people speaking the same language, but also forms the bridge between two people speaking different languages. All that has to happen is for one of these to learn the language conventions of the other. Then all possible sharable meanings can be transmitted between them. The same thing is true in receiving communication from people who lived in a bygone age, whose language no one speaks today. In the case of the Bible, all we need to do is learn the conventions of the languages its authors used; then we can recognize the meaning these ancient authors willed to share with their contemporaries.

Contrary to Gadamer, then, the first task of textual interpreters, like that of conversational translators, is to gain understanding of what is being said. Just as translators must first grasp the intended meaning of the persons they are translating, so interpreters must first grasp the intended meaning of the text they are working on. Just as translators can understand the persons they are translating only by construing them in the terms those persons use, so interpreters must confine themselves solely to the terms an author used to convey sharable meaning. "Verbal meaning," argues Hirsch, "can be construed only on the basis of its own presuppositions, which are not given from some other realm but must be learned and guessed at—a process that is entirely intrinsic to a particular social and linguistic system" (H 134). It is obvious, then, that serious interpretation of the Bible, originally written in Hebrew and Greek, can be carried out only by those willing to learn the conventions of those languages.

But just as translators, after they have construed and understood an utterance in its own terms then restate this in the conventions of another language, so too interpreters, after we have understood a text in its own terms, will almost always want to set forth an exposition of this understanding in conventions most suitable to the particular historical situation of the particular group to which we address ourselves. Besides expounding, we will also want to show the application or significance of a text in relation to something else. In Hirsch's terminology *understanding* involves a recognition of just the meaning an author intends to convey, whereas *interpretation* is making this clear and applying it to others. Hirsch points out that "the historicity of interpretation is quite distinct from the timelessness of understanding" (H 137). In other words, what an author intended to say will never change, but we will explain and expound what that person meant in different ways to various audiences depending on the particular historicity of a given audience (e.g., we would explain and apply John 3:16 differently to elementary age children than we would to a group on a college campus).

Certainly, in this rejection of Gadamer's paradigm, there is no rejection of his insistence on making ancient texts meaningful and vital for today. Hirsch says, "I recognize the validity of Gadamer's insistence that a vital, contemporary understanding of the past is the only understanding worth having, and [I recognize] his rightness in insisting on the differentness in the cultural givens and shared attitudes between a past age and a present one. What is wanted [however] is to preserve these truths without committing contradictions and abolishing logically necessary distinctions" (H 255).

The great emphasis that we need to preserve in order to clear up the contradictions in Gadamer's system is that understanding is not the same as exposition. Only by insisting that we must first gain understanding before giving exposition does it become possible for a text out of the past to mold and shape the all-too-provincial horizon of our present historicity, for only when we discipline ourselves to construe the meaning of others in their own terms does an horizon emerge for us which is fundamentally different from our own, and therefore able to change it.

As we insist on the changelessness and timelessness of understanding, it becomes clear how the Bible can indeed function as an infallible rule of faith and practice. What the biblical writers meant, what they intended to say as they composed the books of the Bible, is something that cannot change. It is perfectly realistic, then, for us to have as our goal for interpreting Scripture that of recognizing the faith once for all delivered to the saints. Therefore, the first part of our efforts as biblical interpreters is to learn how to understand an author's intended, sharable meaning by recourse to his own terms. But we do not want to be antiquarians who simply rediscover what people in the past wanted to say and let it go at that. We also want to know the significance of these things for today. The greatest question we can raise concerning a text's significance is whether or not what an author meant is true, and it is to this question that we now address ourselves.

Chapter Two—Grammatico-Historical Interpretation

No matter how far writers may be from us in time and culture, we may still grasp their intended meanings if we have learned their language conventions. This involves knowing their linguistic system and the characteristics of the society which this language binds together. Some of the language will be a reflection of customs, ways of viewing life, and attitudes that are distinctive to this society; and until we know about these, this language will be somewhat obscure.

In the Old Testament, for example, the word for "cut" is used to designate the action involved in instituting a covenant. The Hebrew of Genesis 15:18 and 21:27 will not be very understandable to us when it speaks of "cutting" a covenant until we become aware of the ceremony that often accompanied the making of a covenant. In Genesis 15:17 and Jeremiah 34:18–19 the authors mention an animal's being cut in two and the parties to the covenant passing between the severed portions; and thus we gain some understanding of why they describe the institution of a covenant in this way.

Then too, as we interpret texts, we listen in, as it were, to what authors wanted to share with their original audiences and notice that they make allusions to things which were common knowledge to both of them, but which mean very little or nothing to us third party readers without further research. In Philippians 1:5 Paul speaks of his readers' sharing (κοινωνία) with him in the furtherance of the Gospel from the first day until the day he wrote his letter. We grasp more of what the readers understood by this from Philippians 4:10, 14–16, which tell us that one reason Paul had for writing this letter was to thank his readers for their latest in a series of gifts to him which began from the day they were converted.

These two examples illustrate how a reader's attention must be directed not merely to the words of a text but to the particularities of the society of that language and to any special knowledge that the readers and authors shared in common. Attention to the words of the text is, in hermeneutical parlance, the *grammatical* aspect of interpretation, while attention to particular things in the authors' and readers' society and circumstances which may provide an explanation for why certain words were used is the *historical* aspect of interpretation. In this chapter we want to consider what constitutes the data for these two aspects of interpretation.

The Data for Grammatical Interpretation

We interpreters must direct our efforts in three ways to be sure that we are dealing only with those signs that authors decided were adequate to convey their intended meaning to their readers.

First, we must take pains to learn the language conventions which existed between the author and the original readers. H. G. Gadamer, referred to in the preceding chapter, made it clear that a translation is always an exposition. Although a translator expends every effort to represent, in another language, just what the original speaker intended to communicate, the translation never fully achieves this goal. "Where there is need of a translation, the distance between the genius of the original wording of what is said and its reproduction must be taken as part of the bargain, for the overcoming of this distance never succeeds fully."[33] Sometimes greater clarity comes out in the translation than was meant in the original; sometimes an important implication that is present in some succinct way of speaking in the original cannot be reproduced in the translation without a very tedious circumlocution, and therefore is simply omitted. The contours of the words of a translation never correspond fully to those of the original, and this is why the intention of authors is best construed simply by recourse to their own terms, to the language conventions which they knew would evoke in the original readers' minds the meaning they wanted to transmit from their minds.

One example of this comes from the parable of the Rich Fool, Luke 12:15–21. In verse 20 God speaks to the man who has laid up treasure for himself and is not rich toward God, saying, "Fool! This night your soul is required of you." The word "required" is ἀπαιτέω, which for such a context in the Greek signifies the demand that a loan be paid back. In the Greek the implication is clear that life is considered as a loan which God has given to each person, but that the day comes when this loan must be repaid. Since a translation cannot be as lengthy as a commentary, this implication is not carried over into the English translation.

The best we can do in studying the Bible in a translation is to construe the intended meaning of the translator. But we believe that in the Bible God spoke through holy men who were inspired by the Holy Spirit (2 Peter 1:21); thus, those fortunate enough will welcome the chance to learn the language conventions of Hebrew and Greek. When studying the Bible in these languages, we have the security of handling the words the authors themselves selected to create the meaning they wanted to share with their readers. These words will call up the same meaning in our minds to the extent that we have mastered the Greek and Hebrew language conventions.

The second way we interpreters gain optimum certainty that we are dealing only with the authors' own terms, and therefore will use only what stemmed from them in construing their intended meanings, is by applying the techniques of textual criticism. Like all ancient documents, the texts of the Bible in their original languages have come down to us through a long history of textual transmission. In the centuries before the invention of printing, these texts were copied and recopied by hand many times, and as we compare these manuscripts, we note that there are minor variations between them which were due either to a scribe's unintentional error or to his attempt to correct what he thought was either unclear or objectionable in the text. We interpreters must therefore know something of the science of textual criticism, so that as we work in the Greek New Testament or the Hebrew Old Testament, we will be able to handle the respective textual apparatus of each volume and thus achieve an optimal assurance of what the authors'

---

[33] Hans-Georg Gadamer, *Wahrheit und Methode* (Tübingen: J. C. B. Mohr, 1964), p. 362.

words really were. A knowledge of the history of the Greek and Hebrew texts is essential for understanding the symbols used in these apparatuses.

As regards the text of the Old Testament, we should understand that in the centuries just prior to Christ, this text appeared in several families, each of which was competing for supremacy. But people, and especially religious people, do not enjoy seeing a conflict in what is their authority. Consequently, in about the second or third century after Christ, one text (generally the text found in our Hebrew Bibles today) was made to prevail over the competing texts. Then, sometime after 500 CE, when Hebrew was no longer spoken, those perpetuating the scribal tradition, now called the Masoretes, added vowel points to the consonants of this prevailing text, so that the way of pronouncing the ancient Hebrew would not be lost and the Hebrew Old Testament could continue to be read in the synagogues. Hence in handling the present Hebrew text, we must realize that the vocalization does not necessarily stem from the original authors. Instead, it may be possible in some instances that the same set of consonants for a word should receive a different pointing which would give a different meaning to that word. Some criticism of the Masoretic text is possible, since evidence for the families suppressed by this text is still extant in the readings of the Samaritan Pentateuch and in the Septuagint. The manuscripts discovered at Qumran also provide evidence for these other families of texts, as well as evidence of the antiquity and consequent authority of the Masoretic text.

In general, the policy by which to proceed in carrying out Old Testament textual criticism is to consider the Masoretic text as basic and allow its readings to be emended by evidence from these other textual families only (1) when a variation from the Masoretic text is not the sort scribes were apt to make either unintentionally (misreading, miswriting, omission, or dittography) or intentionally; (2) when the other reading is the harder reading and it is seen how it could have given rise to the simplification found in the Masoretic text; and (3) when the other reading represents a simplification of the Masoretic text, but the difficulty in the Masoretic text can be explained as an *unintentional* scribal error.[34]

As regards the text of the New Testament, textual critics have concluded that it is represented by four major families. There is the Koine or Byzantine text, symbolized by K in the Nestle-Aland Greek text. The great majority of manuscripts belong to this family, but it is of little value, since it stems from a fourth-century recension, made as an attempt to reconcile the many variations that had appeared between the texts of the New Testament. The remaining three textual families are pre-Koine. They are the Western text, whose chief representative is the Codex Bezae, or D, as it is symbolized in Nestle; the Caesarean text, whose chief representative is Θ; and the Alexandrian text, whose most easily remembered representatives are א and B. We interpreters should come to know all the chief representatives of these texts and the way in which they are symbolized in

---

[34] E. Würthein, *The Text of the Old Testament*. Tr. By P. Ackroyd (Oxford: Blackwell, 1957), pp. 70–82. Cf. O. Eissfeldt, *An Introduction to the Old Testament*. Tr. By P. Ackroyd from 3rd German edition (New York: Harper & Row, 1965), Section V.

the Nestle apparatus. We should also learn the other symbols used to set forth textual evidence in this apparatus.[35]

In general, the method for carrying out New Testament textual criticism is to give the greatest weight to readings supported by the Alexandrian text. But our decision must also be influenced by internal evidence, for the worth of a reading must always be weighed against the well-known fact that scribes desired to clarify things, and therefore the harder and shorter reading is to be preferred over the easier and longer one. But sometimes a reading can be so hard that is it impossible to suppose that it could have been used by the original author. Then another reading will be preferred which is well attested and which does not clash with the characteristics of an author's style.

The third procedure that ensures that we interpreters are working exclusively with the author's own semantic symbols is differentiating between the actual wording of the text and the various punctuation marks by which subsequent editors have sought to facilitate and clarify the reading of the text. An examination of ancient documents reveals that authors in those days used few, if any, marks to signify how words grouped themselves into clauses, sentences, paragraphs, and larger units. Parchment and papyrus were difficult to come by as material upon which to write; so, in many ancient texts of both the Greek New Testament and Hebrew Old Testament copyists used the space-saving device of *scriptio continua*, that is, continued writing in which there are not even spaces between words or sentences. Of course, we do not possess any of the original autographs of the biblical books, but it is safe to infer from the evidence of the most ancient extant manuscripts that the autographs likewise contained little, if any, punctuation. Even question marks were not used commonly in Greek manuscripts until the ninth century CE.[36]

However, with the passage of time, the need arose to delimit the sections of the biblical texts that were about the size of large paragraphs, both because of the necessity to be able to readily locate a passage in the text and because of the desirability to have units of this magnitude stand out clearly. Thus, in the Old Testament texts, even as far back as the time of Qumran, the text was divided into sections called *parashoth*. Larger sections were denoted by beginning a new line, or by omitting an entire line, and smaller sections were denoted by leaving a gap within a line. Such sectioning, historically related to the practice evident in the Qumran texts but not identical with it, continued on in the Masoretic texts and is present in our Hebrew Bibles today. A *sammech* (ס) between sentences indicates a paragraph break of smaller degree, while a *pe* (פ) between the ending of a sentence on one line and the beginning of a new sentence on another indicates a larger break. Verse divisions with these *parashoth* came in during the Mishnaic period (c. 200 CE) when it was necessary to intersperse the Hebrew reading with an Aramaic translation so the hearers could understand. The amount of Hebrew that was read before the translation was given in Aramaic became the verse divisions in the Old Testament,

---

[35] See: B. Metzger, *The Text of the New Testament* (New York: Oxford University Press, 1963); and F. Kenyon, *Handbook of the Textual Criticism of the New Testament* (Grand Rapids: Wm. B. Eerdmans, 1951—reprint of second edition).

[36] B. Metzger, *op. cit.*, p. 27.

and around 500 CE these were signified by the *sôph pāsûq* (:) that still appears in the Hebrew text.[37]

Divisions of paragraph magnitude were also the first punctuation marks that came into the New Testament texts. The earliest such divisions were the *kephalaia* indicated in the Nestle text by a single number in italics in the inner margin. Smaller divisions are indicated by a large Roman script number in this inner margin. A good bit of the function of these early textual divisions was for reference rather than for indicating the author's units of composition, and their use has not been carried over into our modern versions.

The present chapter divisions in our Bibles were invented in 1205 by Stephen Langton, a professor in Paris (he later became Archbishop of Canterbury), who put these into a Vulgate edition of the Bible. These chapter divisions were first used by the Jews in 1330 for the Hebrew Old Testament in a manuscript, and for a printed edition in 1516. This system of chapter divisions likewise came into the Greek manuscripts of the New Testament in the 1400s.

It was Robert Stephanus, a Parisian book printer, whose versification of the Bible has prevailed to the present. He took over the verse divisions already indicated in the Hebrew Bible by the *sôph pāsûq*, and assigned numbers to them within the chapter divisions already assigned by Stephen Langton. While riding on horseback from Paris to Lyons he assigned his own verse divisions to the New Testament and numbered them within Langton's chapter divisions. Consequently, the quality of his work was not the best. Von Soden complained:

> The verse divisions of Stephanus which he, according to an incidental remark by his son, made during a trip from Paris to Lyons, frequently do not do service to the sense of the text. There is no consistent method at work in this system. The verses sometimes coincide with a single sentence, and sometimes they include several sentences; sometimes a single sentence is divided into two verses, with the result that the reader is led to consider the second verse while forgetting the point of view of the first verse. Especially objectionable is the way in which words introducing a direct quotation sometimes belong to the preceding verse and sometimes to the verse in which the quotation is found.[38]

But through Stephanus the versification for the Old Testament found its way into the Hebrew Bible printed first in 1571. Then Theodor Beza's use of Stephanus' verse and chapter divisions in his edition of the *textus receptus* of the New Testament (1565) assured them the permanence that they enjoy in our Bibles today.[39]

---

[37] R. Pfeiffer, *Introduction to the Old Testament*, rev. ed. (New York: Harper & Row, 1948), p. 80.

[38] H. von Soden, *Die Schriften des Neuen Testamentes* (Göttingen: Vandenhoeck, 1911), I, 484.

[39] See also *Die Relgion in der Geschichte und der Gegenwart* (3rd ed.), III, 1141 f.

From this brief survey of the history of the Bible's chapter and verse divisions, it is only too apparent that these are nothing more than a handy method of reference. They do not necessarily represent those units of composition present in the author's mind as he strove to impart his thoughts. Nevertheless, it is utterly impractical to think of expunging them from our Bibles. "There is no doubt," said von Soden,

> that the chapter divisions which we have inherited from Langton leave much to be desired. These divisions do not rest upon a comprehension of the literary structure of the biblical books ... But it is utterly impractical today to think of trying to correct this system of chapter divisions. From practical considerations, this system must be kept as the means for designating individual passages. All that we can do is to realize that this system falls far short of doing justice to the inherent units of Scripture. Therefore, if future editions want to aid rather than hinder a reader's understanding of the New Testament, it should be realized that the time is ripe to cause both the verse and chapter divisions to disappear from the text and to be put on the margin in as inconspicuous a place as possible. Every effort must be made to print the text in a way which makes it possible for the units which the author himself had in mind to become apparent.[40]

The Nestle edition of the Greek New Testament did as von Soden recommended and placed the chapter and verse divisions on the margin. So did the text of Tasker.[41] The Greek text put forward by the American Bible Society for use in Bible translation kept these references within the text,[42] but possibly this would be more helpful to Bible trans-lators. It is unfortunate that the *Biblia Hebraica* of Kittel has both chapter and verse divisions in the text. But whatever the text that we are using, we should follow the advice of A. T. Robertson: "The first step in interpretation is to ignore the modern chapters and verses."[43]

But what about the punctuation marks, inserted by more recent editors, as an attempt to delimit the author's own units of thought? Indeed, we interpreters should acquaint our-selves with the system of punctuation used in these texts, and we should seek to discern the reasons why the various editors divided the texts as they did. However, no two edi-tors agree fully on where these units begin and end, and this means that interpreters themselves must make the final decision as to the all-important matter of the delimitation of the larger and smaller literary units. Using a system of sentence diagramming will be helpful for detecting the author's units of thought which were about the size of sentences, and there are other methods (e.g., Chapter Four, below) for determining the limits of larger units.

---

[40] Von Soden, *op.cit.*, p. 482.

[41] R. Tasker, *The Greek New Testament* (New York: Oxford University Press, 1964).

[42] K. Aland, M. Black, B. Metzger, A. Wikren, eds., *The Greek New Testament* (New York: American Bible Society, 1966).)

[43] A. Robertson, *An Introduction to the Textual Criticism of the New testament* (Nashville: Broadman Press, 1925), p. 101.

The Data for Historical Interpretation

After focusing attention solely upon the symbols the authors themselves used, we begin to construe them sentence by sentence, keeping especially on the lookout for indications of the purpose they were trying to achieve; for nothing will be understood properly until we grasp this purpose. But the farther we interpreters are removed historically and culturally from being like those readers the authors had in mind as they wrote, the more we will need to familiarize ourselves with certain elements in the culture of the original readers which reflect themselves in statements which seem strange to their ears. This is the historical aspect of interpretation, and the following are some examples of it.

In Matthew 12:38 the Pharisees and scribes asked Jesus for a sign, but in verse 39 Jesus rebuked them by replying, "An evil and adulterous generation seeks for a sign; but no sign shall be given to it except the sign of the prophet Jonah ..." It seems strange that Jesus extends his rebuke, directed to the Pharisees, and makes it include the whole generation of Israel. Why should all of the people of Israel be guilty because the Pharisees and scribes had asked for a sign? The Jewish historian Josephus, in his *Antiquities of the Jews*, XIII, 10, 5, gives an insight into the relationship between the Pharisees and the great masses of the people of Israel which clears up this difficulty. Josephus remarked, "[The Pharisees] have so great a power over the multitude, that when they say anything against the king, or against the high priest, they are presently believed." In other words, the Pharisees were the controllers of public opinion. They were regarded as the conservators of orthodoxy, and what they taught, the people felt obliged to believe. This tendency for the Jewish people to listen to the Pharisees was one of Jesus' chief problems. Even his own disciples were under their spell (Matthew 15:12; 23:1 ff.), and consequently, in rebuking the Pharisees, Jesus found it necessary to rebuke the whole generation of Israel which had allowed its thought to be controlled by the Pharisees. The original readers of Matthew would have had no difficulty understanding why Jesus extended his rebuke to the whole nation. But we who are far removed from the situation of those days have to take pains to learn about this facet of the historical situation from whatever source may be available.

Another example is Matthew 3:8–9, where John the Baptist declares to the Pharisees and scribes who came to receive baptism from him that they should "bear fruit that befits repentance, and do not presume to say to yourselves, 'We have Abraham as our father,' for I tell you, God is able to raise up children to Abraham from these stones." An investigation of Jewish thought reveals that it was very common to suppose that physical descent from Abraham insured a person of God's favor. The Jewish Midrash *Rabba* on Numbers 8 (150b) explains how a proselyte who became a Jew could not find any favor with God because of physical descent from Abraham, but must rather depend wholly upon his good works.[44] Thus those who could trace their descent from Abraham regarded this as a virtual guarantee of salvation. Justyn Martyr also alludes to this feeling in Judaism when he says, "The Jews beguile themselves and you [Trypho, a Jew], supposing

---

[44] H. Strack and P. Billerbeck, *Kommentar zum Neuen Testament* (München: C. H. Beck, 1926), I, 119 f.

that the everlasting kingdom will be assuredly given to those of the dispersion who are of Abraham after the flesh, although they be sinners, and faithless, and disobedient towards God …"[45] When we know the Jews were prone to think this way, the meaning this statement must have had for the original readers of Matthew becomes clear.

The baptism John the Baptist administered in the Gospels offers one of the best examples of how historical knowledge, derived from a non-biblical source, provides a key for understanding the biblical text. John's baptism is referenced in the New Testament without any explanation as to its meaning. Neither is it the continuation of anything in the Old Testament, for we look in vain there for any regulation regarding the necessity for baptism. What then was the significance of this baptism? From the Mishnah *Yebamot* 47a, b (written in the second century CE, but speaking of a practice that had begun much earlier), we learn that baptism by immersion was one of the rituals through which a Gentile had to pass in order to become a member of the fellowship of Israel. After being instructed from the law and being circumcised and healed, the proselyte then "immerses himself and when he comes up, he is in all respects an Israelite."[46] Thus, it becomes clear that the significance of John's baptism lay in the fact that Israelites who submitted to it acknowledged that being a member of their race was itself of no value and that to prepare themselves for the announced coming of the kingdom of God, they were no different than the Gentiles but must likewise do what is required in order to join the commonwealth of Israel. This all fits, of course, with what was said above about John's emphasis that Jews must not consider their lineage from Abraham as giving them any special advantage. To the original readers of the Gospels, such matters were common knowledge, but today we are a long way from the New Testament world, and to understand such allusions, we must engage in historical investigation.

We must not think that the historical data necessary for understanding one passage of the Bible cannot come from anywhere else in the Bible but only from some non-biblical source. To the contrary, there are a number of places where scriptural allusions to some historical aspect of the times provides a way to understand some other passage. An example of this is Matthew 5:34–35, where Jesus said, "But I say to you, do not swear at all, either by heaven, for it is the throne of God, or by earth, for it is his footstool, or by Jerusalem, for it is the city of the great king." Some help for understanding this passage comes from Matthew 23:16–18, where Jesus, citing the Pharisees' practice of having a number of things by which to swear, said to them, "Woe to you, blind guides, who say, 'If anyone swears by the temple, it is nothing; but if anyone swears by the gold of the temple, he is bound by his oath.' … And you say, 'If anyone swears by the altar, it is nothing; but if anyone swears by the gift on the altar, he is bound by his oath.'"

From these statements in Matthew 23, it becomes clear that by his statement in Matthew 5, Jesus was alluding to the Jews' practice of differentiating between binding and non-

---

[45] J. Martyr, *Dialogue with Trypho*, 140.

[46] C. Barrett, *New Testament Background: Selected Documents*, Harper Torchbooks (New York: Harper & Row, 1961), p. 165f.; G. Moore, *Judaism* (Cambridge: Harvard University Press, 1954), I, 333f.

binding oaths. If we take the command of Matthew 5:34, "Do not swear at all," by itself, we might think Jesus forbade all taking of oaths. But data regarding the historical context to which Jesus was speaking indicates that in saying "Swear not at all," Jesus was simply condemning the whole practice of exonerating lies uttered under certain conditions. His purpose was to condemn lying, and it would be pressing this verse too far to read it as forbidding all oath-taking.

Thus, it becomes clear that the sources for historical interpretation can comprise every bit of evidence that in any way casts light upon the world of the authors and their original readers. Valuable information for the understanding of the Old Testament can be gleaned from the cuneiform tablets written in the Akkadian and Ugaritic languages. For example, the Ras Shamra texts, in the Ugaritic language, reveal the religion of the Canaanites, which the Old Testament prophets attacked so vigorously. Likewise, parallels to the Pentateuchal laws may be found in the Babylonian law code of Hammurabi, written in the eighteenth-century BCE. Records from the kingdom of Assyria complement the history of Israel recorded in 1 and 2 Kings. An introductory survey of the historical data possibly relevant for the interpretation of the Old Testament is available in a book by D. Winton Thomas (ed.), *Documents from Old Testament Times*.[47]

A similar introductory survey of the literature containing historical data possibly relevant for the interpretation of the New Testament is C. K. Barrett's *The New Testament Background: Selected Documents*.[48] The writings of Josephus, Jewish Rabbinical literature, the Qumran scrolls, the Old Testament Apocrypha and Pseudepigrapha, and the Papyri are a few of the classifications of pertinent literature available in this book. A veritable goldmine of historical data useful for the interpretation of the New Testament is also available in Strack-Billerbeck's *Kommentar zum Neuen Testament*.[49] Here citations are made from the Rabbinical literature for each statement in the New Testament for which there is a parallel.

Any archeological evidence of an unwritten sort which throws light upon the times in which a biblical writing originated can also be useful, as well as knowledge of the geography, topography, and climate of the place where it was written. Of course, not all the materials are extant for every detail of ancient life. But there is a great deal that is in place, and our ability to think God's thoughts after him from Scripture will depend on the extent to which we take pains to think as the original readers of the biblical books thought.

Oscar Cullmann recounts how as a student at Strasbourg he repudiated orthodoxy for liberalism so that the facts might speak for themselves more freely. But then Schwei-

---

[47] D. Thomas (ed.), *Documents from Old Testament Times*, Harper Torchbooks (New York: Harper & Row, 1961).

[48] C. Barrett, *The New Testament Background: Selected Documents*. Harper Torchbooks (New York: Harper & Row, 1961).

[49] H. Strack and P. Billerbeck, *Kommentar zum Neuen Testamen aus Talmud und Midrasch*. 4 vols. (München: C. H. Beck, 1922–28).

tzer's *Qwest for the Historical Jesus* proved to him that liberalism could also be guilty of making the evidence fit an *a priori*. Therefore, he espoused the methodology of form criticism as the best way to rediscover the faith of the early church. Then he relates, "As I prepared my lectures, I sought to hold every modern or personally cherished idea regarding the nature of Christianity at a distance. Through this purely *scientific* approach, I came gradually to a deeper theological understanding of those concepts in the NT, which at the outset had been foreign to my ways of thinking."[50] We do well to follow his example.

---

[50] O. Cullmann, "Neuses Testament und Geshcichte der Alten Kirche," *Lehre und Forschung an der Universtät Basel* (Basel: Birkhäuser Verlag, 1960), p. 26.

Chapter Three—Understanding Propositions

In the preceding chapters we made certain generalizations about understanding a text. Now we become more specific by indicating the point at which the process of understanding actually commences. The whole of a text is, of course essential for grasping its parts, but an understanding of a whole cannot be accomplished without first attending to the parts.

What, then, are the parts with which we begin? While letters and words are the smallest elements of a text, they are not, by themselves, the basic building blocks of a text. They begin to convey determinate meanings only as they interact as parts of propositions; and it is the propositions which are a text's basic building blocks. The meanings which words begin to have as they comprise a portion of a proposition are determined, in part, by their syntax, that is, by the way the words relate to one another to make up a proposition.

Essentially, a proposition makes an assertion about something. This assertion is the predication and the "something" is the subject. Basically, then, a proposition consists of a subject and a predicate. The shortest verse in the Bible, "Jesus wept" (John 11:35), consists of two words, the first being the subject, and the second, the predicate. A proposition can even consist of only one word, as in the imperative "Run!", where the subject who is to do the running is already understood. Usually, however, a proposition consists of more than two words. A subject will often consist of more than one word, and it will usually have phrases and clauses, as well as single words, for modifiers. Sometimes a predicate will include a transitive verb which often has one or more direct objects and one or more indirect objects, to say nothing of various modifiers of these objects, as well as of the verb itself. At other times a predicate consists of a word or clause joined to a subject by a copulative (usually some form of the verb "to be")—as in John 1:1, "The Word was God"—and very often this predicate nominative construction, as it is called, will have a number of modifiers.

When we have located the subject and the whole predication, as well as all of the words that may modify both, then we have delimited one of the text's smallest building blocks; and in seeing how all of its words make their contribution to the one proposition, we grasp what this whole proposition is saying; and each of the words becomes significant in relation to this one assertion. Then we execute the same process for the next proposition, and so on through the text, proposition by proposition. The only words in a text which are not themselves parts of propositions are the conjunctions that link propositions together.

We greatly enhance our ability to grasp how words function to form propositions by using the visual presentation afforded by sentence diagraming. The discipline of diagraming sentences is a means of enabling us to make syntax the basis of our ability to read the text—we will do so in Greek here; but we could also do this in Hebrew, English, or any other language, necessary changes being made. Since each syntactical phenomenon is represented in its characteristic way, it is certain that when we have diagramed a sentence, we have grasped its syntax. The diagrams of the following propositions in the Greek will show the various forms which the subject and predicate and their modifiers can take.

Sentence Diagramming

1. Basic Sentence Structure

The basic parts of a sentence are placed on a straight horizontal line. The verb is the center, preceded by the subject and followed by the direct object, predicate nominative, or predicate adjective (if the sentence contains any of them). Note that the vertical slash preceding the verb passes *through* the line, and any slashes following the verb rest *on* the line.

A. Simple subject and predicate

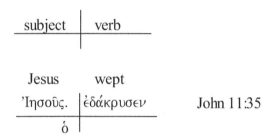

John 11:35

B. Simple sentence with direct object. Note that the slash preceding the direct object is vertical.

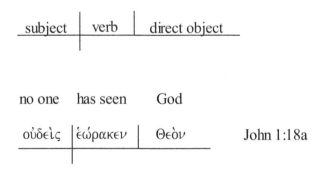

John 1:18a

C. Simple sentence with double accusative.

Some Greek verbs take two accusatives, one of which, in English, usually becomes an indirect object. Both accusatives are diagrammed *on* the line. They are separated by a second vertical slash.

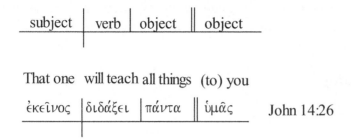

subject | verb | object ‖ object

That one will teach all things (to) you

ἐκεῖνος | διδάξει | πάντα ‖ ὑμᾶς   John 14:26

D. Simple sentence with an objective predicate

Certain transitive verbs can take a second object which completes the meaning of the first object. Verbs of calling, choosing, naming, making, and thinking often take objective predicates. The objective predicate is preceded in the diagram by a slash leaning back toward the direct object.

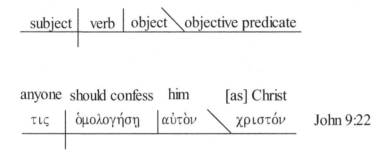

subject | verb | object \ objective predicate

anyone should confess him [as] Christ

τις | ὁμολογήσῃ | αὐτὸν \ χριστόν   John 9:22

E. Simple sentence with predicate nominative or predicate adjective.

The slash preceding the predicate nominative or predicate adjective leans leftward—back toward the verb and the subject.

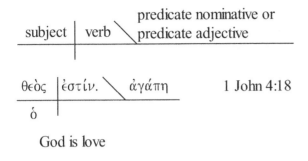

subject | verb \ predicate nominative or predicate adjective

θεὸς | ἐστίν. \ ἀγάπη   1 John 4:18
ὁ

God is love

ἐκεῖνος | ἦν \ ἀνθρωποκτόνος   John 8:44

This one was a murderer

F. Periphrastic construction

The periphrastic use of the Greek participle is diagrammed as follows:

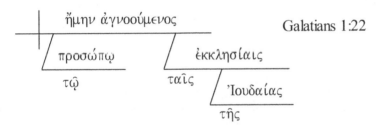

ἤμην ἀγνοούμενος   Galatians 1:22
προσώπῳ   ἐκκλησίαις
τῷ   ταῖς
                'Ιουδαίας
                    τῆς

I was unknown by face to the churches of Judea.

G. Modifiers

Modifiers are placed directly below the words they modify. Genitive modifiers are treated like prepositional phrases (see example F above and more in section 2 below).

H. Many times sentences are written with words "missing." We readers are expected to supply the missing words in our own minds as we read. Sentences with ellipses are diagrammed without supplying the missing words. (See the section on clauses below for examples.)

2. Prepositional Phrases

Prepositional phrases consist of a preposition, its object, and the modifiers of the object, if any. Prepositional phrases always modify other words and behave either as adjectives or adverbs. They are diagrammed on a horizontal line which is connected to the modified word by a line slanting downward and leftward. Often words in the Greek accusative, dative and genitive cases are not governed by expressed prepositions. These are diagrammed simply. When the preposition is expressed, it precedes a vertical line which is followed by the object of the preposition.

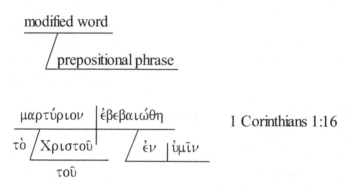

1 Corinthians 1:16

The testimony about Christ was confirmed among you.

Since some prepositional phrases modify the objects of other prepositions, the diagram can show a whole "string" of prepositional phrases tied together. Sometimes several prepositional phrases modify the same word. In order to avoid running lines together, the phrases are diagrammed in a "chain," by connecting each phrase to the previous preposition. For an example see 3–A–3. But cf. 5–A.

3. Infinitives

Infinitives are verbals which may act either as substantives or as modifiers. The verbal quality of the infinitive allows it to take a subject and/or an object. As a substantive, the infinitive may stand in a place where a noun or pronoun could stand. As a modifier, the infinitive acts as an adjective or adverb.

A. Infinitives as substantives

1. Infinitive as subject

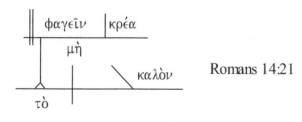

Romans 14:21

Not to eat meat (is) good

2. Infinitive as direct object

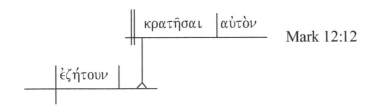

Mark 12:12

They were seeking to arrest him

Cf. John 14:2 and Acts 18:10 below to see why this is not a complementary infinitive.

Infinitives in indirect discourse are diagrammed similarly.

3. Infinitive as the object of a preposition

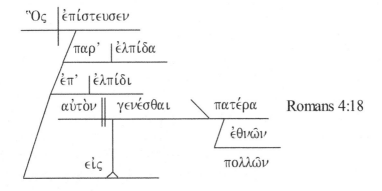

Romans 4:18

[Abraham] against hope, on the basis of hope,
believed in order to become the
father of many nations

In the above example the infinitive takes a subject. The subject of the infinitive is placed ahead of the double slash which precedes the infinitive. Also, in this example, when the slanted lines do not come off of the object of the preposition (as here), each prepositional phrase is understood to come off of the main verb.

B. Infinitives as modifiers

Infinitives which modify in the ordinary fashion of adjectives or adverbs appear in this way:

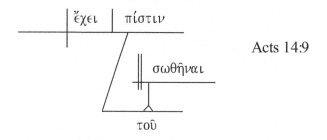

Acts 14:9

he had faith to be healed

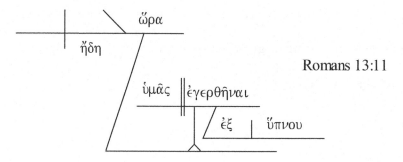

Romans 13:11

[It is] already [the] hour [for] you to awaken from sleep.

Complementary infinitives are considered to be a special type of modifier. A complementary infinitive completes the meaning of the verb it modifies—a verb whose meaning would not be complete without the infinitive. The complementary infinitive is connected to the main verb by a *vertical* line. No stilt is necessary for complementary infinitives.

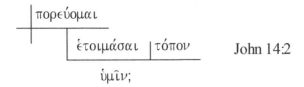

John 14:2

I go to prepare a place for you

Acts 18:10

No one will attack you to harm you

If an infinitive following a finite verb can possibly be construed as the object of that verb, it should be diagrammed as such and not as a complementary infinitive.

4. Participles

Participles, like infinitives, are verbals. Participles often function as adverbial clauses (see below), and we should be ready to show which of the nine different adverbial clauses the participle is like. However, participles may also be used as adjectives and as nouns. A participle always stands on its own line. Like the infinitive, the participle may stand alone or it may take an object and be attended by modifiers.

A. Participles as substantives

The participle may function as a subject, direct object, or predicate nominative. Whenever a participle is used as a substantive, its definite article is considered to be a noun and the participle is considered to modify the definite article.

ὁ | ἐστιν. \ δεκτὸς
αὐτῷ
φοβούμενος | αὐτὸν

Acts 10:35

The one who fears him is welcome to him

B. Participles as modifiers

Participles which modify other words are connected to the words they modify by *vertical* lines.

1. A participle as an attributive adjective

```
Ἡρώδης | ἠκρίβωσεν | χρόνον                    Matthew 2:7
           |                  τὸν / ἀστέρος
                                   τοῦ | φαινομένου
```

Herod determined the time of the star's appearing

2. A participle as appositive

Many participles fulfill both a substantival and a modifying role. Notable is the appositive, diagrammed here.

```
οὗτός | ἐστιν \ ἄρτος     =    ὁ                John 6:50
          |          ὁ
                           | καταβαίνων
                              / ἐκ | οὐρανοῦ
                                      τοῦ
```

This is the bread that comes down out of heaven

3. A participle as an adverb

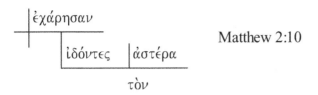

Matthew 2:10

Beholding the star, they rejoiced

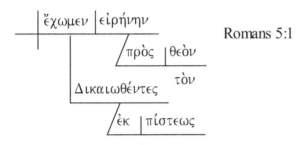

Romans 5:1

Having been justified by faith,
let us be at peace with God

Note: Whenever a participle can be paraphrased as an adverbial clause, it will modify the verb, not the noun, even though its inflection derives from the implied subject of the verb. Thus, in the first example above a more accurate construal is, "*While* they beheld the star, they rejoiced."

5. Clauses

A clause is a group of words containing a subject and a predicate. All clauses are given their own lines in sentence diagramming.

A. Noun clauses

Noun clauses may be found at any place in a sentence where a simple noun might occur. Noun clauses are placed on stilts.

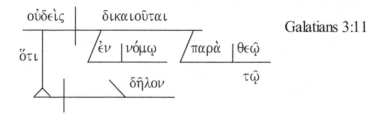

Galatians 3:11

That no one is justified by law before God is evident

B. Adjective clauses

Adjective clauses behave as simple adjectives, modifying substantives. They are connected to the words they modify by *broken* lines.

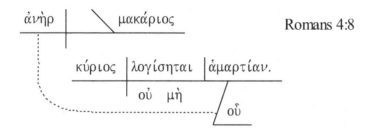

Romans 4:8

Fortunate is the person whose sin the Lord does not count.

C. Adverbial clauses

Adverbial clauses are connected to the words they modify by a *solid* line *slanting* either to the right or to the left. There are nine kinds of adverbial clauses: causal, result, purpose, concessive, conditional, modal, comparative, locative, and temporal. For purposes of exegesis it is of utmost importance to know the exact kind of an adverbial clause that is under consideration.

θεὸς | ἠγάπησεν | κόσμον
ὁ   ὥστε   τὸν

John 3:16
(Result)

ἔδωκεν | υἱὸν = μονογενῆ
τὸν   τὸν

God so loved the world that he gave his one and only Son.

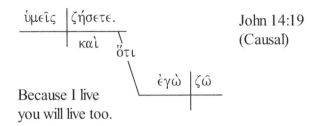

ὑμεῖς | ζήσετε.
καὶ
ὅτι

ἐγὼ | ζῶ

Because I live
you will live too.

John 14:19
(Causal)

Note: The example of John 3:16 contains an appositive. Appositives are diagrammed as shown, connected to the words they explain by an "equal" sign.

6. Special Problems

A. Coordinate and subordinate clauses

Ἀλλά (but/rather), γάρ (for/because), δέ (but/and/now), διό (therefore/for this reason), καί (and), and οὖν (therefore/consequently) are the usual conjunctions used to introduce coordinate or subordinate clauses. The general procedure with such clauses is to put the conjunction above the clause without attaching it to anything. But there is one particular combination of conjunctions in Greek, the combination of μέν...δέ, that should join the coordinate clause by a dotted line.

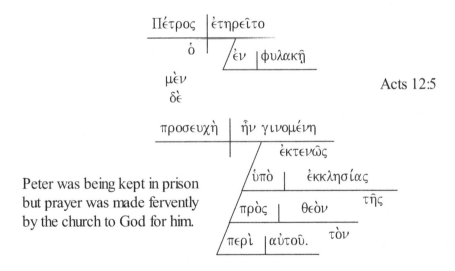

Πέτρος | ἐτηρεῖτο
ὁ
ἐν | φυλακῇ

μέν
δέ

Acts 12:5

προσευχὴ | ἦν γινομένη
ἐκτενῶς
ὑπὸ | ἐκκλησίας
τῆς
πρὸς | θεὸν
τὸν
περὶ | αὐτοῦ.

Peter was being kept in prison
but prayer was made fervently
by the church to God for him.

B. Multiple sentence parts

Sentences containing compound subjects, verbs, etc., are diagrammed according to the following example.

Acts 15:32

Judas and Silas exhorted and strengthened the brothers.

C. The genitive absolute

The genitive absolute is connected to the main part of the sentence by a *broken* line. Genitive absolutes should be classified according to one of the adverbial categories.

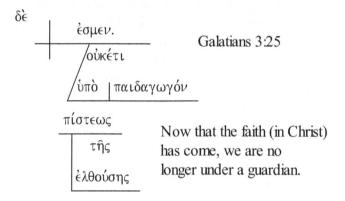

Galatians 3:25

Now that the faith (in Christ) has come, we are no longer under a guardian.

D. The reciprocal relative

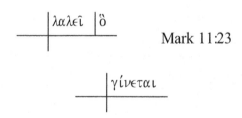

Mark 11:23

... what he says will happen ...

44

Chapter Four—Relationships Between Propositions

Just as we must grasp the syntactical relationships between words in a proposition in order to understand it, so, in order to grasp the text as a whole, we must see how propositions relate as they succeed one another. John Calvin spoke of the need to trace out *le fil du texte* (the thread of the text).[51] We stand no chance of grasping what authors intended until we have thought their thoughts after them, proposition by proposition, and have seen how successive propositions join together.

The purposes of this chapter are first to present a way to classify the various relationships that can exist between propositions, and then to demonstrate a method for visualizing the thread of a text by examples from Philippians, Genesis and Luke.

A Classification of Relationships

A good starting point for understanding the ways propositions can relate to one another is to discern the fundamental difference between a coordinate clause and a subordinate clause within a sentence. Consider the following example of a compound sentence containing a main clause and a secondary clause: "This morning I am going to the market and then I will get the car washed" is a *compound* sentence comprised of a pair of coordinate clauses. Each of these clauses is a part of what constitutes a plan for the morning, and together they state the entire plan. They are coordinate clauses in that one does not support the other in some way, but each makes its own distinct contribution to the whole. A *complex* sentence, on the other hand, would be "I am going to market this morning because company is coming for dinner tonight." The two clauses in this sentence are not of equal rank. They do not both make their separate contribution to one thing. Rather, the second clause, "because company is coming for dinner tonight," states the cause or ground for the proposed action of the first clause, "I am going to market this morning." In that the second clause supports the first clause, it is subordinate to it and not coordinate with it. Just as clauses other than the main clause in a sentence are either coordinate or subordinate, so propositions relate to one another in either a coordinate or subordinate way.

A. Coordinate Relationships

There are three kinds of coordinate relationships: series (S), progression (P), and alternative (A). S, A, and P are shorthand ways to signify these relationships. These symbols and the various symbols for subordinate relationships will be used in the method we will introduce at the end of the chapter to visualize a text.

---

[51] See his commentary on Ephesians 1:10.

Description	Conjunctions	Examples
Series (S) The relationship between clauses each of which makes its independent contribution to the whole	And, likewise, moreover furthermore, etc.	Everyone who asks receives, <u>and</u> the one who seeks finds, <u>and</u> to the one who knocks it will be opened. Matthew 7:8
Progression (P) Like series, but each proposition is a further step toward a climax	Then, plus the ones for S	Those whom he predestined, he also called; <u>and</u> those whom he called, he also justified; <u>and</u> those he justified, he also glorified. Romans 8:30
Alternative (A) Each proposition expresses an opposite possibility arising from a situation	or, but, while, on the other hand	Some were convinced by what he said, <u>while</u> others disbelieved. Acts 28:24

B. Subordinate Relationships

We have already seen how it is the essential nature of a subordinate clause to play a supportive role. An analysis of the several kinds of subordinate adverbial clauses shows that support is rendered in three different ways: by restatement, by distinct statement, and by contrary statement.

(1) Support by restatement

A MODAL clause, for example, supports a main clause by restating it. In the sentence, "God did not leave himself without a witness, in that he did good and gave you rains from heaven and fruitful seasons" (Acts 14:17), the clause introduced by "in that ..." repeats the statement of the main clause in a more detailed way. By giving us rain, springtime and harvest, God witnesses to his existence. The mention of rain and fruitful seasons supports the first proposition because it is not independent of it but stands in the service of the first proposition, spelling out in more detail the "way" God gave witness, that is conveying "how" he accomplished this. The symbols that represent this relationship of action and manner is (Ac/Mn —sometimes this relationship is also referred to as "way/end").

A COMPARATIVE clause also restates the main clause. In Paul's command, "Be imitators of me, even as I also am [an imitator] of Christ (1 Corinthians 11:1), the clause introduced by "even as ..." makes clearer the meaning he intends by the main clause "Be imitators of me." A comparative clause restates, and in so doing, makes the meaning of the main clause more precise. (__/Cf ; the "__" in this and some following symbol sets refers to the member of the set that receives no symbol when indicating the

46

relationship that exists between the two propositions). Whereas a modal clause details the meaning of the main clause by telling us 'how,' a comparative clause makes the meaning of the main clause more specific by citing the model after which it is patterned.

A *negative* comparative clause provides another nuance in the way one clause or proposition can restate an adjacent proposition. An example of such a clause is found in Acts 2:25, "These people are not drunk, as you suppose [they are drunk]." Here the comparative clause states what is the exact opposite of the main clause, and, at first sight, seems to do anything but restate the main clause. Yet restatement is really what is happening. The two clauses set forth alternative possibilities for explaining how the apostles are speaking in tongues: (1) that they are inebriated, and (2) another reason which Peter later specifies as the infilling of the Holy Spirit. But while these two possibilities are opposites, the relationship between these clauses is not alternative (A—described above). Note that one of the alternatives is denied in order to enforce and emphasize the truth of the other, whereas in the (A) relationship, both sides stand without either being negated. What we have in Acts 2:15 is not an alternative but a POSTITIVE-NEGATIVE relationship (+/–); that the apostles are drunk is denied in order to enforce the truth of the alternative that their speaking in tongues comes from being filled with the Holy Spirit.

Sometimes we must classify a comparative clause that states a greater or lesser degree than the action of the main clause. In 1 Corinthians 15:10 Paul said, "I worked harder than all of them [worked]." Here the comparative clause "than all of them worked" is not a restatement of "I worked harder" because it talks of work that is less energetic than Paul's. Perhaps the best classification for this sort of a comparative is progression (P), because the same category of thought is in both propositions (i.e., working in ministry), but the main clause's proposition has an ascendency over that of the subordinate clause. If Paul had said he worked less hard than any of them worked, then the subordinate clause would be in progression or ascendancy over the main clause.

In the following table of restatements, the first three are relationships we have already illustrated from two subordinate clauses, the modal and the comparative. The remaining one is a nuance of restatement which finds no counterpart in a subordinate clause.

Description	Conjunctions	Examples
Action-Manner (Ac/Mn) An action and a more precise statement indicating the way or manner in which the action is carried out. (Also called Way-End.)	in that, by, (participles)	[God] has given assurance [that he will judge the world through Christ] in that he raised him from the dead. (Acts 17:31)
Comparison (__/Cf) An action and a statement that clarifies	even as, as...so, like, just as	As my father has sent me, so I send you. (John 20:21)

47

Description	Conjunctions	Examples
that action by showing what it is like.		Cf. 1 Corinthians 11:1; 1 Thessalonians 2:7
Negative-Positive (–/+) Two statements, one of which is denied so that the other is enforced. This is also the relationship implicit in contrasting statements. Sequence can be reversed.	Not ... but	Do not be foolish, but understand what the will of the Lord is (Ephesians 5:17). Cf. 1 Corinthians 4:10 for an example of contrast.
Idea-Explanation (Id/Exp) The relationship between a statement and another clarifying its meaning. The clarifying proposition may expound on, or specify, only one word of the associated proposition or its entirety.	That is, in other words, for,[52] specifically	Jacob has supplanted me these two times: he took my birthright and now he has taken my blessing. (Genesis 27:36) They drank of the rock that followed them, and the rock was Christ. (1 Corinthians 10:4)

(2) Support by Distinct Statement

A causal clause supports a main clause by setting forth a proposition distinct from the main proposition. In the sentence "I thank my God through Jesus Christ for all of you, because your faith is proclaimed in all the world" (Romans 1:8), the clause introduced by "because ..." is not supporting the main clause by clarifying its meaning in some way, but rather by citing a distinct and separate proposition as support for it. The reason that Paul gives thanks is the fact that the faith of the Roman church is so vital that its fame has spread widely. The same is true when the causal clause comes first, as in the following instance: "Since you thrust [the word of God] from you and judge yourselves unworthy of eternal life, behold, we turn to the Gentiles" (Acts 13:46). When this relationship exists between propositions separated by a period, the conjunction introducing the second proposition is "For" when the cause comes second and "Therefore" when the cause comes first. Whether in the same sentence or not, when the causal clause precedes the main clause, we label the relationship as INFERENCE (__/∴); when the causal clause follows the main clause, we label the relationship as GROUND (__/G).

A RESULT clause distinguishes itself from a causal clause by stressing how the proposition of the main clause necessarily leads to a certain result, as in the sentence, "There

---

[52] 'For' usually introduces a ground clause. However, sometimes, it introduces an explanation to clarify what has proceeded. E.g., Ephesians 2:8 "For by grace you have been saved ..." John 4:9 "For Jews have no dealings with Samaritans."

as a great earthquake, <u>so that</u> the foundations of the prison were shaken" (Acts 16:26). There is a subtle difference between a main ... result clause relationship and a causal ... main clause relationship. Acts 16:26 could be reworded so it would have a causal clause, and then it would read, "Since there was a great earthquake, the foundations of the prison were shaken." But this causal ... main clause sequence does not stress so much the effectuality of the earthquake in shaking the prison foundations as does the main ... result clause sequence. The symbol for the action-result relationship is Ac/Res.

A CONDITIONAL ... main clause sequence is a close cousin of the action ... result clause sequence. By saying, "<u>If</u> you walk by the Spirit, you will not fulfill the desires of the flesh" (Galatians 5:16), the inescapable tie-in between the cause and effect is maintained, but the reality of the cause leading to such a result or effect is viewed as potential rather than actual. The symbol for representing the conditional relationship is If/Th.

A main ... PURPOSE clause sequence is the fourth instance of a subordinate clause that falls into the category of support by distinct statement. This sequence differs from the main ... result clause sequence in that the result of the action of the main clause is something more hoped for or intended than what automatically results from such action. In saying "to the weak I became weak, <u>that</u> I might win the weak" (1 Corinthians 9:22), Paul was stressing his intention, rather than what would inescapably result in winning the weak. The symbol for representing the action ... purpose relationship is Ac/Pur.

A TEMPORAL clause is another subordinate clause which renders support by distinct statement. Sometimes this support consists of little more than the occasion for the action of the main clause, as in Acts 1:13, "<u>When</u> they had entered, they went up to the upper room." However, often there is a causal note in it, as in Luke 6:22, "Fortunate are you <u>when</u> people hate you." The temporal relationship is represented __/T

A LOCATIVE clause supports the action of the main clause (L/__) by declaring the confines within which an action takes place, as "<u>where</u> two or three are gathered in my name, there I am in their midst" (Matthew 18:20). The causal idea appears in this subordinate clause so that it constitutes one more nuance of a support by distinct statement.

The following table summarizes the various ways one proposition can support another by distinct statement.

Description	Conjunctions	Examples
Ground (__/G) The relationship between a statement and the argument or basis on which it stands. G is used when the supporting argument follows the proposition being supported.	For, because, since	Fortunate are the poor in spirit, for theirs is the kingdom of heaven. (Matthew 5:3) Cf. Philippians 2:25–26

49

Description	Conjunctions	Examples
Inference (__/∴) The relationship between a statement and the supporting argument or basis on which it stands. ∴ is used when the supporting argument precedes the proposition being supported.	Therefore, wherefore, consequently, accordingly	The scribes and the Pharisees sit in Moses' seat. <u>Therefore</u>, pay attention to what they tell you and do it. (Matthew 23:2–3) Cf. 1 Peter 5:5b–6
Action-Result (Ac/Res) An action and a consequence or result which accompanies that action. (Also called Cause-Effect.)	So … that, so that, that	God <u>so</u> loved the world <u>that</u> he gave his one and only Son. (John 3:16)
Conditional (If/Th) Like Ac/Res, except the cause's actual existence is only a potential and the result is contingent upon that action. Sequence can be reversed.	If … then, if, provided, except	<u>If</u> you love me, keep my commandments. (John 14:15) Cf. Galatians 5:16; Romans 8:9
Action-Purpose (Ac/Pur) An action and its intended result. (Also called Means-End.)	In order that, so that, that, lest	I long to see you, <u>that</u> I might impart some spiritual gift to strengthen you. (Romans 1:11) Cf. 1 Corinthians 9:22, 27
Bilateral (BL) A proposition that supports two other propositions, one preceding and one following.	because, therefore, so, for	At that time Menahem sacked Tiphsah and all who were in it ... <u>because</u> they did not open it to him. <u>Therefore</u>, he sacked it. (2 Kings 15:16)
Temporal (T/__) A statement and the occasion when it is true or can occur.	When, after, before, whenever	<u>When</u> you fast, do not look dismal. (Matthew 6:16) You are fortunate <u>when</u> people hate you. (Luke 6:22)
Locative (L/__) A statement and the place where it is true or can occur.	Wherever, where	<u>Where</u> you go, I will go. (Ruth 1:16)

(3) Support by Contrary Statement

The only one of the nine adverbial clauses yet to be mentioned is the CONCESSIVE clause. An example of it is Hebrews 5:8, "<u>Although</u> he was a son, he learned obedience through what he suffered." The concessive clause presents an obstacle to the proposition of the main clause, but because the main clause stands despite this obstacle, the conces-sive clause actually supports it by highlighting the strength it has to stand against oppo-sition. We consider the main clause to be adversative to the subordinate, concessive clause. The sequence can be reversed; and we should be careful to distinguish this type of clause from the alternative (A) and the negative-positive (–/+) relationships.

There are two more relationships which are peculiar in that they can function either in a concessive way or as one of the two kinds of supporting roles. These relationships are the QUESTION/ANSWER and the SITUATION/RESPONSE.

Description	Conjunctions	Examples
Concessive (__/Csv) A main clause that stands despite a contrary statement. (Also called Adversative.)	though, yet, nevertheless, but, although, however	<u>Though</u> you may have ten thou-sand guardians in Christ, you do not have many fathers. (1 Corin-thians 4:15) Cf. 9:19; Hebrews 5:8
Question-Answer (Q/An) When the answer is opposite to that implied or expected by the question, a Q functions as a concessive clause	(question mark)	Shall we continue in sin that grace may abound? Absolutely not! (Romans 6:1–2)
Question-Answer (Q/An) When an answer contains no surprise, it functions as a re-statement of the question		What does Scripture say? Abra-ham believed God. (Romans 4:3)
Situation-Response (Sit/R) When a person responds in a way not intended by the situa-tion that another creates the Sit functions as a concessive.		How often I have longed to gather your children together as a hen gathers her chicks under her wings, but you would have none of it! (Matthew 23:37) Cf. Jere-miah 25:4–7
Situation-Response (Sit/R) When the response accords with the situation that has cre-ated it, Sit/R functions like Ac/Res		I did one deed, and you all mar-vel at it. (John 7:21)

From the fact that clauses were used in the foregoing to illustrate the relationships that can exist between propositions, we must not infer that standard subject/verb clauses are the only forms in which propositions can appear. Participial phrases, infinitival clauses, prepositional phrases, and (rarely) relative clauses can convey propositions whenever the sense of the passage would allow these to be restated as adverbial clauses. Thus, the participial phrase appearing in this sentence, "He who doubts is like a wave of the sea *driven and tossed by the wind*" (James 1:6), has no adverbial function because it does nothing more than describe "wave." But many participial phrases, while linked up grammatically with the substantive they modify (in Greek having the same gender, number, and case as the substantive), nevertheless have a syntactical adverbial relationship that modifies the predicate. These can be restated as adverbial clauses with no change in meaning. "A participle, though a modifier of the subject, has at the same time a peculiar relation to the predicate, because it may take the place of an adverbial clause ... This dual office of the participle comes from its twofold nature as (1) an adjective and (2) a verb."[53] "The adverbial participle logically modifies some other verb of the sentence in which it stands, being equivalent to an adverbial phrase or clause denoting time, condition, concession, cause, purpose, means, manner, or attendant circumstances."[54]

In the following instances where participial phrases behave adverbially, a literal rendering appears that preserves the Greek participle which is sometimes lost in our English translations. The words in brackets show how the participial phrase can be restated as an adverbial clause without changing the meaning.

Conditional (Th/If) "Nothing is to be rejected, *being received with thanksgiving* [if it is received with thanksgiving]" (1 Timothy 4:4).

Concessive (Csv/__) "Who, *being in the form of God* [though he was in the form of God], did not think equality with God as a thing to be grasped" (Philippians 2:6).

Action-Result (Ac/Res) "*Having been justified by faith* [because we have been justified by faith], let us be at peace with God" (Romans 5:1).

Action-Manner (Ac/Mn) "You killed him *hanging him on a tree* [in that you hung him on a tree]" (Acts 5:30).

Temporal (T/__) "*They speaking these things* [As they spoke these things], Jesus himself stood in their midst" (Luke 24:36). Note: The grammatical form in the Greek is a genitive absolute. This form usually functions adverbially.

Similarly, infinitives function adverbially.

"God sent him *to bless you* [that he might bless you (Ac/Res)] [to bless you (Ac/Pur)]" (Acts 3:26). While the infinitive modifies the direct object (him) grammatically in the Greek, it sustains an adverbial relationship to the predicate. As we see from the brackets, the infinitive clause can function as either a result clause or a purpose clause.

---

[53] G. L. Kittredge and F. E. Farley, *An Advanced English Grammar* (Boston: Ginn and Company, 1913), p. 194.
[54] Ernest De Witt Burton, *Syntax of the Moods and Tenses in New Testament Greek* (Edinburgh: T & T Clark, 1989), p. 169.

"God gave them up to a reprobate mind, *to do* the things which are not fitting [so that they would do the things which are not fitting]" (Romans 1:32). This is another example of an infinitive clause that sets forth a separate proposition, in this case as a result clause (Ac/Res).

Prepositional phrases can also contain all the meaning of an adverbial clause. In Ephesians 4:18 the Gentiles are spoken of as being darkened in their understanding "*because of* the ignorance that is in them, *because of* the hardening of their hearts" [*because of* is a one-word preposition in the Greek]. It is plain that these phrases would mean exactly the same thing if we read them as adverbial clauses: "because they were ignorant, because their hearts were hardened." Philippians 1:5 is another example. In verse 4 Paul had declared how he prayed for the Philippians with joy, and then in verse 5 he went on to say, "on the basis of your fellowship in the gospel from the first day until now." Stated as an adverbial clause, these two verses would read, "I pray for you with joy (vs 4) because you have worked together with me for the gospel from the first day until now." In tracing through the thread of a text, it is more important to restate some prepositional phrases as adverbial clauses than some others which might also, conceivably, be thus restated. Experience in exegesis will give us a feel for when we should do this.

Before illustrating how propositions are delimited and related in a paragraph of Scripture, we need to consider the nature of indirect discourse. Noun clauses introduced by verbs of telling, thinking, knowing, perceiving, and feeling are statements in indirect discourse. As an example, the italicized words in Job 19:25, "I know *that my redeemer lives*," are indirect discourse. The italicized words are really the proposition, whereas the "I know" simply states the source, and often the mood, of the proposition.

Relating the Propositions of Philippians 1:3–11[55]

In verse 3, "I thank my God in all my remembrance of you," the prepositional phrase can be restated as an adverbial clause so that this verse would yield two propositions: "I thank my God" (3a), and "as/when I remember what is true about you" (3b). Thus, the second clause functions as a temporal clause modifying the first, or main, clause.

A literal rendering of verse 4 is "always in every petition of mine for you all, with joy making the petition." ("In every petition of mine" is a prepositional phrase that could be reworded as an adverbial clause, but we do not bother to do so because it does not have as vital a function for what follows as 3b does.) The emphasis in this verse is the joy which Paul experiences even when he prays about things in the Philippian church which are not right. It is not difficult to see how verse 4, then, gives a clearer understanding of the thanksgiving that Paul has for the Philippians (3a). Verses 3a, and 4 can then be rephrased as follows: "I thank my God ... <u>in that</u> I make every petition on your behalf

---

[55] The translations of the various parts of this passage in what follows are based on my understanding of the Greek and do not follow any standard English version.

with joy." Verse 3 relates to verse 4 as Action to Manner, since verse 4 functions as a modal clause.

What then shall we do with verse 5, "on the basis of your participation in the gospel from the first day until now"? It provides a cause for the joy Paul has for the Philippians even when he is petitioning God to correct things that are not right. We can reword it as a causal clause without changing its sense: "Because you have participated in the [spreading of the] gospel from the first day until now," and as such it provides the ground/cause for verse 4.

We can visualize all of this by doing the following: (1) Represent the propositions as a chain of arcs on a straight line. (2) Put references for each arc just beneath the line. (3) Place the various relationship symbols, listed above, under the arcs so that they will signify the way each proposition relates to what precedes—some propositions that relate only forward are exceptions to this rule. (4) Beneath all of this, compose an exposition of the text in which the relationship between each proposition becomes explicit by using appropriate, underlined, connective words. (5) It is helpful to represent each proposition by a straight line of about the length of the arc's diameter and placed directly below its corresponding arc. Those which support by a restatement of what precedes will go on the same level; those supporting by distinct statement will go one notch below what they support. Those supporting by contrary statement will go somewhat beneath what they support but will have a slant line going back to the end of their support to signify that they are opposite to it.

A visual representation of Philippians 1:3–5 will then appear as follows:

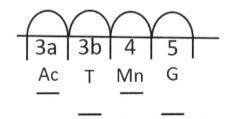

3a   I thank my God
3b   when I remember all that is true about you
4   in that I make every petition on your behalf with joy
5   because you have participated in the [spreading of the] gospel from the first day until now.

The participle that introduces verse 6 does more than just tell interesting details about the Paul who petitions in verse 4. Along with verse 5, it presents a cause, a more basic cause, for the joy Paul experienced even as he petitioned God to correct the wrongs in the Philippian church. Together verses 5 and 6 constitute what is involved in the "remember" of 3b. (This is why we took the trouble to make a proposition out of 3b.) The Philippians' faithfulness in helping Paul with the gospel (vs 5) caused some of his joy, but a far greater cause was that Paul was "persuaded of this very thing, namely, that God who had begun a good work among them would go right on perfecting it until the day of Jesus Christ."

In verse 7 Paul justifies this confidence that God will complete his perfecting work with a clause saying "even as it is right for me to have my thoughts on your behalf so disposed." "Even as" often introduces a comparative phrase, but here it introduces a causal one. The Greek attaches to this clause a prepositional phrase, "on account of my having you in my heart," which gives the basis upon which Paul can justify this confidence regarding God's work among the Philippians. Because this prepositional phrase gives the basis for his purported "rightness," it is important enough that we rephrase it as a causal clause: "because I have you in my heart" (7b). What then should we do with the three prepositional phrases that follow, and the "fellow participants with me of grace all you being" with which verse 7 concludes? Do the prepositional phrases modify "I have you in my heart" or do they modify "fellow participants ... being"?[56] The latter is more preferable because it would be strange for Paul to say he has the Philippians in his heart only when he is in prison and when he is being tried for his stand for the gospel. Much better sense comes by construing these phrases to modify "fellow participants ... being," for then Paul has the Philippians in his heart precisely because the Philippians (not Paul), both in his bonds and in his defense and consequent confirmation of the gospel, have been fellow participants with him of the grace that comes from God. That is, they have not despised his plight when he has been imprisoned and tried (as now) for the gospel but have rather been moved by the grace of God to share with Paul in his sufferings by sending him money (cf. 4:15–16). Consequently this last part of verse 7 would provide a reason why Paul has the Philippians in his heart: "I have you in my heart (7b) because both in my imprisonment and in the confirmation that results from my defense of the gospel, you are fellow participants with me in the grace that comes from God" (7c). (Note that 7c is an example of how a participle modifies a direct object which also has an adverbial function in that it provides a cause for the preceding proposition.)

For Paul to have the Philippians in his heart (7b) is an expression of his deep affection for them, but if this is all that it means, it would be difficult to see how this would justify the confidence (7a) that he expressed in verse 6. (Just because Paul has deep affection for some people is not a very good reason why God will cause them to persevere to the end.) How could Paul's deep affection for the Philippians (7b), caused by their sharing in his sufferings (7c), support the confidence that God will go on perfecting his good work until Christ's judgment day? It is verse 8 that provides this confidence: "For God is my witness how deeply I long for you all with the tender mercies that stem from Jesus Christ." Since the deep affection Paul has for the Philippians stems from the very heart of Jesus Christ, and thus is an expression of the love that Jesus himself has for the Philippians, then surely Christ will go on working for them. Thus, if Jesus, who lives in Paul's heart through the Holy Spirit, has such love for the Philippians, then, not only will Paul experience a deep affection for them but Jesus, because he loves them so, will surely complete his work so they can pass muster on his judgment day. Thus, verse 8,

---

[56] For more on how to ask and answer this type of question, see Chapter Five "Reading As Asking Questions."

along with 7c, is a cause for 7b, but unlike 7c, the cause stated in verse 8 makes Paul's affection something that does justify the confidence he expresses in verse 6.

A visual representation of Philippians 1:6–8 will appear as follows:

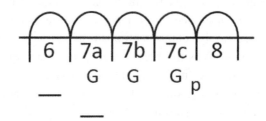

6   (I rejoice over you even when I petition God about your failings—vs 4)
6   and for the even greater reason (than vs 5) that I am convinced that God will complete the good work he began among you
     (I have this conviction—vs 6)
7a   because it is right for me to have it
          (It is right for me to have it—vs 7a)
7b   because I have a deep affection for you
              (I have this deep affection—vs 7b)
7c   because, in helping me, you share with me in God's grace, which enables me to stand for the gospel
8   and, even more, because Christ's own compassion inspires this affection (thus, since Jesus loves you so, therefore—vs 6—God will keep on working for you).

Verses 9–11 are a prayer which follows naturally from Paul's intense longing that he just mentioned in verse 8. The "and" which connects verses 8 and 9 signifies the connection between this longing and the prayer that immediately follows. This longing is so intense that prayer must necessarily result; so, verse 8 is to verse 9 as Ac to Res. The prayer of verses 9–11 consists of two successive noun clauses, which are in apposition to the "this" (vs 9) and are the indirect speech introduced by "I pray." Therefore, we should not consider the verb "pray" as a rallying point for a proposition; that honor belongs to the first predicate of the first noun clause. The first proposition of verse 9 is that "the love of the Philippians might abound more and more in knowledge and all discernment."

This abounding should then result "in their approving the things that are excellent" (verse 10a). This prepositional phrase, which has an infinitive clause as the object of the preposition, establishes the basis upon which the next clause stands, and therefore, we should reword it as an adverbial clause, "so that you might distinguish between the things that really excel and those which are merely good." Thus, 10a relates to verse 9 as result clause (Res) to action clause (Ac). The ἵνα in the middle of verse 10 cannot be coordinate with the first ἵνα back in verse 9 because the purpose clause which it introduces is not something that could stand alongside of the clause in that verse. Instead, love must abound in all wisdom and knowledge (9), so that the Philippians will have discernment (10a), and then *the purpose and intent* of this discernment is to make them ready to be genuine and without offense at the day of Christ (10b).

Verse 11 commences with a participle that modifies the predicate of the last proposition of 10b. "Having been filled with the fruit of righteousness ..." is the same as "being genuine and without offense ..."; thus, the participle that introduces verse 11 has the adverbial function of being a modal restatement of 10b: the Philippians will be genuine and without offense at the day of Christ, in that they have been filled with the fruit of righteousness (11a). But lest they be discouraged in thinking they must struggle to be filled with this fruit by their own unaided efforts, Paul adds that the fruit of righteousness comes from Jesus Christ: "You will have been filled with the fruit of righteousness" (11a), says Paul, "in that Christ causes this fruit to abound" (11b). Christ is the one who does this work (11b), in order that all credit might go to God (11c).

This last phrase, reworded as a purpose clause, is not necessarily supported by the prior clause, for often a purpose is cited as a supportive argument for what precedes. In dealing with the Ac/Res, Ac/Pur and S/R type of relationships, we must always try to detect *from the context* whether a purpose or a result have been presented as arguments in support of a proposition or whether they themselves are supported by their counterparts. It is plain from the context of this passage that while Paul exhorts the Philippians to increase in discernment, he does not want them to conclude that they must do this by their unaided efforts. So, in verse 6 as well as in 11b he stresses that it is God who enables them to succeed. As an *argument* for this he cites the fact that his readers will accept, namely, that God works so as to receive all credit for their success. Therefore, in the diagram for verses 9–11, the 11c line goes below the 11b line.

What then of the line for the purpose clause of 10b? Should it be above or below 10a? In answering this question, we must remember that the more specific, determinate idea will represent the high point of Paul's prayer, while general ideas, such as being ready for the day of Christ, are more suited for an argument. Verse 4 indicates that Paul is making specific petitions for the Philippians, and therefore, the most specific thing in the prayer of verses 9–11 is the high point, while the rest of the text is supportive. For this reason, we consider 10a to be the main point of Paul's prayer, for it is the statement that is least general.

The following is a visualization of this prayer. Note that in the pairs Ac/Pur, Ac/Res and S/R we will circle the member of the pair that is supported, that is, the member that is on a higher logical level.

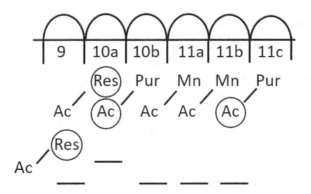

9 <u>Therefore, as a result of Christ's love for you</u> (cf. vs 8) <u>and because I am so thankful</u> (cf. vs 3a, 4) for how you have lived, I pray that your love might abound increasingly in mature knowledge and all discernment.

10a <u>so that</u> you will be able to distinguish between what is best and what is merely good.

10b <u>in order that</u> (<u>for</u>, in so doing)[57] you will be genuine and without offense at the judgment

11a <u>in that</u> you will have been filled with the fruit of righteousness

11b <u>in that</u> Christ causes it to abound
   (Christ causes righteousness to abound—vs 11b)

11c   <u>in order that</u> (<u>for</u>, in so doing) God gets all of the credit.

Thus by (1) delimiting the successive propositions, (2) determining the relationships between them, and (3) determining (in certain cases) which of two propositions supports the other, we are able to follow a paragraph's train of thought.

The next diagram is a visualization of all of Philippians 1:3–11. In this diagram all of the arcs have been joined together into larger and larger ones, until one arc covers the entire paragraph. The basic principle on which we construct this diagram is that when we join two arcs, the one idea the resulting larger arc is saying is what the *supported* unit is saying, not the supporting unit. Notice how relationships corresponding to subordinate clauses go up underneath the apex of an arc. Study the following representation of Philippians 1:3–11 to see how *all* of the relationship underneath a line find their proper place above the line. Since not all relationships have a *pair* of symbols (e.g., G, ∴, Csv, as well as S, A, P), not every arc has a symbol under it. Finally, note that since verse 8 supports both what precedes as well as what follows, we cannot combine it with arcs representing the propositions it supports in both directions. It is appropriate that verse 8 should stand alone under the largest arc, because it is the keystone of the whole passage.

---

[57] When either the result or purpose clause argues for what would correspond to the main clause, we should make clear in the exposition of the text its function of providing support for the main clause.

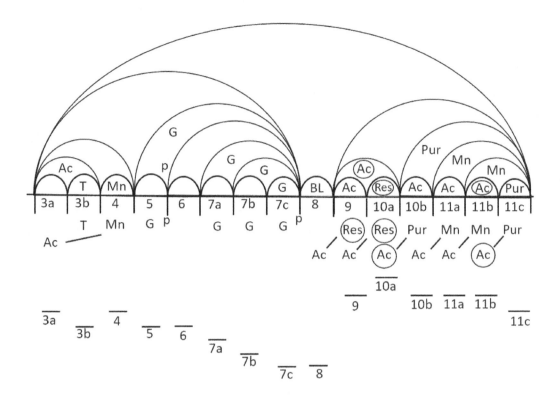

3a   I thank my God

3b   when I remember all that is true about you

4   in that I make every petition on your behalf with joy

5   because you have participated in the [spreading of the] gospel from the first day until now.

6   and for the even greater reason (than vs 5) that I am convinced that Christ will complete the good work he began among you
(I have this conviction—vs 6)

7a   because it is right for me to have it
(It is right for me to have it—vs 7a)

7b   because I have a deep affection for you
(I have this deep affection—vs 7b)

7c   because, in helping me, you share with me in God's grace, which enables me to stand for the gospel

8   and, even more, because Christ's own compassion inspires this affection (thus, since Jesus loves you so, therefore [vs 6] he will keep on perfecting you).

9   Therefore, as a result of Christ's love for you (cf. vs 8) and because I am so thankful (cf. vs 3a, 4) for how you have lived, I pray that your love might increasingly abound in mature knowledge and all discernment.

10a   so that you will be able to distinguish between what is best and what is merely good.

10b   in order that (for, in so doing) you will be genuine and without offense at the judgment

11a	<u>in that</u> you will have been filled with the fruit of righteousness
11b	<u>in that</u> Christ causes it to abound
	(Christ causes righteousness to abound—vs 11b)
11c	<u>in order that</u> (<u>for</u>, in so doing) God gets all of the credit.

Further instructions for drawing the larger arc:

1. The major problem in drawing the larger arcs is determining where to begin to connect two of the smallest arcs together. We do not join a supporting arc with a supported arc (or, in other words, a secondary arc with a primary arc) until we know that the supporting arc is not itself supported in some way. If we join a secondary arc with a primary one, the one idea the resulting larger unit will be saying is simply what the supported (primary) arc is saying, not what the supporting (secondary) arc is saying (except in cases of restatement when supports by restatement inform the primary arc with the meaning supplied by their restatement). We should always begin with the lowest level relationships. If we join a secondary arc with a primary one when that secondary arc has its own support, we then rule out relating that secondary arc's support to the higher secondary arc, for that secondary arc no longer figures in the one idea that the arc of which it is now a part is saying.

2. Bi-Lateral support: Verse 8 in the preceding set of arcs must stand by itself because it has the peculiar function of supporting both 7b and 9. It must stand by itself, since if it were linked up in either direction, it would no longer be able to express its relationship (except by the symbols under the line) in the other direction. Thus, we call such units bi-lateral units. They are *bi*-lateral in that they support in *two* directions, forward and backwards.

This section is followed by more examples. For even more instruction and examples, see Appendix B at the end of the book. For help construing the remainder of Philippians 1–2, see Appendix C.

Video instruction and computer-aided arc drawing is available at www.biblearc.com.

Examples and Hints

Philippians 1:12–18 In the section below is my rewording of this passage in propositional format. Copy this onto a separate sheet of paper and practice relating and arcing the propositions in this paragraph before looking at my solution that follows.

12   My imprisonment has resulted not in a hindrance but in an advance of the gospel.

13   <u>One way this has happened</u> is that my imprisonment for Christ has resulted in a testimony that has gone to all the Praetorian guard and others.

14a   <u>Another way</u> the gospel has been advanced is this: <u>Because</u> of my example,

14b   many of the brethren have had the courage to preach the Word of God

15a   <u>That is,</u> <u>even though</u> there are those who preach Christ from a spirit of envy

15b   Others do it from a spirit of good will.

16a   <u>Let me tell you what I mean:</u> Some people preach Christ through love

16b   <u>because</u> they know that I am set for the defense of the gospel;

17a   <u>but</u> others preach Christ through strife

17b   <u>because</u> they hope they might make it more difficult for me.

18a   How do we summarize all of this?

18b   Christ is being preached here at Rome regardless of motive.

18c   <u>My response</u> to Christ's being preached is to rejoice.

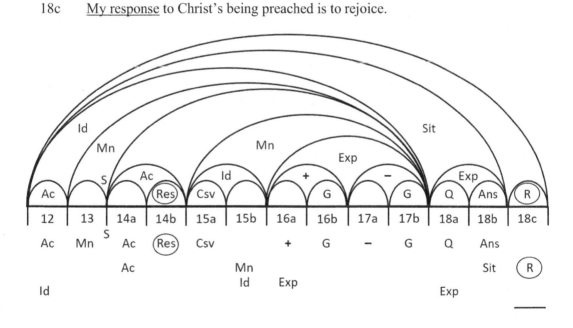

Genesis 32:10–12

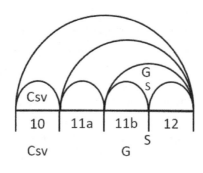

10   <u>Although</u> I am not worthy of the least of your benefits,
11a   <u>Nevertheless,</u> I am asking you to deliver me from Esau
11b   <u>For</u> I fear lest he slay all of us
12   <u>And</u> you have promised to preserve me and my posterity.

Note that verse 10 concludes with two sentences. These do not receive arcs because they only function to expand the subordinate part of the predication of the first part of 10; namely, they detail what God's extraordinary kindness and faithfulness to Jacob consist in.

In verse 12 "lest" often introduces negative purpose clauses. Here, however, it functions like the conjunction "that", introducing a noun clause, which is the direct object of "fear." Therefore the "lest" in this case does not introduce a new predication.

Luke 12:4–7

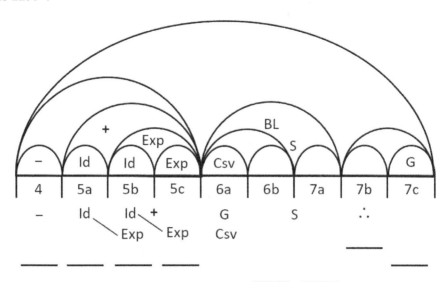

4   Do <u>not</u> fear those who kill the body and that's all they can do,

5a   <u>but</u> I will warn you whom to fear.

5b   <u>I mean</u> you are to fear the One who kills and casts into hell.

5c   <u>I really mean</u> you are to fear him!

6a   <u>For</u>   although sparrows are of very little value

6b   <u>yet</u> God is concerned about every sparrow;

7a   <u>and</u> God even counts the number of your hairs.

7b   <u>Therefore,</u> do not fear anyone but God

7c   <u>For</u> you are worth more than the sparrows

Luke 12:22–31

Here is the text for Luke 12:22–31 from the English Standard Version (ESV). This time before you look at the arcing for this passage, rewrite this text according to the models we have presented above; then prepare your own diagram of this text. Two suggestions as you do this: (1) Regard the imperative "consider" merely as a verb introducing indirect discourse. (2) Rhetorical questions are not followed by an explicit answer; they require that we rephrase them as declarative statements before they can be paraphrased, related and arced.

> ... Do not be anxious about your life, what you will eat, nor about your body, what you will put on. [23] For life is more than food, and the body more than clothing. [24] Consider the ravens: they neither sow nor reap, they have neither storehouse nor barn, and yet God feeds them. Of how much more value are you than the birds! [25] And which of you by being anxious can add a single hour to his span of life? [26] If then you are not able to do as small a thing as that, why are you anxious about the rest? [27] Consider the lilies, how they grow: they neither toil nor spin, yet I tell you,

even Solomon in all his glory was not arrayed like one of these. [28] But if God so clothes the grass, which is alive in the field today, and tomorrow is thrown into the oven, how much more will he clothe you, O you of little faith! [29] And do not seek what you are to eat and what you are to drink, nor be worried. [30] For all the nations of the world seek after these things, and your Father knows that you need them. [31] Instead, seek his kingdom, and these things will be added to you.

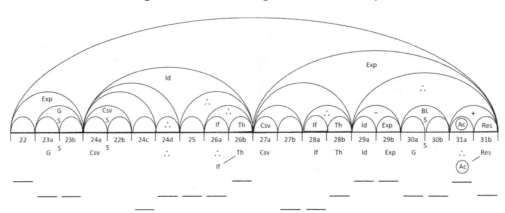

22	Do not be anxious about what is needed to sustain your animating principle or your body,
23a	for your animating principle (given by God) is far greater than the food needed to support it,
23b	and your body is something far greater than the clothes it needs to wear [in other words, if God does the greater, he will surely do the lesser.]
24a	Although the ravens do not cultivate
24b	nor do they build barns,
24c	yet God feeds them.
24d	Therefore, God will feed you who are of more value than birds.
25a	None of you by being anxious can prolong your animating principle's life span at all
26a	If you are so devoid of power to sustain your animating principle,
26b	Then you ought not be anxious about getting what is needed to sustain it.
27a	Although lilies do not labor to achieve their beauty,
27b	Yet they are more glorious than Solomon.
28a	If God clothes short-lived grass so luxuriantly,
28b	then he will surely clothe those who trust him.
29a	Therefore, do not seek things need for life's support;
29b	That is, don't seek them anxiously
30a	because God's people are supposed to be different than the world's people,
30b	and God knows perfectly well what you need;
31a	but seek his kingdom,
31b	for then all of these things will be yours as well.

64

Chapter Five—Reading as Asking Questions

People generally agree that the objective they want to attain when they read (or listen) to what other people have to say is to think the communicators' thoughts after them. As Mortimer Adler put it in his *How to Read a Book*, "Successful communication occurs … where what the writer wanted to have received finds its way into the reader's possession."[58]

When someone other than ourselves seeks to impart not only information but a different way of looking at things (from that to which we are accustomed), then we read in order to gain understanding and insight. This sort of reading requires the hardest sort of work. As Adler put it,

> The most direct sign that you have done the work of reading is fatigue. Reading that is reading entails the most intense mental activity. If you are not tired out, you probably have not been doing the work. Far from being passive and relaxing, I have always found what little reading I have done the most arduous and active occupation. I often cannot read more than a few hours at a time, and I seldom read much in that time. I usually find it hard work and slow work.[59]

The reason that reading for understanding is so difficult is that it requires thinking. "The art of thinking," says Adler, "is the art of learning through being taught or through unaided research."[60] Our concern here is not the art of thinking through research but the thinking involved in learning what someone else has to teach us.

Since reading for understanding (and not merely for information or diversion) produces such fatigue, people have devised many excuses for side-stepping the task. As James Bryce (1838–1922) put it,

> To the vast majority of mankind nothing is more agreeable than to escape from the need for mental exertion … To most people, nothing is more troublesome than the effort of thinking.[61]

We often quickly fling aside authors whose thoughts are not immediately clear with the remark, "Why can't that person write clear English?" But whenever authors are imparting understanding, or insight, or a new way of looking at things, they will always say things which seem strange and, at the outset, incoherent with other things that they are saying. But if we work to pick up the clues that indicate the peculiar way in which they are looking at the world, or a certain segment of it, and then piece all of those clues together (indexing and trying to draw schematic diagrams are an essential part of real

---

[58] Mortimer J. Adler, *How to Read a Book* (New York: Simon and Schuster, 1940), p. 24.
[59] *Ibid.*, p. 110.
[60] *Ibid.*, p. 82.
[61] James Brice, *Studies in History and Jurisprudence* (New York: Oxford University Press, 1901), Vol. II, p. 7–8.

reading), then the moment arrives when our mind, in its indefatigable quest for coherence, lights upon a way of grasping that new, but coherent, way of viewing a subject. Then we receive that most gratifying "lift" that comes from seeing coherency where there was only apparent chaos.

The philosopher, John Dewey, pointed out one of the best ways to subject ourselves to the hard work of thinking in order that we might then attain that "lift" which makes the effort worthwhile. He said, "We never think until we are confronted with a problem." Adler said much the same thing.

> You need to see how essential a part of reading it is to *be perplexed and know it*. Wonder is the beginning of wisdom in learning from books as well as from nature. If you never ask yourself any questions about the meaning of a passage, you cannot expect the book to give you any insight that you do not already possess. ... The heart of the matter [is reached] by stating the one simple prescription for active reading. It is: *Ask questions while you read—questions that you yourself must try to answer in the course of reading.*[62]

In Chapter Three we considered how diagraming sentences will enable us to engage with the basic building blocks of written communication: propositions. Sometimes this task is not so straightforward as it appears. The same is true for relating and organizing collections of propositions, which we described in Chapter Four. Frequently, we will need to do the "hardest sort of work," which will require us to invest large amounts of time looking at the text. Indeed, when we read the Bible, or any other books that are designed to impart understanding/insight, we must look at a portion of text repeatedly, over an extended period, until we begin to become uneasy about something, and then commence the task of translating this initial, vague uneasiness into a question that will focus our minds on the problem so that we will find it impossible to escape the "troublesome effort of thinking."

How to Ask Good Questions

1. We must make what troubles us evident. E.g., Galatians 1:1 The "not-but" antithesis in this verse stresses how Paul's apostleship was derived exclusively from God and not human beings. But when Paull affirms, positively, that his apostleship is from God, he does not use the preposition "from" but "through," which is the weaker preposition in that it does not stress God as the source of his apostleship as much as "from" would have. Why does Paul use the weaker preposition, when his obvious purpose is to state the divine origin of his apostleship in the strongest possible way?

2. Avoid asking a question whose answer is quite obvious and which appears to provide an occasion for bringing out some insight that we might have for a verse or passage.

---

[62] Mortimer J. Adler; Charles Van Doren, *How to Read a Book* (New York: Simon and Schuster, 1972), p. 123

3. Avoid vague, abstract language. Such language is often an indication of not having pondered what is vaguely troubling us long enough for it to become sharpened, so that our minds are forced to home in on something very specific.

4. Substantiate what troubles us by pinpointing the problem from data in the text, or in its pertinent historical background. Note how the example in 1 above calls attention to the fact that the apparently weaker "through" follows the apparently stronger "from." Sometimes it is helpful to reduce a question to two alternatives.

5. Avoid verbosity. A question that takes too many sentences to formulate arouses the suspicion that what troubles us is still vague, which means we need to ponder the text some more.

6. Avoid asking questions that involve a curiosity about something that is peripheral or incidental to the main line of thought in the text. In the question point out why it is crucial for grasping the main line of thought in the text.

Criteria for Good Answers

1. One part of the answer (often the first statement) should be a direct affirmation that answers the question.

2. The answer should contain persuasive (not merely plausible) arguments based on (1) the philological data in the text, (2) and/or pertinent historical background information, and (3) possibly some axiom (self-evident, or highly probable statement that has an appeal to universality). E.g., Answer to the question about Galatians 1:1—Paul's opponents might have granted that his ministry came ultimately from God, as does the ministry even of non-apostles. But what they were not willing to grant was that Paul's ministry was not through other human beings—that he had never been ordained through a human agency for the gospel ministry. Since the matter of Paul's ordination was the root problem, the preposition "through" is really the stronger one to use and deserves to occupy the climactic position after "from."

3. Avoid verbosity in the answer. Say enough, but just enough, to give the answer and to support it. If the question contained an alternative that has been rejected, then it would be good to show how the rejection of that alternative does not pose an objection to the affirmed answer.

4. Avoid the use of strange words, abstractions, and extraneous material that would make someone reading the question and answer wonder what the point really is.

Examples of Questions and Answers

Philippians 1:7 Because the prepositional phrase "on account of my having you in my heart," gives the basis for the purported "rightness" of Paul's conviction that Christ will complete his work among them (7a), it is important enough that we rephrase it as a causal clause: "because I have you in my heart" (7b). What then should we do with the three prepositional phrases that follow, and the συγκοινωνούς μου τῆς χάριτος πάντας ὑμᾶς ὄντας ("fellow participants with me of grace all you being") with which verse 7 concludes? Do the prepositional phrases modify "I have you in my heart" or do they modify "fellow participants ... being"?

> ANS The latter is more preferable because it would be strange for Paul to say he has the Philippians in his heart only when he is in prison and when he is being tried for his stand for the gospel. Much better sense comes by construing these phrases to modify "fellow participants ... being," for then Paul has the Philippians in his heart precisely because the Philippians (not Paul), both in his bonds and in his defense and consequent confirmation of the gospel, have been fellow participants with him of the grace that comes from God. That is, they have not despised his plight when he has been imprisoned and tried (as now) for the gospel but have rather been moved by the grace of God to share with Paul in his sufferings by sending him money. Consequently this last part of verse 7 would provide a reason why Paul has the Philippians in his heart: "I have you in my heart (7b) because both in my imprisonment and in the confirmation that results from my defense of the gospel, you are fellow participants with me in the grace that comes from God" (7c). (Note that 7c is an example of how a participle modifies a direct object which also has an adverbial function in that it provides a cause for the preceding proposition.)

1 John 1:1–5[63] Why should John use the *neuter* relative pronoun ὅ ("that which/what") five times in relative clauses in this prologue (1:1 [4 X], 3 [1 X]—see also the neuter ταῦτα ("this") in 1:4—while all the time he is obviously referring to the incarnation of the living person, Jesus Christ, who would usually be represented by a masculine relative pronoun?

> ANS. The neuter relative pronoun ὅ was used because the most important thing in John's thinking about Jesus Christ was his spoken message regarding eternal life. [Here is the answer to the question in one sentence right at the beginning. Next comes the evidence purporting to support the validity of this answer.] That John deliberately intended to place primary stress on the message that came from the incarnate Jesus, and only secondary (yet essential!) emphasis on his personhood, is supported by several *facts*: (a) John speaks of a "what" rather than a "who" as existing from the beginning, v. 1; (b) hearing comes before seeing in 1:1; (c) even the seeing of v. 1 is a "seeing" of *what*, a pronoun whose referent[64] is the *message* which has to be supplied as the direct object of the ἀπαγγέλλομεν ("we proclaim") up ahead in 1:3a, the main clause of this complicated sentence of 1:1–3; (d) the "beholding and touching" of 1:1 have as their direct object not the visible and palpable Jesus, as would be expected from such verbs, but again the fourth occurrence of the

---

[63] See my *Walking in the Light: Step by Step Through 1 John* for a question and answer approach to understanding the entire letter.

[64] A constant task in exegesis is the determining of a pronoun's *referent*, the precise word or entity that the pronoun represents.

pronoun "what," whose referent is again that message of 1:3a; (e) also this 4th "what" of 1:1, that was beheld and touched, is modified by "concerning the word ...," and a "word" has to be heard rather than beheld or touched in order for it to convey knowledge; (f) indeed, verse 2 speaks of the life which was manifested and seen, but then the verbs switch to the actions of witnessing and proclaiming, and these require hearing in order for knowledge to be received; (g) and the first element of this message in 1:5[65] is the very abstract and difficult-to-construe concept that "God is light." Since knowledge of an abstraction can come only from words, the abstraction of 1:5 is further evidence that John's concern was to give pre-eminence to propositional revelation, rather than a "personal" revelation.

1 John 1:6 Does walking in darkness (1) consist only of putting up the false front of saying we have fellowship with God, when we don't have it, (so that being candid about our sins means that we would no longer walk in darkness), or (2) or does it involve some other essential, so that walking in darkness consists in sinning in many different ways, even though one is candid about such sinfulness?

ANS. Walking in darkness consists of alternative (2) rather than (1). In other words, hypocrisy is not the root of walking in darkness. I[66] advance two reasons (my "appeal to universality") for affirming that the essence of walking in darkness is something different from hypocrisy (although this other meaning of "walking in darkness" can involve, among many other things, putting up the false front of being a hypocrite). First, if hypocrisy were the root meaning of walking in darkness, then we would be involved in the absurdity of saying that someone who was a flagrant sinner could nevertheless walk in the light so long as that person was candid about all his or her sinning and did not claim to have fellowship with God. Second, verse

---

[65] In exegesis the preference is always to determine meanings from the *immediate context*. Usually the immediate context is the preceding three or four verses. Its exact boundaries are imprecise, but the shorter the distance the exegete goes to get evidence for how to gain a determinate understanding (one thing and not another!) of the meaning of a word or phrase, the less chance there is that his or her conclusion will be mere plausible subjectivity. The immediate context can also, as in this last "fact," lie just one or two verses ahead, when it is obvious that the train of thought remains the same, as here. Beyond these boundaries of the immediate context lies the remote context. We will see examples of special situations where arguments for a word or phrase's meaning can be drawn from it, but usually we ignore it in exegesis, since its size and distance from the word or phrase to be construed open the door for so many plausible possibilities for interpretation, that exegesis would become subjective and lose all claim to validity.

[66] The meaning advanced for every complete unit of communication is only what various individual's minds have construed that meaning to be. In any communication transmitted to a more or less specific audience at a specific time and place, the author of that communication has only one *determinate meaning* (that is one thing and not another) that he or she wants to share with a target audience. The proof of this comes from observing that each time anyone of us speaks or writes, we mean only one thing by each proposition (basically a subject and predicate) which makes up what we say to an audience. This is the basic philosophy of hermeneutics controlling the exegetical principles that I have been advocating in this book. We must advance only those meanings that are based on arguments that have, as Michael Polanyi (*Personal Knowledge*, Routledge and Kegan Paul, 1962) put it, "an appeal to universality." We can never appeal to spiritual illumination as the validation of a construction we put on a biblical passage.

69

7, which states the negative of verse 6 positively, declares that to walk in the light rather than in darkness we must behave in some way that is similar to God's behavior. But it is axiomatic that God's righteousness consists in far more than his just being candid and "up front" about himself.

1 John 4:17 Does the ἐν τούτῳ ("in this"), which tells how God's love is perfected/completed in us, relate (a) back to what is involved in abiding in God's love (4:16), or (b) forward to having boldness in the day of judgment?

ANS. (a), because abiding in love by believing in the love God is expressing toward us will produce a sense of rest, confidence, and boldness which could properly be termed as his love's being made perfect/complete. *Since* this love is the love God has for us and appears not only in his comforting us inwardly but also in his doing good things for us in outward circumstances, it is proper for John to speak of this love as being *with us* (v. 17) as well as in us (v. 16). The ἐν τούτῳ could not connect forward (b) because it is nonsensical to say that an already perfected love (see perfect tense) could give us boldness only in the future day of judgment. But since God perfected his love toward us by expressing it in the past, and since he still operates this way today, this experience can also give us boldness to face the day of judgment in the future.

Job 1:9–11; 2:4–5 What charge does Satan level at God during their conversations?

ANS. Satan accuses God of securing Job's loyalty and affection by means of material benefits. While God compliments Job's righteous lifestyle (1:8; 2:3), Satan counters, not by blaming Job of wrong-doing, but God. By asserting that Job lives righteously only because God makes his physical life pleasant, he implies that God is deficient in some way so as not to be worthy of Job's allegiance.

Job 1–2 By using negative assertions, the author strongly affirms Job's responses to his situation as both appropriate (1:22—his speech was not "distasteful" to God) and righteous (2:10). Someone might object that God was terribly cruel to Job to divest him of wealth and health in this life, since he had done nothing to deserve such catastrophes (2:3), and since nothing visibly worthwhile was accomplished by his remaining true to God despite such losses (the thinking of Job's wife, 2:10). What most worthy end was attained by Job's response to what God permitted Satan to do to him?

ANS. In his response Job loudly and clearly extolled the wisdom, goodness and justice of God's sovereignty in the affairs of men to a world (symbolized by his wife) which did not hold this view. By responding this way, Job demonstrated that maintaining fellowship with God was the most valuable privilege a person could have—more desirable than wealth, children, and even health in this life. To affirm this to be the case in such a world surely amounted to achieving a highly desirable end. But the worthy end achieved by Job's response was the justification of God. Job's response upholds God's contention that he was not guilty of bribing him; Satan's accusations were unfounded. So even though Job was unaware of the drama taking place in God's council, Job's response testifies to the justice of God's dealings with him. In that God can now be seen as righteous, a worthy end has been attained for the reader.

Romans 2:13 Should the statement, "The doers of the law shall be justified," be understood (1) as an abstract possibility of how people will be saved if they keep the law perfectly (though no one ever does), or (2) as signaling the obedience to the law that begins with repentance and banking one's hope on God's kindness (2:4)?

ANS. (2), the latter, because:

(a) The point made in the preceding train of thought is that enjoying God's favor depends on doing righteousness (2:2–3; 6–7; 10–11).

(b) All repentance from sin must be a compliance with the law, because the repentance of 2:4 is a repentance from wickedness (1:32–2:3) to the doing of good works (2:6–7, 10–11), which the law enjoins (2:13).

(c) God's forgiveness of sins is necessarily implied in the kindness he extends to sinful people in urging them to repent. 2:4 makes it clear that repentance is a turning to this kindness and that would be possible only by being assured of God's forgiveness for one's sins.

(d) The "doing of the law" to be justified does not have to mean perfect compliance here anymore than in Romans 8:4, which speaks of the righteous demand of the law as being *fulfilled* in those who walk in the Holy Spirit. But it surely does mean a compliance with the law made possible only by being indwelt by the Holy Spirit (Romans 8:7), for those not indwelt by the Spirit are in such rebellion against God that they cannot even begin to be subject to his law. According to Romans 8:13 only those living according to the Spirit, and not the flesh, will live.

(e) Such repentance is a decisive aspect of gaining acceptance with God, for Paul proceeds to say in 2:14–15 that as a result of the recently-inaugurated Gentile mission, certain Gentiles, not exposed to the law like the Jews, have had a change of heart ("nature"—v. 14) because of the law's being written on their hearts by regeneration (cf. Jeremiah 31:31–34). This repentance is as effectual in bringing them to God as it is for any Jews doing the same. Such Gentiles have had the secrets of their hearts judged and laid bare as they have heard the preaching of the Gospel (v. 16; cf. 1 Corinthians 14:24–25) and so have responded with repentance.

Romans 3:21–22 How shall we construe the genitive phrase πίστεως Ἰησοῦ Χριστοῦ, as an objective genitive (= faith whose object is Jesus Christ) or as a subjective genitive (= the faith/faithfulness of Jesus himself)?

ANS. As a subjective genitive. In v. 21 Paul declares that God's being righteous has been manifested (perfect passive), that is made clearly visible, in the past so all can now see it. He includes at this point an adjectival participial phrase describing this righteousness and then resumes his thought on how God's righteousness was manifested. He says it is made evident by means of the πίστεως Ἰησοῦ Χριστοῦ. Those toward / unto / for whom his righteousness was made clear are those who are characterized by faith—whether Jew or Gentile. Using the objective genitive construction makes Paul say that God's righteousness is currently being manifested to those who believe by their believing in Jesus. But this contradicts the fact stated in 21 that the manifestation occurred in the past. Using the subjective genitive construction as Jesus' faithfulness (cf. 3:3) during his life here on earth enables God's righteousness to be truly and objectively manifested in the past so that it can be seen now, and such a manifestation can be said to have been witnessed by the law and prophets. This construal also coheres with Jesus as the summation of the law in 10:4. Another argument for the subjective genitive is that when πίστις takes a personal genitive it is almost never an objective genitive (e.g., just in Romans 1:8, 12; 3:3; 4:5, 12, 16).]

Romans 5:1 The textual evidence for the hortatory subjunctive ἔχωμεν is supported by "strong evidence" (Barrett), "stunningly testified to" (Käsemann), and the indicative ἔχομεν is "a good deal less strongly attested" (Cranfield); Black says, "The textual evidence is overwhelmingly in favor of the subjunctive," and Metzger (*A Textual Commentary* ...) says that the subjunctive has "far better textual support than the indicative;" nevertheless every one of these expositors and all other commentators and translators, except Sanday & Headlam and Lietzmann, affirm that the indicative form should nevertheless be chosen. Are there persuasive reasons to affirm Paul's use of the hortatory subjunctive in this situation?

ANS. Yes, there are. Cranfield argues that there could be no meaning in saying, "Let us have peace with God," for it is something we already have in that, according to vs. 10f. we have reconciliation as a present possession, and that surely involves having peace with God. But the problem with Cranfield's argument is that the idea of justification at the beginning of vs. 1 already involves having peace with God. And this being the case, an understanding of the "have" in the main clause as an indicative would produce the tautology ("saying the same thing") of having the main clause saying nothing different from the subordinate causal clause "... because we have been justified by faith." Barrett complains that understanding the "have" as "let us have" implies the un-Pauline idea that a man may choose whether or not to have peace with God, but in Colossians 3:15 Paul commands us to let the peace of God rule in our hearts." (Barrett does not seem aware of this subjective, experiential meaning of "having peace with God.") Surely this faith is to be a faith in what God did through Jesus Christ (3:21f.), and as such it must be a faith and an assurance of sins forgiven because of his blood which effected a propitiation for our sins (3:25). But this faith in Jesus Christ must also be a faith directed toward God's promises, which are summed up in Christ (2 Corinthians 1:20 and Romans 15:8). And one such promise is indicated by the "let us have peace" of 5:1, for this hortatory subjunctive has to imply being at rest in the confidence that God will take care of us and that we need not fear. A further argument for honoring the "overwhelming" textual evidence for the ἔχωμεν reading is that it makes much better sense to understand the καυχώμεθα's of vs. 2 and vs. 3 as imperatives rather than as indicatives. Surely we do not just automatically rejoice in hope of the glory of God, and still less do we glory in tribulation—which is the way all these commentators have to read these καυχώμεθα's, since the way one construes the "have" of vs. 1 determines the way these other two verbs will be interpreted, since they are parallel to one another.

So, like Abraham, we have to exercise faith and keep walking in the "steps of Abraham's faith" (4:12) in order that at various points in our lives, as in Abraham's, we might be justified (there were 4 times in Abraham's life when he was justified by an act of faith: when he left Ur; Genesis 15:6; Genesis 17:7 which Paul links up to Genesis 15:6 again in Romans 4:22; and in offering up Isaac, James 2:21, where James quotes Genesis 15:6 to prove that a faith completing itself in works justifies). So, we must glory in tribulation, because otherwise we will not be justified, just as Abraham would not have been justified, if he had persisted in not believing in God's promise that he would have an heir by Sarah. With the emphasis upon this futuristic component in faith, we can understand better why Paul saw no difference in Abraham's futuristic faith and ours (4:22ff).

Chapter Six—Finding the "Whole"

To grasp an author's intended meaning, we must understand the assertion of each of his propositions (Ch. 3), and see how these propositions relate to one another (Ch. 4). But full understanding comes only when we readers grasp the "whole" of all that an author is saying. Without knowledge of this, our grasp of the meaning of each proposition is incomplete, and yet knowledge of the "whole" can only be attained after we have achieved some understanding of the meaning of the propositions and the relationships between them.

This interdependence of the parts and the "whole" is what the term "hermeneutical circle" means. At the outset we must understand that the "whole" does not refer to the aggregate sum of the meanings of each proposition, but rather to the point that an author is trying to get across. The purpose of this chapter is to explain how to break the hermeneutical circle, and then use the way the "whole" of Philippians 1:1–11 completes the meaning of each of its parts as an illustration.

Breaking the Hermeneutical Circle

So long as we use the terms "parts" and "whole" in the statement of the hermeneutical circle, it would seem that all of our attempts to interpret a text necessarily involve us in a vicious circle. In the statement of the hermeneutical circle—that we can fully understand the parts only by reference to the whole they are in, but we can grasp the whole only from the parts—there is the denial of any fixed knowledge that will provide a basis for further knowledge, and all seems quite hopeless. Yet experience proves that we constantly break the hermeneutical circle. People do succeed in understanding us, for their consequent actions accord with our intended meanings most of the time. How then can we state the hermeneutical circle in a way that shows how this is possible?

Mortimer Adler tries to take the viciousness out of the hermeneutical circle by proposing that we can grasp a text's "whole" before we have examined scarcely any of the parts. He declares that "the first stage of analytical reading has been accomplished when you … [can] tell what a book is about and [can] outline its structure."[67] According to Adler, we grasp what a book is about by considering the "front matter"—the title, the subtitle, the table of contents and the preface. But he concedes that even books which have this "front matter"—he passes over the problem that ancient texts usually do not have it—sometimes do not help us very much in catching on to what the book is about. Adler then suggests a system of categories for the various purposes for which books are written, and he tries to show the distinctive kind of language that characterizes each purpose. Thus, by skimming a book we could detect whether, for example, its purpose is to impart practical knowledge, telling us *how* to do something, or to impart theoretical knowledge,

---

[67] Mortimer J. Adler and Charles Van Doren, *How to Read a Book*: rev. and updated ed. (New York: Simon & Schuster, 1972), p. 96.

telling us *that* something is the case. His own book, Adler declares, "is practical, not theoretical,"[68] and of course we should sense this from the title *How to Read a Book*.

But Adler would, no doubt, be the first to admit that it is a long step from knowing that his is a practical book to grasping his understanding of what real reading is. Knowing that his book is about how to gain skill in reading is a long way from understanding the basic point of his concept (the "whole") that gives coherency and brings to life all that he says about how to read. Then too, there is the problem that the purpose of books cannot be fitted into any neat system of categories. Adler complains that "you will find authors who do not know the difference between theory and practice, just as there are novelists who do not know the difference between fiction and sociology. You will find books that seem to be partly of one sort and partly of another ..."[69] Thus, a cursory sampling of a book's language may give us a wrong idea of what a book is about. Therefore, Adler's attempt to get an initial grasp of the "whole" so the parts may be more meaningful does not present a viable way for breaking the hermeneutical circle.

After reading the "front matter," Adler proposes that we engage in what he calls a "second reading." In this "second reading," we begin with an author's key terms[70], then move on to understanding his propositions and the way these relate to one another to support a book's thesis.[71] Since grasping a book's thesis is virtually to know what it is about, it would seem that Adler's "second reading" has more promise of getting through to a knowledge of the whole. But he still leaves unsolved the problem of how to break the hermeneutical circle, for how can we grasp the meaning of the parts at the beginning of the "second reading" until we know the purpose an author is trying to accomplish?

E. D. Hirsch, Jr., regards the traditional statement of the hermeneutical circle as not doing justice to what actually happens in interpretation because of the unfortunate use of the terms "parts" and "whole." "To define the hermeneutical circle in terms of "genre" and "trait" instead of whole and part not only describes more accurately the interpretive process but also resolves a troublesome paradox."[72] Genre, or better, "intrinsic genre," is the term Hirsch uses in place of "whole," and "trait" is his term for "part." The traits of language with which a text is composed are really the same as language conventions. "Our chances," argues Hirsch, "of making a correct preliminary guess about the nature of someone's verbal meaning are enormously increased by the limitations imposed on that meaning through cultural norms and conventions."[73] Thus, as we start at a text's beginning and work through it proposition by proposition, the language conventions the author selected will progressively narrow our understanding of what the writer was up to. Each of the traits of the language conventions the author selected have some rela-

---

[68] *Ibid.*, p. 66.

[69] *Ibid.*, p. 70.

[70] *Ibid.*, chapter 8.

[71] *Ibid.*, chapter 9.

[72] E. D. Hirsch, Jr., *Validity in Interpretation* (New Haven: Yale University Press, 1967), p. 77.

[73] *Ibid.*, p. 262.

tionship to what he was trying to say. So, at some point during the reading of a text, these traits will trigger in our minds a hypothesis regarding the author's intended meaning.

It is really the quest to find some unity around which all the traits of a text cohere that impels our minds to keep grappling with the traits until they all become meaningfully related to an author's purpose. "The meaning of a text (or anything else)," says Hirsch, "is a complex of understandings or parts which hang together. (Whenever parts do not cohere, we confront meaninglessness or chaos, not meaning.)"[74]

Instead of "whole," Hirsch uses the term "intrinsic genre" to denote the purpose that motivates an author. Unlike Adler, who tries to fit different texts into a ready-made system of categories which are, in reality, extrinsic genres, Hirsch insists that the task of an interpreter is to press toward an author's *intrinsic* genre, that is, toward the controlling concept that caused an author to put pen to paper, that controlled the language conventions he used to communicate it, and even helped him to determine the order in which the propositions and paragraphs appear. In this way we readers grasp the text's particularity, what is intrinsic to it, so that we succeed in thinking its author's thoughts after him, rather than imposing alien ideas on it. The intrinsic genre is not the final determinate meaning of every proposition in the text, but is rather that understanding of a text's purpose which itself informs every trait with the final, determinate meaning it should have. What Hirsch means by discovering the intrinsic genre is the same as what Adler means when he talks about going beyond a mere factual knowledge of a text to gain an understanding of it. "To be informed is to know simply that something is the case," says Adler, but "to be enlightened [to gain understanding] is to know, in addition, what it is all about: why it is the case, what its connections are with other facts, in what respects it is the same and different."[75] All this happens when we grasp an author's intrinsic genre. In other words, the intrinsic genre is the "whole" which gives final meaning to the parts.

Indeed, it is well known that even interpreters who are experts in the conventions of a text's language still disagree about its meaning. There are two reasons for this. In the first place, many traits in a text are vague enough to be employed in the service of several hypotheses. Then too, hypotheses regarding a text's meaning have a self-confirming power in them, for they indicate, a priori, the particular meaning content that an otherwise vague trait should have. Thus, it is hard to shake loose from an interpretation of a text, once it has been lighted upon; for a given interpretation, which has already determined the ways many traits in it should be understood, likes to proceed, by circular reasoning, to cite these ways as incontestable proofs for its validity.

Were all of a text's traits equally vague, there would be no possible way to arbitrate between different interpretations and the hermeneutical circle would indeed be a vicious one. But interpreters do indeed change their minds about a text's meaning. The reason

---

[74] *Ibid.*, p. 258.
[75] Adler, *op. cit.*, p. 35.

for this is that further scrutiny of the text, and/or the consideration of the objections that discussion with those holding to different interpretations bring to light, reveal certain traits in the text that simply will not bow the knee to a certain interpretation but resolutely insist upon an alternative one. Hirsch talks about how some traits have an "invariant aspect ... which characterizes one aspect of meaning rather than another."[76] These "invariant traits" make it possible to test different hypotheses regarding a text's meaning and achieve consensus regarding the one that has the higher probability of being valid.

> Note: It is an oversimplification to characterize the interpretive process as "inductive." Induction occurs as we let a text's traits limit the range of possible purposes an author might have had, and as the mind makes the "leap" of proposing a plausible hypothesis for giving coherency to all the traits. But the whole process of testing a proposed hypothesis against the traits has overtones of "deduction." Hirsch thus prefers to characterize the process as "hypothetico-deductive."[77] Perhaps it is best to say that the interpretational process is a dialectic between the traits of the text and the hypotheses of the reader.

As such, this process is not limited to the interpretation of texts but finds an analogy in the way the naturalist Agassiz taught his students to observe nature:

> "In his autobiography, Nathaniel Southgate Shaler tells of his initial experiences when he went to Harvard to study science under Agassiz. The famous Swiss scientist assigned him to a small pine table with a rusty tin pan on it in a room crowded with other students. 'When I sat me down before my tin pan,' says Mr. Shaler, 'Agassiz brought me a small fish, placing it before me with the rather stern requirement that I should study it, but should on no account talk to anyone concerning it, nor read anything relating to fishes, until I had his permission so to do. To my inquiry, "What shall I do?" he said in effect: "Find out what you can without damaging the specimen; when I think that you have done the work, I will question you." In the course of an hour I thought I had compassed that fish; it was rather an unsavory object, giving forth the stench of old alcohol, then loathsome to me, though in time I came to like it. Many of the scales were loosened so that they fell off. It appeared to me to be a case for a summary report, which I was anxious to make and get on to the next stage of the business. But Agassiz, though always within call, concerned himself no further with me that day, nor the next, nor for a week. At first this neglect was distressing ... but I set my wits to work upon the thing, and in the course of a hundred hours or so, I thought I had done much—a hundred times as much as seemed possible at the start. I got interested in finding out how the scales went in series, their shape, the form and placement of the teeth, etc. Finally, I felt full of the subject and probably expressed it in my bearing ... but no attention came from my master except his cheery "Good morning." At length on the seventh day, came the question "Well?" ... At the end of an hour's telling, he swung off and away, saying, "That is not right." ... I went at the task anew, discarded my first notes, and in

---

[76] Hirsch, *op. cit.*, p. 77.
[77] *Ibid.*, p. 264.

another week of ten hours a day labor, I had results which astonished myself and satisfied him. I shall never forget the sense of power which this experience brought to me. I had learned the art of comparing objects, which is the basis of the naturalist's work.'

"Samuel H. Scudder, another of Agassiz's pupils, testifies that his teacher's repeated injunction, 'Look, look, look,' had an equally rewarding effect upon him. Agassiz's training in the method of observing facts and their orderly arrangement was ever accompanied by the urgent exhortation not to be content with them. 'Facts are stupid things,' he would say, 'until brought into connection with some general law.' To gain the ability to detect relations between particular objects of attention the individual must learn to see not only intensely but also impartially."[78]

The "Whole" of Philippians 1:3–11

The form in which the intrinsic genre of this passage is illustrated is that which has proven useful in church classes designed to encourage their members to study the Bible for themselves, so they won't be so dependent on others for an understanding of what the Bible says. This form consists of questions which stimulate a class to accomplish four tasks: (1) Become acquainted with the passage's content and larger units. (2) Find the point of the passage—really the "whole," or the intrinsic genre. (3) Show how this point informs the meanings of all the parts. (4) Apply the point, enforced by all of the parts, to their own lives. Of course we who lead a class such as this must have done the kind of ground level exegetical work indicated in the preceding pages and chapters, for only then will we be able to figure out a "lesson strategy" that will enable us to show others something of how the Bible speaks for itself to them; and only then will we know enough to react to the unexpected answers we will get in a way that will lead the class discussion toward what the passage is really saying.

Lesson Strategy—Philippians 1:3–11

I.   Find the content and larger units.

    1.   What block of material stands out most clearly in this passage?
ANS The prayer of verses 9–11

    2.   What different things is Paul doing in verses 3–8 (Indicate references where he is doing each activity?
ANS Thanking God (3a), rejoicing while praying for the Philippians (4), remembering their past (3b, 5, 6a, 7c), telling of his love for them (7b, 8), announcing what God will do for them in the future (6b).

---

[78] Howard T. Kuist, *These Words Upon Thy Heart* (Richmond: John Knox Press, 1947) pp. 77–78.

3. If you had to reduce the material of verses 3–8 to the two most essential things, what would they be?
   ANS Joy over the Philippians (3a, 4) and *reasons* for this joy (3b, 5–8).

4. What essential difference do you notice between the mood of the verbs in verses 3–8 and 9–11?
   ANS Verses 3–8 indicative; verses 9–11 some subjunctives. This question asks us to observe the contrast between the statements of what *is* true (3–8) and what Paul desires to *become* true (the subjunctive mood is easier to detect in the Greek; we identify it in English by the use of auxiliary verbs, such as 'may'.).

II. Find the point of the passage.

1. Since the point of the passage is what the author argues for, rather than any one of the arguments, would you expect to find the point of the passage in verse 3–8 with their factual statements or in verse 9–11 with their statements of desire? Which are better suited for argument, facts or desires?
   ANS The facts of verses 3–8, because arguments must consist of what is actually true.

2. Which of the desired states presented in 9–11 can be realized only in the distant future, at the 'day of Christ,' and which can be realized in the near future?
   ANS *Far Future*: sincere and blameless unto the day of Christ, 10b; filled with the fruit of righteousness, 11a; fully glorify God, 11c. *Near Future:* your love abounding more and more in knowledge and all discernment, 9; being able to distinguish between the best and the merely good, 10a.

3. Would you expect to find the point of a passage in what can become a reality here and now or only in the future?
   ANS What can *now* become a reality, with things coming to pass in the future cited as inducements to change conduct in the present. Therefore, the point of the passage is either 9 or 10a. 10a is the main point of the passage because it is the ultimate thing that can become true here and now; verse 9 being a precondition for it. Also, notice that 10a is the most specific thing, and we would expect Paul's purpose to consist in what is most specific.

4. Focus attention on 10a. Our problem is that we tend to avoid living for what is best, all the time justifying our lives by the merely good things that consume our time and energy. Our great need (9) is for discernment and mature knowledge so that we will live for the best (10a).

III. Relate this point to the rest of the passage.

1. Verses 9–11

a. How does a prayer for a more knowledgeable and discerning love work to encourage Paul's readers to approve what is most valuable?
ANS The prayer lets the readers know that God will be working on their behalf, which gives them hope of being able to obey the command to approve what is excellent.

b. How would a more knowledgeable and discerning love enable the approval of what is most excellent?
ANS Because love—both the affection and the action—is a function of viewing something as valuable, Paul wants them to have a greater ability to set our affections on what is truly valuable. This ability will allow them to come to grips with reality—particularly from God's point of view—to see clearly the truth about the issues of life and to be able to accurately assess their value.

c. How does 10b induce them to live for the best and not the merely good?
ANS Only by so living will they pass muster at the judgment seat of Christ. [Note how the general supports the specific.]

d. How does verse 11 encourage them to fulfill 10a?
ANS This verse lets them know the righteousness of their success at choosing what is excellent because Christ has answered the prayer for more knowledge and discernment as they express their love. This must be so; otherwise God would not get full credit (11c).

2. Verses 3–8

a. Why is Paul so happy about the Philippians that even as he prays for them, he rejoices over them?
ANS He remembers how they have helped him in furthering the Gospel ever since they were converted. His joyfulness shows how much he is interested in them and their salvation. Cf. 4:15–16 with 1:5.

b. What is the ultimate reason why the Philippians have helped Paul in this task all along?
ANS God has been at work among them. Cf. 2:14 with 6a.

c. How does the truth of 6a encourage us now to live more for the best and not merely for the good?
ANS Realizing that God is for us should encourage us. What we are supposed to do in the future will be but a continuation of the work that God has already been doing for us in the past.

d. What other indications does Paul give that God has enabled them to help him further the gospel?

ANS Verse 7 shows that they have been partners in grace. Just as Paul has been able to stand for the Gospel, he implies that they will also. Also, he says that he "has them in his heart" which means that Christ has given him an affection for them. If Christ is so concerned for them that he gave Paul a love strong enough to write this letter and to pray for them, then they should be encouraged about Christ's own interest in seeing that they appear before him blameless.

e.   Paul says he's sure that the Philippians will continue to benefit from God's grace because he has them in his heart (7b). What does he mean by this?
ANS In verse 8 he indicates that he has them in his heart in the sense that he has a longing for them that stems from the very heart of Jesus Christ himself. If Christ is so anxious for their improvement, then they can be assured that he will continue to work for it.

f.   Why does Paul present the material in verse 3–8 before verses 9–11?
ANS He does this to lay a groundwork of encouragement by informing them of what God will enable them to do in carrying out the desires expressed in 8, 10a.

g.   What is the one thing that Paul seems to value more than any other?
ANS The furtherance of the Gospel.

IV. Application

Stress how we have nothing less than the gracious resources of God himself to enable us to give ourselves to those things that are best, and particularly to furthering the Gospel (the very best).

Chapter Seven—The Narrative Form

Up to this point we have concerned ourselves with some of the problems that arise in connection with interpreting expository texts—that sort of communication in which the author speaks directly to his readers. Indeed, there are many genres which would fall under this general heading (e.g., poetry, proverbs, prophetic declarations, epistles, and liturgical instructions—as in Leviticus), but we have been content to use the epistolary genre of Paul as he commences his letter to the church in Philippi as an illustration of the basic way to approach exposition.

To be sure, each of the other genres that are in the category of exposition will require a certain modification of this approach in order to grasp the author's intended meaning. It has been the custom for hermeneutics books to provide several illustrations of how to handle the sort of problems encountered in each of the easily differentiated literary genres encountered in Scripture, in the hope that the reader would then know how to interpret any part of Scripture. The difficulty, however, is that each specific literary unit that can be classified under some basic genre has its own peculiar set of interpretational problems, because each piece of literature has (to use Hirsch's language) its own "intrinsic genre." So, an illustration of how to interpret the foreword to Philippians cannot show the reader how to solve some of the special problems encountered in almost every paragraph in the remainder of Philippians and in the rest of the Pauline corpus. (So, too, illustrations of how to interpret several proverbs or several psalms will not equip anyone for handling all of the interpretational problems in Psalms and Proverbs.)

Furthermore, we cannot lift, for example, a parable out of Matthew's gospel and show how to interpret it, because this parable is just one part of all that Matthew wanted to say and cannot be interpreted apart from that larger literary whole of which it is a vital part. Neither can the interpretation of one such parable, or several parables, provide an adequate paradigm of how to interpret all of the parables. Each of Jesus' parables is of a slightly different genre; so, each parable will require a slightly different interpretational procedure. A hermeneutics book, therefore, cannot show all that needs to be done in interpreting each parable without becoming a commentary on the gospels—in which case it would no longer be a hermeneutics book.

Therefore, instead of trying to show proper interpretational techniques for as many problem passages in as many genres as possible in Scripture, the strategy in Chapter Four was to show, generally what is involved in interpreting the direct speaking that characterizes exposition. Now, in this chapter, we will examine some of what is involved in the indirect speaking that characterizes the narrative form. A narrative is an indirect form of communication because the writers of narratives hold themselves in the background and let the words and actions of the people in the narrative convey the message. Sizeable portions of Scripture (Genesis, portions of Exodus and Numbers, Joshua through 2 Chronicles, the Gospels, and Acts) are devoted to the narrative form; so, some of the principles for interpreting this form should be included in a book of hermeneutics.

The Theory of the Narrative Form

A narrative is a record of certain events arranged in a particular order, whereas an exposition is the articulation of an idea by means of elucidation and argumentation. The narrative form differs from exposition in that it is built upon the framework of the time sequence rather than on a framework that arises from the demands of logic and rhetoric. This basic difference gives rise to two features of the narrative form which control the procedure for representing it by means of arcs.

A. The narrative form is largely comprised of a concatenation of situations and responses.

When we examine any narrative, we see that it presents essentially the way two or more people or groups of people interact with each other. One party says or does something, and this leads another party to respond in some way. To this either the first, or a third, party makes a response, and so on it goes until some climax occurs. To be sure, within the narrative form we often find an extended description of certain places, things, and people. We also find sections which simply describe what someone did, said, or thought during a protracted interval (the saying and thinking will appear to be expository in nature); but sooner or later the author records how someone responded to what was said or done, or how someone responded to something that happened.

Let us consider how to relate the propositions for a typical situation-response sequence, such as we find in John 4:47–50.

> [47] When this man heard that Jesus had come from Judea to Galilee, he went to him and asked him to come down and heal his son, for he was at the point of death.[48] So Jesus said to him, "Unless you see signs and wonders you will not believe." [49] The official said to him, "Sir, come down before my child dies." [50] Jesus said to him, "Go; your son will live." The man believed the word that Jesus spoke to him and went on his way.

Verse 47 tells of the situation that presents itself to Jesus when a nobleman comes beseeching him to heal his son. Jesus' apparently tart rebuff in verse 48 is his response. It also becomes the situation to which the nobleman responds in verse 49, as he continues to insist that Jesus come to heal his son. In turn, this response becomes the situation to which Jesus responds in verse 50a by bidding the man to go his way because his son lives. To this situation the nobleman responds in verse 50b by believing Jesus' word and going his way. We would represent such a sequence by arcs in the following manner:

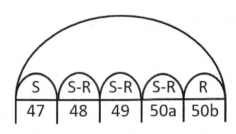

S	S-R	S-R	S-R	R
47	48	49	50a	50b

Arcs for each of the individual propositions within this sequence are not shown; only those arcs are drawn which represent all of what one party said or did at one time. Notice how easy it is to delimit these larger units: they begin where a person begins to act or react and they end where the action he began at that particular time stops. In actual practice, rather than putting the symbols S and R under the various arcs, it is helpful to assign a distinctive color for each arc representing the actions of one person. Thus, for the preceding narrative, we might give a blue color to each arc in which the nobleman acts/speaks: verse 47, 49 and 50b. We would assign some other color—for example, red—to each arc in which Jesus acts/speaks: verse 48 and 50a. It is amazing how much easier it is to get a grasp of a lengthy narrative involving the actions of many people by simply assigning a distinctive color to the arcs representing the actions of each individual. Without assigning such colors, all we see is a series of little arcs grouped under some larger arcs, and it becomes difficult to recall the narrative to mind as we view the arcs that we have drawn.

The question naturally arises, What justification is there in lumping a series of situations and responses under only one arc? Since each successive action arises from the preceding action, it would seem that we should draw an arc joining these two together. Since the resulting primary idea would be the second action, we could then join this larger arc to the next action and so on until we had represented the entire series. Indeed, such a procedure would adhere strictly to Chapter Four's theory for drawing arcs, but the drawing of so many arcs tends to obscure the basic simplicity of the narrative form which is that of one party's response to what another has done. We are able to grasp the content of a narrative more easily by simply drawing an arc for each entire action and by joining these together by nothing more than one arc that covers the entire sequence.

Happily, it is usually a very simple matter to find where the entire sequence ends. We join chains of situations and responses because they are actions that occur between the same people, at the same place, and during a single period of time. Therefore, changes in time, place, and/or persons are often the indicators of where the break between chains occurs. Thus, in the narrative of the healing of the nobleman's son, the chain of situation-responses breaks between verses 50 and 51. Up to verse 50, the nobleman is interacting with Jesus, but from verse 51 to verse 53, he is interacting with his servants. A new chain of situation-responses also commences whenever we encounter an action that does not arise from the immediately preceding action. For example, the action of Jesus in John 5:14 and that of Yahweh in Jonah 1:17 are the beginnings of new series of arcs because these actions arise *de novo*.

As an author records events in time, it is often necessary to introduce the readers to the place and circumstances in which the incident occurs. This introductory word is called the setting, and we should consider it as having equality of support with the incident that follows. In the paragraph about the healing of the nobleman's son, verse 46 is the setting for what happens in verse 47–53. Though there are different kinds of settings, all of them fall between these two possible extremes: (1) a setting which tells simply the time, place and persons involved in the incident that follows, and (2) a setting which acts as the prime mover, in that it is the basic situation for the chain of situation-responses that comprises the occurrence.

Hence, unlike the expositional form, the narrative form, by virtue of the fact that it is built upon a framework of time sequence, permits the interpreter to draw many of the larger arcs without first drawing the smaller ones. But now the question of how to group the chains of sequences together under larger arcs arises, and to answer this, we must consider a second feature of the narrative form which also arises from its being based on a time sequence.

B. The meaning which the narrator intends to communicate is given indirectly by the events which he records.

A mere account of events in chronological sequence does not necessarily impart meaning. It is possible to conceive of such an account that would convey nothing more than the facts themselves. But when authors undertake to record a series of incidents occurring either in actuality or imagination, they usually work to impose a form upon them so that they may do more than simply impart factual knowledge. Thus, humorists compose stories in ways that cause their readers to laugh. "Whodunits" are designed to challenge the readers to discover the guilty party on the basis of the evidence adduced. Then there are those stories composed for the serious purpose of communicating ideas to enlighten the readers. John Steinbeck, in *Grapes of Wrath*, records the events befalling the Joads as they move from Oklahoma to California. By means of his selection and arrangement of events, he tries to cause his readers to understand that a society that destroys food to maintain the profit margin while some of its people starve is doomed to suffer the "grapes of wrath."

The biblical narratives are also composed for the purpose of imparting meaning, for they are a record of things said and done as God revealed himself in history. Composed by men inspired by God, these narratives were shaped so that, in addition to imparting factual knowledge, they also imparted meaning.

The narrative form, however, has an inherent disadvantage which tends to hinder the communication of the author's message. The disadvantage is that the message must be expressed indirectly through the medium of events. This is overshadowed, though, by the great advantage which the narrative form possesses in comparison with the discourse form. While the latter tends to use abstractions that are difficult for our minds to grasp, the narrative form deals with the concretions of what people do and say in real life. Because of this, the narrative form can be a very effective way to communicate meaning.

The answer to the question, "Who is my neighbor?" comes home with much greater power through the parable of the good Samaritan than it would through an abstract exposition. Furthermore, the narrator has ways of handling narrative so that its inherent disadvantage becomes almost negligible. We have already indicated that the narrator may break into his account to give an interpretation of the events he is relating. But the skillful narrator does not depend chiefly on this device. There are two other ways to use the narrative itself to overcome the disadvantage of indirection so that we may perceive the message.

1. The narrator employs selectivity to convey the basic thrust of his meaning. The concept "meaning" implies a homogeneous, unified idea. Therefore, if events are to impart meaning, they must have an underlying unifying element. When we think of the totality of events occurring at a given place during a given period of time, however, we conceive of what is little more than a heterogeneous, unrelated group of facts. For example, let us recall the things that happened to Jeremiah while he was shut up on the court of the guard during the closing months of the siege of Jerusalem. The record of what befell him is in chapters 32–33 and 37–39 of the book bearing his name. Chapters 32–33 tell how Jeremiah obeyed the command to fulfill the office of the kinsman-redeemer and buy from his cousin a piece of land in Anathoth. This sequence of events serves as the vehicle for conveying a message regarding the future restoration of Israel. Chapters 37–39 tell of the various stages of Jeremiah's imprisonment during the latter days of the siege, and how he was delivered to freedom in contrast with Zedekiah, who met doom at the hands of the Chaldeans. Though made up of events transpiring at the same place and during the same period of time as those in chapters 32–33, this narrative conveys the distinct message that obedience to God leads to deliverance, whereas disobedience results in doom. To have related the totality of these events, that is, to have put chapters 32–33 and 37–39 together in one narrative, would have provided an informative record of what happened to Jeremiah during his imprisonment, but this would have failed to impart any coherent message, or meaning, for the reader to grasp. Jeremiah, however, made these events the vehicle for coherent messages by separating them into groupings surrounding separate themes. In short, Jeremiah employed selectivity to communicate the thrust of his message.

But selectivity means more than simply selecting the events the author will use to convey his message. It also involves the manner in which he recounts these events. By choosing specific incidents, the author is like the director who chooses the actors for his cast. Once selected, the director works with the members of the cast so they will know how to act in the way that will best communicate the director's interpretation of the play. Likewise, the author selects details from each event which will function to impart the meaning he wishes to convey.

As an example of this process of selectivity, let us examine one of Paul's few narrative sections, found in Galatians 1:13–2:10. Bible students have often been troubled by this passage, because Paul fails to mention one of his visits to Jerusalem, which is recorded in Acts. In Galatians 1:18–24 Paul speaks of the first visit he made to Jerusalem, about three years after his conversion. In Galatians 2:1–10 he speaks of another visit, one that occurred after a fourteen-year interval. If, as seems highly probable, the visit of Galatians 2:1–10 occurred at the time of the Jerusalem Conference of Acts 15, then Paul omitted the visit recorded in Acts 11:30, when he and Barnabas carried an offering to Jerusalem to help the saints who were suffering from famine. But this difficulty disappears when we understand the function of selectivity in the composition of the narrative. Paul omitted mentioning the famine visit because it was not useful as a vehicle for imparting the message he wished to convey.

The message, or the meaning, which he wished to convey through these accounts was not that he had been to Jerusalem a certain number of times; rather, his purpose was to provide a refutation for the arguments the Judaizers had used to dissuade the Galatians from being loyal to Paul. Their first argument was that Paul was not a true apostle because he had received his message secondhand, namely, from the apostles at Jerusalem. Paul refutes this by what he writes in 1:13–24, in which he tells what actually did happen during the days when he might have received his message from other people. Their second argument was that Paul's message was a perversion of the true Gospel taught by the Jerusalem apostles. Paul refutes this in 2:1–10 by showing the way Peter, James and John received him when he presented the Gospel he preached among the Gentiles. The famine visit, however, did not affect the question of whether he received his message firsthand from the Lord or secondhand from men. Neither did it have any theological implications which would help to refute the second argument, for the purpose of the famine visit was to do good works rather than settle theological issues. Therefore, when Paul omits the famine visit in this narrative passage in Galatians, we understand that he is using the process of selectivity.

Selectivity also accounts for the details that Paul included in each unit of the narrative section. As we examine Galatians 1:13–17, we find that instead of telling every interesting detail about the days surrounding his conversion, Paul stresses only (1) that he was completely involved in the Jewish religion before his conversion, and (2) that he was in places far removed from Jerusalem immediately after his conversion. It is obvious that he cites these facts because they serve as telling blows against the assertion that he received his message from men. The points he makes in 1:18–24 are likewise well-aimed blows against this assertion. In the same way we could demonstrate that each detail in Galatians 2:1–10 serves to refute the second argument of the Judaizers.

Though selectivity does not tell everything, it does work for the best interests of truth. This can be seen when we remember that a portrait can be a better representation of the truth than a photograph. In discussing the differences between the birth narratives in Matthew and Luke, J. Gresham Machen shows that while the differences arose from the separate purposes of the two authors, these different purposes did not affect the historicity of the two accounts. He reasons as follows:

> … Although a portrait is different from a photograph, it may be just as faithful a
> representation of the person it depicts. In many cases a portrait would be spoiled by
> the addition to it of the wealth of details that a photograph contains. Those details

belong truly to the person whose portrait is being made; yet they would detract not merely from the artistic beauty of the picture, but also from the faithfulness of its representation. A portrait, in other words, as distinguished from a photograph, is selective; by omitting some details it enables the eye to grasp those details that remain; and thus it brings us into far closer and far truer spiritual contact with the person whom it sets forth.[79]

In an article entitled "I Owe My Thanks," the great historian Arnold J. Toynbee tells of the influences in his early life that were decisive in his career. Among these was learning the lesson that selectivity is the servant of truth. Speaking of himself in the third person he recalls:

The occasion on which the present writer had learnt this rule [speaking of selectivity as the fundamental rule of art] had made an indelible mark on his memory. He recalled a day in July, 1894, on which he was intently watching his mother painting a water-color sketch of a ruined church. When his mother had finished the sketch and they were looking at it together, he pointed out to her that it was incomplete because she had put in only the ruined church walls and the seascape visible through its glassless windows, and had left out the luxuriant dock leaves and nettlebeds sprouting through the church's dislocated pavement (as sordid witness to Man's ephemeral occupation of the site). His mother answered quietly, but without hesitation, that the secret of sketching was to know what to leave out. Her son's first thought was that, in leaving out the dock leaves, his mother had shown something less than an absolute faithfulness to the truth. His second thought was that she had lifted a veil from his eyes and shown him the truth behind it.[80]

Thus, we do well to observe this principle at work in our study of the Bible, for when we see why an author said what he said, we have grasped the mind of the author.

2. The narrator employs arrangement to organize events so that they will make an impact upon the mind of the reader. While 'selectivity' provides the basic materials for communicating meaning, 'arrangement' assembles these materials so that the meaning may be readily grasped. Arrangement is of such importance in communicating meaning that an author occasionally allows the pattern of arrangement to take precedence over the chronological sequence of events. For example, the message that Luke apparently wished to impart in Luke 3:1–20 was that Jesus' appearance at the scene of John's baptizing was the great climax to and termination of the Baptist's ministry. Arrangement of materials, therefore, played so crucial a role, in getting this idea across, that Luke first records the imprisonment of John the Baptist, and then, as the grand climax, the baptism of Jesus by John! But the usual manner in which arrangement is achieved is to have the

---

[79] J. Gresham Machen, *The Virgin Birth of Christ* (New York: Harper & Bros., 1930), p. 199.
[80] Arnold J. Toynbee, "I Owe My Thanks," *Saturday Review of Literature*, 37 (October 2, 1954), p. 14.

material selected so that units occur in some sort of pattern. The following are the various patterns of arrangement.

a. The pattern of repetition. This is used when it is essential to emphasize one crucial thought. The indication of this structural pattern is the recurrence of a crucial idea in two or more units. When we determine that these units have been arranged for the repetition of this idea, then we consider these units as being in a series with one another. An illustration of this pattern is Jeremiah 40:2–12. The ultimate outcome of Jeremiah 40:2–6 is Jeremiah's return to Gedaliah at Mizpah. Verses 7–12 tell of the scattered remnants of Judah who are likewise returning to Gedaliah. Consequently, we see that the author is employing selectivity and arrangement to convey to the reader the idea that the remnant of Judah is now secure because they are under Gedaliah, the governor appointed by the Chaldeans, and because they have Jeremiah, God's appointed spokesman, in their midst.

b. The pattern of progression. Narrators use this arrangement when they wish to show the way a certain theme progresses to a climax. We would see an indication of this pattern when we see the repetition of an idea that moves towards a goal. Each successive unit that shows a certain stage of development should be related to the preceding unit by the symbol for progression. For example, each of the three units of 1 Samuel 1:21–2:11 (1:21–23; 1:24–2:10; and 2:11) shows with heightened emphasis the theme of the parent's willingness to give Samuel for the service of the Lord.

c. The pattern of contrast. This scheme of arrangement serves to make one particular idea stand out by aligning it with a contrasting idea. The indication of this arrangement, then, is a salient contrast between two adjacent units. Thus, in the example we will explore in more detail at the end of this chapter, we note the contrast between the way the Babylonians treat Zedekiah and the people of Jerusalem and the way they treat Jeremiah and Ebed-melech. The relationship between the units containing the contrasting ideas would be that of alternatives.

d. The pattern of interchange. This pattern is an extension of the preceding pattern in that it emphasizes a contrast by repeating the contrast several times. Authors use this pattern either when they wish to stress a contrast by setting it forth in several ways, or when they wish to show that two apparently contradictory themes must be thought of as complementary to each other. To illustrate, in Matthew 16:13–17:23, the theme of Jesus' glory as the Messiah and Son of God is stated alongside the theme of his suffering three times. The following is an example of the way this unit's relationship symbols would be represented:

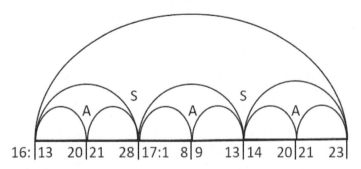

16: |13 20|21 28|17:1 8|9   13|14 20|21 23|

e. The pattern of inversion. This pattern is used to show that a certain event is pivotal or crucial for what occurs at the climax of a sequence of events. Authors use this pattern when they wish to emphasize that one theme holds the key to all that happens. Though this pattern occurs primarily in the narrative form, the best illustration on a scale small enough to depict in this book is the arrangement of the seven proverbs of Proverbs 6:16–19. In Proverbs 6:16 we read, "There are six things that the Lord hates, seven that are an abomination to him." Verses 17–19 enumerate these seven things, and these seven sins are arranged in the following pattern:

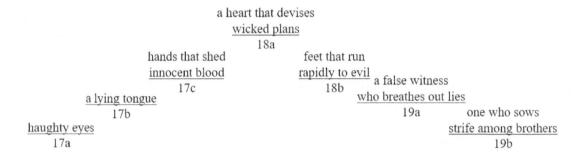

Note the correspondence between the third and the fifth elements and between the second and sixth. It is not difficult to see that correspondence also exists between the first and seventh, for is not pride the chief motive behind all of the ways people sow discord? The pivotal point is the fourth element. The heart is the source of six other sins which God hates. It is also noteworthy that the sins mentioned after this pivotal point are expressed more in terms of the whole person's involvement in them than are those to which they correspond on the left-hand side of the inversion. For example, the idea of the involvement of the entire person is indicated more in "a false witness who breathes out lies" than in the "lying tongue." "Feet that run rapidly to evil" implies that the whole person is engaged more than "hands that shed innocent blood." Note that the climax comes in sowing discord among the community, for now the sin of one has spread to become the sins of many. This inversion is thus used to get the following idea across: Though committed by specific members of the body, sin stems from the heart so that it involves the whole person and incites others to sin as well.

The arcs for Proverbs 6:16–19 would be drawn as follows (the 'inv' in parentheses indicates that the units within this arc are arranged in an inverted pattern):

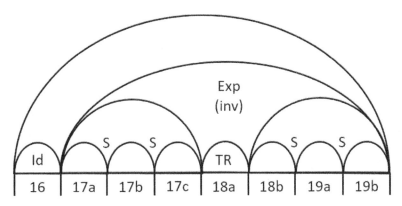

The essential indicators of the pattern of inversion are: (1) a contrast or correspondence between the first and last events, the second and next to last events, and so on; (2) a common idea between the events leading up to the transition, and a corresponding idea for the events leading from the transition; and (3) the middle unit's acting as a transition between that which characterized the first half of the unit and that which characterizes the second half. For further examples of this pattern, consider Mark 2:1–3:6 and 7:24–8:30.

f. The patterns of symmetry. These patterns are modifications of the pattern of inversion, but since they serve the different purpose of showing contrast between two ideas, they occupy a separate category. The symbol "Sym" should be placed beneath the arc denoting the sequence that is arranged in either of the two patterns of symmetry:

One type of symmetry is found in a sequence of events in which the first contrasts with the last, the second with the next to last, and so on, but there is no pivotal event in the center. The arrangement would thus be: A′ – A′′ – A′′′ / B′′′ – B′′ – B′. The author's purpose in using this arrangement would be to contrast the idea common to A with that common to B.

Another type of symmetry is a unit arranged in the following manner: A′ – B – A′′. In this arrangement the first and last events in the sequence convey a similar idea, while the central event is in contrast to this idea. The author's purpose in such an arrangement is to stress the theme common to A′ and A′′ by placing it in contrast to the theme of B.

The use of repetition, either in the form of words or themes, is the means for detecting these patterns, and the relationships assigned between units that are equals in these patterns are for units having equality of class. However, there may be units within a narrative that are related to one another by equality of support. Such units will not fall into any of these patterns of arrangement.

The question thus arises, "How can we sense whether we are dealing with units related by equality by support or by equality of class?" As a general rule, repetitions will indicate units which are arranged in the patterns cited above and which will have equality of class. Consequently, in working through a narrative, we first look for repetitions that are indicative of the patterns of arrangement and delimit the larger units that become apparent. In some narratives such a procedure will enable us to draw all the larger arcs. But sometimes after the patterns of arrangement are determined, some relationships still need to be determined and their arcs drawn. Two adjacent chains of situation-responses may yet need to be related, or the larger arcs that embrace the entire narrative may need to be related to one another so that the whole unit may come beneath one arc. When such is the case, we are probably dealing with units related by equality by support. Then, the procedure we should follow is to summarize the basic thought of each in a concise statement, align the basic thrust of each side by side, and then discern the logical relationship that exists between them.

In setting forth the theory of the narrative form, we have also indicated the procedure to follow in analyzing and synthesizing a narrative. We first draw arcs for the smallest complete thoughts and delimit the obvious units into which these fall. Next, we observe repetitions between these units so as to determine the larger units into which they group themselves. If patterns of arrangement do not appear, we then seek for units related by equality by support. In this manner the entire narrative can be seen as a whole comprised of its parts, and thus we can grasp the message the author wished to impart.

Jeremiah 38–39: An Example of Working with the Narrative Form

The following narrative of Jeremiah 38:28b–39:18 is brief and has a simple structure. The defect in this illustration is that the termination of the unit is more obvious than it is in most instances of the narrative form. But this example's advantages for the purposes of illustrating the procedure for working with the narrative form far outweigh its defects.

A. Step #1: Work into the narrative for a sufficient distance and draw arcs for each proposition; then group these into the larger arcs which are immediately apparent.

> [28b] The following events occurred when Jerusalem was captured. [39:1] (King Nebuchadnezzar of Babylon came against Jerusalem with his whole army and laid siege to it. The siege began in the tenth month of the ninth year that Zedekiah ruled over Judah. [2] It lasted until the ninth day of the fourth month of Zedekiah's eleventh year. On that day they broke through the city walls.) [3] Then Nergal-Sharezer of Samgar, Nebo-Sarsekim, a chief officer, Nergal-Sharezer, a high official, and all the other officers of the king of Babylon came and set up quarters in the Middle Gate. (38:28b–39:3 NET)

The proposition begun in 38:28b ends in 39:3. This proposition cites the fact that the leaders of the Babylonian army had won such a victory over Jerusalem that they were able to sit at one of its chief gates. To be able to do this was clear proof that the city had been overwhelmed. The material in between the conclusion of chapter 38 and the third verse of chapter 39 tells of those events which led up to the capture of the city. Though 39:1–2 does not come at the very beginning of the narrative, yet its function is that of a setting for the happening in the following narrative. Thus 38:28b and 39:3 tell of the first situation which sets off a concatenation of actions that are recorded in the verses that follow.

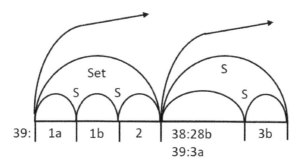

⁴ When King Zedekiah of Judah and all his soldiers saw them, they tried to escape. They left the city during the night. They took a path through the king's garden and passed out through the gate between the two walls. Then they headed for the Jordan Valley. ⁵ But the Babylonian army chased after them. They caught up with Zedekiah in the plains of Jericho and captured him. They took him to King Nebuchadnezzar of Babylon at Riblah in the territory of Hamath and Nebuchadnezzar passed sentence on him there. ⁶ There at Riblah the king of Babylon had Zedekiah's sons put to death while Zedekiah was looking on. The king of Babylon also had all the nobles of Judah put to death. ⁷ Then he had Zedekiah's eyes put out and had him bound in chains to be led off to Babylon. (39:4–7 NET)

Verse 4 tells of the response of Zedekiah and his remaining soldiers to the fact that the Babylonians were now seated in the gate of the city. Their response of fleeing from the city to hide in the Arabah then becomes the situation which gives rise to the Babylonian army's response which is to capture them and bring the leaders, in particular King Zedekiah, to judgment before Nebuchadnezzar at Riblah. Verses 5c–7 tell of Nebuchadnezzar's response to his captain's action of bringing these leaders to him. So ends the first chain of situation-responses.

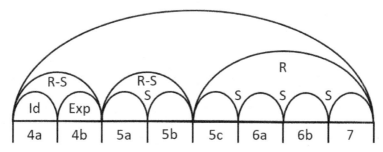

⁸ The Babylonians burned down the royal palace, the temple of the LORD, and the people's homes and tore down the wall of Jerusalem. ⁹ Then Nebuzaradan, the captain of the royal guard, took captive the rest of the people who were left in the city. He carried them off to Babylon along with the people who had deserted to him. ¹⁰ But he left behind in the land of Judah some of the poor people who owned nothing. He gave them fields and vineyards at that time. (39:8–10 NET)

The action of destroying Jerusalem and taking away the captives, recorded in verses 8–10, is not a response from the situation of verses 5c–7, in which Nebuchadnezzar blinds Zedekiah and slays his sons. The destruction of Jerusalem was a part of the Babylonians' policy that they would carry out regardless of what happened to Zedekiah. Another evidence that the first chain of situation-responses has ended with verse 7 is that in verse 8 there is a change in the persons involved. Nebuzaradan and the populace of Jerusalem are the new actors in the storyline who have not appeared since the narrative began. Furthermore, there is a change in place. The action of verses 5c–7 occurred in Hamath, some 275 miles to the north of Jerusalem where the action of verse 8–10 occurred.

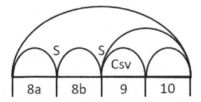

[11] Now King Nebuchadnezzar of Babylon had issued orders concerning Jeremiah. He had passed them on through Nebuzaradan, the captain of his royal guard. He had ordered, [12] "Find Jeremiah and look out for him. Don't do anything to harm him but do with him whatever he tells you to." [13] So Nebuzaradan, the captain of the royal guard, Nebushazban, a chief officer, Nergal-Sharezer, a high official, and all the other officers of the king of Babylon [14] sent and had Jeremiah brought from the courtyard of the guardhouse. They turned him over to Gedaliah, the son of Ahikam and the grandson of Shaphan, to take him home with him. But Jeremiah stayed among the people. (39:11–14 NET)

What happens in verse 11 is likewise not a response from the action of verses 8–10, for in verse 11 the scene shifts back to Hamath. There is also a change in time, for the events of verses 11ff. could not have happened until sufficient time had elapsed for the captives to travel from Jerusalem to Hamath on their way to Babylon. Hence the following arcs are immediately apparent after we have travelled thus far into this passage via step #1.

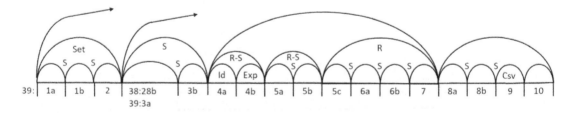

Verses 11–12 tell of Nebuchadnezzar's action in giving a command regarding Jeremiah. Verses 13–14a (down through the words "to take him home with him") record Nebuzaradan's response to Nebuchadnezzar's command to do for Jeremiah whatever he wanted. According to Jeremiah 40:4, Jeremiah could either have continued on with the captives to Babylon or he could have returned to Jerusalem. His response to this offer is recorded in 14b.

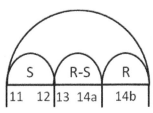

¹⁵ Now the LORD had spoken to Jeremiah while he was still confined in the court-yard of the guardhouse. He had said, ¹⁶ "Go and tell Ebed-Melech the Ethiopian, 'The LORD God of Israel who rules over all says, "I am going to carry out against this city what I promised. It will mean disaster and not good fortune for it. When that disaster happens, you will be right there to see it. ¹⁷ But I will rescue you when it does happen. I, the LORD, affirm it. You will not be handed over to those you are afraid of. ¹⁸ I will certainly save you. You will not fall victim to violence. You will escape with your life because you trust in me. I, the LORD, affirm it."'" (39:15–18 NET)

Verses 15–18 record the Lord's word to Jeremiah regarding Ebed-Melech. This action could not have been God's response to the fact that Jeremiah chose to return to Jerusalem (14b), for what is recorded in these verses happened before Jerusalem had fallen to the Babylonians. That Jeremiah would break the chronological sequence to the extent of putting in this incident at this point is strong evidence that a narrator does arrange his material to impart a message to his readers. These verses should fit together under one arc.

B. Step #2: Find the arrangement of the largest arcs drawn thus far and group them accordingly under larger arcs.

We have already noted that the author's arrangement of his material is indicated by repetitions. Sometimes these crucial repetitions occur in a word or a phrase; at other times they occur in a larger theme or idea. In this passage, the theme of doom and destruction appears in both 39:3–7 and 8–10, and we can consider this as a crucial repetition because it is the salient thought for each unit. The theme we find in common for both verse 11–14 and 15–18 is deliverance, and this is likewise the primary thought for each unit. Consequently, we observe that each of these pairs of units is composed using the pattern of repetition. So, we draw arcs embracing each of these pairs, and we show that each part of these pairs is in series with each other.

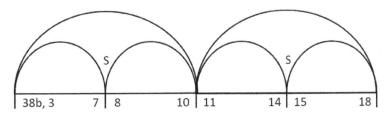

As we examine the resulting two units, we raise the question of whether they are related to each other by equality by support or whether they have equality of class, in which case they conform to one of the patterns of arrangement. We notice that there is a sharp contrast between these two units: the first concerns destruction and the latter deliverance. Therefore, we conclude that they conform to the pattern of contrast, so that we relate them as alternatives and join them under one arc. This one arc becomes the happening which is equal to the setting of 39:1–2. The larger arcs for this narrative should appear thus:

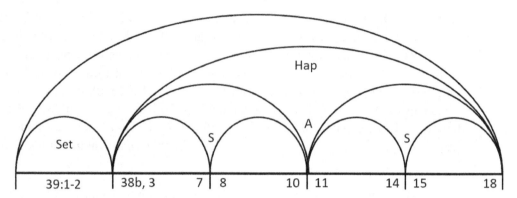

Hence, we come to see the meaning which Jeremiah wished to impart by this narrative. It is that those who were disobedient to God, such as Zedekiah and the populace of Jerusalem, receive nothing but misery. But those who trust God so that they obey him, such as Jeremiah and Ebed-Melech, are granted deliverance.

Ultimately the narrative form has the same purpose as the expositional form: both are means by which authors communicate their ideas to their readers. The only difference is that in the expositional form authors speak directly to the readers and in the narrative form, they speak indirectly, through the medium of recorded events. These are the two great categories into which literature falls. As interpreters, we must handle each literary genre either as exposition or narrative; even poetry. A piece of poetry may function to elucidate and argue for an idea, in which case we draw the arcs as we would with a more straightforward expositional form. Or the poetry may be the record of a sequence of events, in which case we would draw the arcs as in the narrative form. Thus, we are prepared to delimit and interpret the larger units for all literary forms.

Jonah: Asking Questions of, and Expounding, the Narrative Form

Key Questions for Interpreting Jonah

1. Delimiting the text: What is the argument for seeing a major break between 1:16 and 1:17? What factors make it apparent that there is a major break between 2:10 and 3:1? Where (and why [i.e., the reasons for claiming it]) is the major break between 3:1 and the end of the book?

2. What basic inclination / predisposition / preference in Jonah did both (1) the non-destruction of Nineveh and (2) the destruction of the gourd irritate?

3. What is it about this disposition that, when it is frustrated, makes Jonah want to die? Besides the explicit statements of this desire, where is it necessarily implied?

4. Why did God's causing the gourd to grow cater to Jonah's disposition (cf. "Jonah was exceedingly glad …" 4:7)?

5. Precisely what had Jonah "said" (4:2) when he was still in Israel before he left to go, not to Nineveh, but to Joppa and points west? What arguments from the immediate context of 4:2 justify this construal of the content the author intended his readers to understand here?

6. Precisely what was the reason why Jonah was so opposed to God's being gracious, compassionate, slow to anger, and abundant in extravagant kindness (cf. Exodus 34:6–7)?

7. What sort of kindness [חֶסֶד *chesed*] did Jonah approve of when in 2:8, he praises God for the greatness of his kindness?

8. If Jonah hated God's kindness when he was still in the land of Israel, then how is his delight in God and in his kindness, as evidenced by the prayer of 2:1–9, to be accounted for: (1) because Jonah had repented, or (2) because Jonah thought, in chapter 2, that he had succeeded in reforming God to be a more sensible God? (Argue from the text for the answer.)

9. Was Jonah angry at God because God was disposed to be unconditionally gracious, or because God responded to the meeting of (what Jonah thought) were the wrong conditions? (Hint: examine the nature of the response of the Ninevites in 3:5–9.)

10. In what way were the Ninevites' attitudes and actions (3:9)—to which God responded by saving them—radically opposite from the reasons for which Jonah wanted God to bless him and other people?

11. Did Jonah have a missionary zeal? If he did, why was he unwilling to go to Nineveh?

Expounding Jonah's Intrinsic Genre

The basic question in interpreting Jonah is why he was so angry that he wanted to die when he learned that God had decided not to destroy Nineveh (4:1–4). A common answer is that Jonah did not want to be humiliated as a prophet by finding that God did not fulfill his prediction that Nineveh would be destroyed in forty days. The difficulty with this interpretation is that it does not explain why Jonah wants to die just as much after God destroyed the commodious gourd (4:8–9) as he does when he learns that God will not destroy Nineveh after all; but there is nothing in the destruction of the gourd that would imply that Jonah was a false prophet (cf. Deuteronomy 18:22). So, we must search for an interpretation in which both of these acts indicate something in God's nature that is so distasteful to Jonah that he no longer wants to live in a world ordered by such a

God. A further indication that the author intended both of these acts to display the inclination of God that Jonah finds so distasteful appears in (1) Jonah's desire to die expressed immediately after both happenings (4:4, 8), and (2) the author's combining
God's creation and destruction of the gourd with his sparing of Nineveh (4:10–11).

In common with both 4:2–3 and 4:10–11 is God's compassion for those who have acted
so as not to deserve it. In 4:2–3, where there is the explanation for why God did not
destroy Nineveh, God is a "gracious God and merciful, slow to anger and abundant in
kindness [חֶסֶד] and relents concerning calamity." In 4:11 the Ninevites are also described as unable to "discern their right hand from their left hand." This second declara-
tion of compassion for Nineveh comes as the conclusion from an argument that begins
with stating how much Jonah was troubled about the loss of the gourd which God provided to shade Jonah's head from the scorching sun: "You were grieved about this little
plant, something for which you have not worked nor did you do anything to make it
grow. It grew up overnight and died the next day" (4:10). Except for the few hours of
shade which the gourd provided, there was nothing about this gourd to call forth any
sense of attachment in Jonah. This makes the argument for God's having had compassion on Nineveh all the stronger: if this gourd, which had so little to commend it, nevertheless caused Jonah to be exceedingly glad (4:6) about it, then there was ever so much
more reason why *God* [made emphatic in the original] should have compassion on Nineveh.

The emphatic use of "God" in the original implies that while God had indeed brought
forth the gourd, yet *God* was responsible for the existence of the 120,000 inhabitants of
Nineveh, along with their cattle. But the difference between Nineveh and the gourd is
great: whereas there was only a single gourd, belonging to what was created on the third
day (Genesis 1:9–13), there were 120,000 Ninevites, all made in God's image, and their
cattle (another creation of the sixth day). Furthermore, these people had a great need for
God's word (3:2), because they were so blinded by their sins, and thus unable to act
wisely, that it was as if they did not know their right hand from their left. So, the "gracious and merciful God, full of *chesed* [חֶסֶד, a kindness above and beyond what was
required or expected in a relationship]" would certainly be acting inconsistently with his
own nature, if he did not spare these people, when they honored his merciful nature by
repenting with the desire that God would be merciful and not destroy them.

But why, then, had Jonah been so grieved about the gourd? It was certainly not for any
value inherent in the gourd. The reason for his "exceeding gladness" for the gourd was
that it represented what he thought of as his inherent value, an Israelite who, in contrast
to all other peoples of earth, feared (?) "the God of heaven who made the sea and the
dry land" (1:9). Jonah was exceedingly glad for this gourd because Jonah regarded it as
God's acknowledgement of his inherent worth. The gourd represented for Jonah an affection from God that was not pity or mercy, but was rather called forth by Jonah's
distinctive worth. But then when God had destroyed the gourd, God made it plain that
he did not regard Johan's distinctives as an Israelite as having any special inherent worth.
And, certainly, Jonah's distinctives of belonging to a nation whose God had made the

sea and the dry land were of no special worth, for he did not "fear" this God or regard him as meeting special needs in Jonah, for otherwise he would surely have immediately responded to the command to preach to the Ninevites. The *Gentile* Ninevites, on the other hand, demonstrated that they *feared* the God of heaven in that they renounced all of their acts of violence and placed all of their hope for a happy future in the God of heaven.

In that God responded so favorably to the Ninevites when they repented with appropriate works, and yet destroyed the gourd that had sheltered Jonah for a few hours, Jonah was starkly confronted with the fact that God was a merciful God who rendered no praise to humans but only received praise from them for the gracious way in which he treated them. Jonah, however, wanted a deity that was entirely different from the deity of Exodus 34:6–7; but since God was not like this, and Jonah could never extract any praise from him for Jonah's inherent worth, therefore, Jonah wanted to die because there was no chance of ever gaining what he regarded as giving life its greatest joy, namely, getting the God of heaven to worship him by praising him.

Chapter Eight—Our Concern with the Bible

In Chapter One we outlined what is involved in grasping an author's intended, sharable meaning, and since our concern is to understand the Bible, we have used passages from it to illustrate how an author's meaning may be grasped. In Chapter One, however, we stressed that the scope of hermeneutics is larger than simply finding out what some author, writing in a bygone era, wanted to communicate. Indeed, some writers have argued that hermeneutics has no task beyond understanding what an author meant. For example, a Roman Catholic writer said, "Hermeneutics does not investigate the objective truth of a writer's meaning ... It does not inquire what is true or false, but only what the writer intended to say."[81] Adler takes the exact opposite position: "The activity of reading does not stop with the work of understanding what a book says. It must be completed by the work of criticism, the work of judging."[82] In carrying on this second phase of hermeneutics, Adler says, "The reader must do more than make judgments of agreement or disagreement. He must give reasons for them ... Otherwise he is treating a matter of knowledge as if it were opinion."[83]

Certainly, no one who regards the Bible as the Word of God would consider its teachings as mere opinions. Yet, if we do not give reasons for crediting the Bible's claim to be the Word of God, we are in effect treating it as a mere opinion, a point of view that is so lacking in reasons and bases for upholding it that others are quite justified in seeing things differently. A passage of Scripture makes it plain that moral fault attaches to those who do not take the trouble to determine why they believe something in the Bible to be true. The writer of Acts declares that those in Berea were "more noble than those in Thessalonica, for they received the word with all eagerness, examining the scriptures daily to see if these things were so" (Acts 17:11). The Thessalonians had accepted the apostles' teachings uncritically, and in so doing were less noble than the Bereans. According to Acts, wherever the apostles went, they cited reasons why people should believe their message. They themselves had come to believe the truth of the message through the "many infallible proofs" (Acts 1:3) by which Jesus had revealed himself to them as alive, and they did not expect their hearers to credit their message without similar evidence.

Thus, in the first sermon at Pentecost, Peter began with common ground statements that were accepted by both himself and his hearers: the unusual phenomenon of people who were speaking in a variety of different languages at nine o'clock in the morning (Acts 2:12ff.), and from this and an appeal to the Old Testament (which the hearers credited), the empty tomb, and the concerted apostolic witness, he concluded by saying, "Let all the house of Israel therefore know assuredly that God has made him both Lord and Christ, this Jesus whom you crucified" (v. 36). Likewise, when Paul was at

---

[81] A. J. Maas, "Hermeneutics," *The Catholic Encyclopedia*, special ed. (New York: The Encyclopedia Press, 1910), VII, 271b.

[82] Mortimer J. Adler and Charles Van Dorn, *How to Read a Book*, rev. and updated ed. (New York: Simon & Schuster, 1972), pp. 138f.

[83] *Ibid.*, pp. 249f.

Thessalonica, he "argued from the scriptures, explaining and proving that it was necessary for the Christ to suffer and to rise from the dead" (Acts 17:2–3). At Athens Paul declared that his message was true because God had given assurance to everyone by raising Jesus from the dead (Acts 17:30f.). At Corinth Paul "argued/reasoned" (διαλέγετο) in the synagogue every Sabbath and persuaded both Jews and Greeks" (Acts 18:4). He did the same thing at Ephesus (Acts 19:8–9). With Felix Paul spoke about faith in Jesus Christ and "reasoned (διαλεγομένου) about righteousness and self-control and future judgment" (Acts 24:24f.). When standing before Agrippa II, Paul's defense centered on the resurrection of Jesus, and he reminded Agrippa that he really had independent access to knowledge of this, since "none of these things escaped his notice, for this was not done in a corner" (Acts 26:26).

Since the apostles, in giving their message, argued, reasoned, and sought to persuade their hearers, it is plain that they regarded their message as being more than a mere opinion. But if we readers do not carefully examine their arguments to see if they are sound, then we insult them, by implying that what they taught had no more claim to truth than a mere opinion. To borrow Adler's mode of expression, we do not show good manners if we simply understand what the biblical writers were saying but expend no effort to determine whether they are to be credited. We must also read them critically to see whether their understanding represents what is really true.

But this Berean eagerness, while commendable, also carries with it a certain danger. The very fact that we single out the Bible for critical examination may indicate that we are disposed to regard it as true. Why not single out the Koran for critical reading rather than the Bible? In directing our attention to the Bible, are we not thereby signifying our inclination to regard it as the Word of God more than the other books which also claim to be God's Word? If this should turn out to be the main reason for our concern with the Bible, then efforts to show it as true would beg the question. Therefore, we must show, at the outset, that there are sound reasons for selecting the Bible for such an inquiry. This reasoning process involves three steps.

"All Men Seek Happiness"

Paradoxically, the reasonable starting point for justifying concern for the Bible's truth cannot be some rational dictum, but the plain fact that our minds are not controlled so much by reason as by desire. We want things and then afterwards adduce reasons to justify what we want. Langdon Gilkey, in his book *The Shantung Compound*, became utterly convinced of this as he saw the way even Christian missionaries reacted when, during World War II, he along with 2,000 other British and American nationals in China were herded together into a very small school, which, with its small play yards, was to be their prison camp home for three and a half years. For example, it was decided to remodel two rooms, one for teenaged boys and one for teenaged girls, whose parents could then move into smaller rooms and so provide shelter for twenty-four families with smaller children. But people marshalled the most reasonable excuses why their teenaged children should not be taken from them and why they should not be moved to smaller rooms. When Gilkey, who was on the housing committee, asked an American missionary family to move, the husband replied, "You know, Gilkey, I write lots of sermons here. I am asked by the other missionaries to preach in our church services. It is for their sakes, and for that of the camp as a whole, that we need a little extra space in which I can have quiet to think out these sermons."[84]

Bumping up against this kind of thing day after day caused Gilkey to scrap his belief in the innate goodness of men. "My ideas as to what people were like and as to what motivated their actions were undergoing a radical revision," said Gilkey. "People generally—and I knew I could not exclude myself—seemed to be much less rational and much more selfish than I had every guessed, not at all the 'nice folk' I had always thought them to be. They did not decide to do things because it would be reasonable and moral to act in that way, but because that course of action suited their self-interest. Afterward, they would find rational and moral reasons for what they had already determined to do … I asked myself, 'Why has our whole culture, especially its academic life, remained so determinedly unaware of what almost all the evidence clearly indicates?'"[85]

Up until Schopenhauer, philosophers had, almost without exception, regarded man's essence to reside in his reason and consciousness. But Schopenhauer declared that man's will was the driving force. The will "is the strong blind man who carries on his shoulders the lame man [reason] who can see." "Nature has produced [intellect] for the individual will. Therefore [intellect] is only designed to know things so far as they afford motives for the will …" "Nothing is more provoking, when we are arguing against a man with reasons and explanations, and taking all pains to convince him, than to discover at last that he *will* not understand, that we have to do with his *will*."[86]

"All men seek happiness, without exception," affirmed Blaise Pascal. "They all aim at this goal, however different the means they use to attain it. What makes these go to war and those bide at home is this same desire, which both classes cherish, though the point of view varies. The will never makes the smallest move but with this as its goal. It is the motive of all the actions of all men, even of those who contemplate suicide."[87]

But "happiness" is a rather vague and general term, and we do well to define more precisely the basic strategy that humanity pursues in order to be happy. It seems quite evident that we do not seek happiness chiefly in the lower immediacies, through indulging in sensuous pleasures. We only feel comfortable in slumping down in front of a television set, with a drink in one hand, in the evening *after* we have accomplished a good day's work, or on a weekend, *after* we have accomplished a good week's work. Only those who have somehow been quite frustrated in accomplishing their goals and fulfilling their ideals will find it possible to spend the daylight hours of a weekday sipping

---

[84] Langdon, Gilkey, *The Shantung Compound* (New York: Harper & Row, 1966), p. 88.

[85] *Ibid.*, pp. 89f.

[86] Quotations taken from Will Durant, *The Story of Philosophy*. Pocket Library edition. (New York: Pocket Books, Inc., 1954), p. 143.

[87] H. F. Steward, *Pascal's Pensées* (New York: Pantheon Books, 1950), p. 143.

a martini and playing a slot machine in Las Vegas. Sensuous pleasures, then, are either added as frosting on top of the cake of accomplishment or they are taken as an anesthetic to soothe the hurt of failure. Cows may be content to chew the cud all day long, and dogs to embark on no greater plans for the day than to sleep in the sunshine, but human beings distinguish themselves from the animals by craving to accomplish things which will indicate that, more than simply being the reflex of nature, they have been successful in acting creatively to shape their world more to their liking.

Goethe's play "Faust" illustrates this well. In Part I, Faust contracted to sell his soul to the devil, if the devil through any one sensual pleasure, or a combination of them, could give him one moment of pleasure so complete that he would say to it, "Ah, still delay— thou art so fair." Mephistopheles, the devil, then provides Faust with a complete series of all sensual delights, but not one moment is fair enough for him to ask it to tarry awhile. But at the end of Part II, Faust does find a moment which is so fair that he wants to capture it, and that is when he, the civil engineer, sits upon a hillside overlooking a plain, formerly a marsh, which he has made fertile and habitable through a system of dams and drainage ditches. "Then dared I hail the moment fleeing: 'Ah, still delay—thou art so fair!' The traces cannot of mine earthly being, in eons perish—they are there!" Ultimate joy came to Faust, not through sensual pleasures, but through having overcome the limitations of the world by having reshaped a bit of it so that henceforth others would suffer less from life's limitations.

As we consider the late John F. Kennedy's reasons for wanting to be president, we detect that his ultimate desires were actually the same as those of Faust. Soon after he was inaugurated in 1960, he said, "The political world is stimulating. It's the most interesting thing you can do. It beats following the dollar. It allows the full use of your powers. First, there is the great chess game—the battle, the competition. There's the strategy and which pieces you move and all that. And then in government, you can do something about what you think."[88] Both Faust and Kennedy found ultimate enjoyment in being able to reshape the world to their liking. Their example seems to echo Aristotle's statement that "the truly happy man is the man who is happy with himself." We cannot really get excited about ourselves when we have frittered away a day lolling in front of the television set; but after a day during which we have succeeded in shaping a bit of the world so that we and others are less limited, we have fulfilled a most basic urge in our natures. We are happy, because we are pleased with ourselves. The happiness of such a day stems from success in overcoming finitude, in making some progress in belying our sense of inferiority and the limitations that surround our lives. The psychologist Alfred Adler affirmed that human beings distinguish themselves from the animals in that they have an inferiority complex and seek to overcome it in some way.

Thus Donald R. Burgett, in his book *Currahee!*, describing his years as a paratrooper during World War II, declared that he joined the paratroopers initially because his older

---

[88] *Time*, Atlantic edition, November 7, 1960, p. 21.

brother said that "it took a good man to get in, and a better man to stay in."[89] Likewise Heinrich Harrer, a member of the first team to climb the north wall of the Eiger in the Swiss Alps, confessed that his reason for attempting such a climb was to overcome a sense of insecurity. "Self-confidence," he said, "is the most valuable gift a man can possess ... but to possess this true confidence it is necessary to have learned to know oneself at moments when one was standing at the very frontier of things ... On the 'Spider' in the Eiger's North Face, I experienced such borderline situations, while the avalanches were roaring down over us, endlessly."[90] In answering the question, "What is happiness?" Nietzsche replied, "The feeling that power increases, that resistance is overcome."[91] Similarly, Spinoza declared, "Joy consists in this, that one's power is increased."[92]

Thus, we conclude that all people seek the happiness that comes through overcoming finitude. To be sure, the examples cited above are taken from those standing within the culture of rather recent Western civilization, but as we read how Tariri, a native of a stone-age culture in Ecuador, sought to be the best head hunter in his tribe, we detect that he attempted to overcome finitude just as diligently as those conditioned by Western culture, though, to be sure, in a rather un-Western way. Tariri told the missionary who had led him to Christ that "it was the man who killed and took many heads who became greater than all other people. He became a great chief."[93] Tariri recalled that when some young men did not want to go out on raiding parties and learn how to kill, "the older ones would scold the young ones and say, 'How is it that you do not have a heart like mine? Look, your father is a great killer. Why do you want to be a no-killer and just sit around the house?' So, the young ones would think about it some and come to their senses and say, 'All right.'"[94] One day a friend of Tariri's came from a neighboring tribe and told how someone had killed his two brothers and his father. This friend said, "Why shouldn't you help me? If I were a killer like you [Tariri], I would help everybody."[95] So Tariri, wanting to make the world a little more to his and his friend's liking, obliged and in recounting the story said, "And so we left them [he had killed a goodly number of the enemy tribe to be sure to get the right man]. We returned home. My heart was happy."[96] Tariri, in his way, had overcome the fear of the finitude involved in the threat that he would be killed in such a venture, and so as he returned home from his raid, he was happy because he was satisfied with himself for having proven himself in control of a little portion of the world.

Everyone seeks the happiness that overcoming finitude brings. Some may try to prove their ability to overcome by climbing the Eiger, others by joining the paratroops, and

---

[89] Donald R. Burgett, *Currahee!* Reader's Digest Condensed Books, Vol. III, 1967 (Pleasantville, NY: The Reader's Digest Association, 1967), p. 349.

[90] H. Harrer, *The White Spider* (New York: E. P. Dutton, 1960), p. 21.

[91] *Antichrist*, sect. 2.

[92] Quoted by Will Durant, *op. cit.*, p. 180.

[93] E. Wallis, *Tariri: My Story* (New York: Harper & Row, 1961), p. 69.

[94] *Ibid.*, p. 34.

[95] *Ibid.*, p. 42.

[96] *Ibid.*, p. 43.

still others by being the champion headhunter. They greatly desire the praise that comes from such accomplishments, for praise helps overcome any lingering doubt that they have overcome finitude. Those who fail to overcome in some such way may try to assuage the consequent hurt by sensual indulgence, and when this fails to bring much satisfaction, they may even contemplate suicide. But no matter how sharply human behaviors may differ, all people are ultimately seeking happiness by showing themselves capable of overcoming finitude. If our desire for happiness so controls our actions, and even our ways of thinking about things, then this fact must be reckoned with as we account for why we should be particularly concerned with the Bible.

"We Are Far Too Easily Pleased."

We have seen how all people seek happiness, but we should also observe that people do not seem to find what they are looking for. Farther on in *The Pensées*, describing how everyone seeks happiness, Blaise Pascal observed that "for centuries past, never has anyone, lacking faith, reached the mark at which all continually aim. All men murmur: princes, subjects, nobles, commoners; old and young; learned, ignorant; sound and sick; of every clime, of every time, of every age, of every state." [97] None of us ever seems quite to reach the level of happiness which each of us seeks. Surely Alexander the Great found joy in conquering all the territory of Persia, but that was not enough, for he wanted to conquer India too. But his troops, homesick and exhausted from their many battles, refused to ford the Indus River, and Plutarch records that Alexander wept because he could not conquer any more worlds. Sir Francis Chichester, the British aviator and yachtsman who spent his life attempting to establish new navigational records and made a solo sail around the world twice as fast as any previous attempt, tells of the letdown that always followed every triumph: "I felt isolated, and drained of personality, horribly cut off from other people by some sheer gulf of loneliness. I had achieved my great ambition to fly across the Tasman Sea alone, I had found the islands by my own system of navigation, which was dependent on accurate sun-sights worked out while flying alone, something which no one had ever done before and perhaps no one would ever do in similar circumstances. I had not then learned that I would feel an intense depression every time I achieved a great ambition; I had not then discovered that the joy of living comes from action, from making the attempt, from the effort, not from the success."[98]

Such examples which are so representative of life should instruct us that the happiness we crave cannot be found in this world. In Pascal's words, "So long an ordeal [of constantly complaining about life's unfulfillment], so continual and unbroken, ought certainly to convince us of our inability to reach the good by our own efforts; but example teaches little. Example is never so perfectly uniform that there is not some delicate difference; hence it is that we expect our hope will not be deceived on this occasion as on the other. And thus the present never satisfying us, hope cheats us, and from evil to evil leads us on to death, which is an eternal consummation of ill?"[99] Thus even though

---

[97] Steward, *op. cit.*, p. 143.

[98] Francis Chichester, *The Lonely Sea and Sky* (New York: Ballantine Books, 1964), p. 175.

[99] Steward, *op. cit.*, p. 143.

Chichester felt "an intense depression" after flying across the Tasman Sea in 1931, he kept right on seeking to accomplish navigational goals never before achieved; and even though at the end of his life when he wrote his autobiography, he concluded that joy comes "only from the effort, not from the success," he seemed quite content to accept the depression that follows achievement. But was he not too easily satisfied? Why be content to risk life and limb when all that ever finally comes from it is "intense depression"? If our goal is to find happiness, should we be content with such paltry results?

According to Pascal, we should learn from this phenomenon that our true end is to find our happiness in God. In his 250th pensée Pascal continued: "What then is this cry of avidity and impotency [seen in universal murmuring and complaining] except that there was formerly in man a true happiness, of which there remains to him now only a mark, a trace wholly void, which he vainly tries to fill with all that surrounds him. Seeking from things absent the succor which he cannot obtain from things present, but which are incapable of it, because this infinite abyss cannot be filled but by God himself."[100] However, there are several different directions in which we turn in preference to concluding that we can find fulfillment only in God. When it begins to be apparent that life in the world cannot satisfy the heart, people sometimes try to anesthetize the pain through indulgence in the lower immediacies. A song made popular by Peggy Lee expresses this strategy:

> Is that all there is?
> Is that all there is?
> If that's all there is, my friends,
> Then, let's keep dancing.
> Let's bring out the booze and have a ball,
> If that's all … there is.[101]

Another escapist strategy is to try to talk ourselves into believing that life with all its frustrations does satisfy. Longfellow's poem, "Hymn to Life," is a classical expression of this strategy:

> Tell me not in mournful numbers,
> Life is but an empty dream!
> For the soul is dead that slumbers
> And things are not what they seem.
> Life is real! Life is earnest!
> And the grave is not the goal;
> Dust thou art, to dust returnest

---

[100] *Loc.cit.*

[101] "Is That All There Is?" Peggy Lee, (Hollywood, CA: Capitol Studios, 1969), written by Jerry Leiber and Mike Stoller. The song was inspired by the 1896 story "Disillusionment" by Thomas Mann. Most of the words used in the song are taken verbatim from the narrator's words in Mann's story.

Was not spoken of the soul.

Not enjoyment, and not sorrow,
Is our destined end or way;
But to act, that each tomorrow
Find us farther than today.
Art is long and Time is fleeting
And our hearts, though stout and brave
Still, like muffled drums, are beating
Funeral marches to the grave.

In the world's broad field of battle,
In the bivouac of Life,
Be not like dumb, driven cattle!
Be a hero in the strife!
Trust no Future, howe'er pleasant;
Let the dead past bury its dead.
Act—act in the living Present!
Heart within and God o'erhead.

Lives of great men all remind us
We can make our lives sublime,
And departing, leave behind us
Footprints on the sands of Time.
Footprints that perhaps another,
Sailing o'er life's solemn main,
A forlorn and shipwrecked brother,
Seeing, shall take heart again.

Let us then be up and doing,
With a heart for any fate:
Still achieving, still pursuing,
Learn to labor, and to wait.

And we should observe at this point that modern existentialism is trying to say just this.

Some of Longfellow's statements in this poem seem sufficient to indicate the inadequacy of this way of avoiding Pascal's conclusion. If our destined end is not joy; if our heartbeats are a funeral march to the grave; if life is like "sailing o'er a solemn main," and any kind of fate can beset us in life; if the best we can do is leave footprints in sand which will soon disappear; then should we not face the facts and not affirm, as Longfellow did, that "things are not what they seem"? Longfellow is perfectly correct that our hearts, with their unwavering quest for happiness, cannot be content to settle for a world such as ours, but is he not being far too easily satisfied when he recommends flying in the face of reality and living as though the world were different? It would seem that anyone who remains calm and confident, Longfellow-like, in the midst of all this confusion, simply does not understand the situation or is running, full flight, from reality.

Still others try to escape the problem by professing that they do not really care about themselves and their own happiness. C. S. Lewis made the following comment about this very popular mood:

> If you asked twenty good men today what they thought the highest of the virtues, nineteen of them would reply, Unselfishness. But if you asked almost any of the great Christians of old, he would have replied, Love. You see what has happened? A negative term has been substituted for a positive, and this is of more than philological importance. The negative ideal of Unselfishness carries with it the suggestion not primarily of securing good things for others, but of going without them ourselves, as if our abstinence and not their happiness was the important point. I do not think this is the Christian virtue of Love. The New Testament has lots to say about self-denial, but not about self-denial as an end in itself. We are told to deny ourselves and to take up our crosses in order that we may follow Christ; and nearly every description of what we shall ultimately find if we do so contains an appeal to desire. If there lurks in most modern minds the notion that to desire our own good and earnestly to hope for the enjoyment of it is a bad thing, I submit that this notion has crept in from Kant and the Stoics and is no part of the Christian faith. Indeed, if we consider the unblushing promises of reward and the staggering nature of the rewards promised in the Gospels it would seem that our Lord finds our desires not too strong, but too weak. We are half-hearted creatures, fooling around with drink and sex and ambition when infinite joy is offered us, like an ignorant child who wants to go on making mud pies in a slum because he cannot imagine what is meant by the offer of a holiday at the sea. We are far too easily pleased."[102]

The plain fact is that we can no more turn off the desire each of us has for happiness than we can cease to be attracted to the earth by gravity. Jesus, therefore, in his teaching was not so unrealistic as to command people to act contrary to their own self-interest. Rather, he enjoined us to find fulfillment for our craving for happiness in God and in the great blessings he stood ready to bestow on those who turned to him. Then when our hearts are happy in God, we can have love for others that "does not seek its own" (1 Corinthians 13:5), a love without strings attached, a love that gives without seeking anything in return; for when we are happy in God, how could we want to obtain anything at the expense of others?

But controlled as we are by our emotions rather than our reason, we will not own up to the fact that we are finite and not able to overcome our finitude sufficiently so that, contemplating ourselves, we can be happy with ourselves. We do not want to face squarely the inconvertible fact, as stated in 1 Corinthians 4:7, that all of our possessions and abilities have come to us as a gift from outside ourselves, and that there is not one single thing that we are or have for which we can credit ourselves. Instead, we go on

---

[102] C. S. Lewis, *The Weight of Glory* (New York: The Macmillan Company, 1949), pp. 1f.

thinking that happiness is just around the next corner, or we try to make believe we have happiness, Longfellow-like, or we try to think that we can dispense with the need for happiness. Others may try to avoid the problem by sensual indulgence, but to the extent that they realize how utterly unsatisfactory this is, they may find courage enough to end it all. Controlled as we are by our emotions and not by reason, we proceed in these unreasonable ways to try to solve our predicament.

Perhaps these ways would not seem to be unreasonable if there were no other way to go. But if everything we are or have comes to us ultimately from outside ourselves and not from our own doing, we would be acting very reasonably to cease, once and for all, trying through our own efforts and instead seek fulfillment in the direction from which all that we are and have comes. To do this is virtually the same as turning to God and seeking him, for that which distinguishes God most essentially from human beings is that unlike us, he is himself the source of all that we are and have. If all that we are and have comes from God, it just might be that the fulfillment we crave, but cannot gain by our own efforts, might be found in God. Certainly, there would be nothing unreasonable in earnestly seeking how contact might be made with him.

Where Can Enduring Joy Be Found?

Instead of going on stubbornly in the several vain ways we usually seek to find fulfillment, we would do well to consider whether finding God would not answer the cry of this poem by B. Cumming Kennedy:

> Where can enduring joy be found?
> Where is rustless treasure?
> Where is contentment's camping ground?
> Where is deathless pleasure?

People have often tried to find God through philosophical speculation, but Plato, one of the world's greatest philosophers, voiced the basic problem of finding God in this way when he said through Simmias, one of those who held dialogue with Socrates, that "[someone] must take whatever human doctrine is best and hardest to disprove and, embarking upon it as upon a raft, sail upon it through life in the midst of dangers, unless he can sail upon some stronger vessel, some divine revelation, and make his voyage more safely and securely."[103] The quest for enduring joy would be much more fruitful if we could find a sure revelation in which God had taken the initiative to make himself known to human beings than it would be if we were to base our knowledge of God on our own flimsy speculative reasonings. Therefore, in the quest for fulfillment outside of ourselves, the better strategy would be to examine the well-established religions of the world. But even as we narrow down the field of inquiry to the world's great religions, our time and energies are not sufficient for making an exhaustive study of all of them.

---

[103] "Phaedo" 85. *Plato in Twelve Volumes*, Vol. 1 translated by Harold North Fowler; Introduction by W.R.M. Lamb. (Cambridge, MA, Harvard University Press; London, William Heinemann Ltd. 1966).

However, since our aim is to find the happiness after which the heart craves, we can examine each religion in order to learn whether or not its claims, if true, would fully satisfy our hearts.

Any religion whose teachings would fail to do this would be quite irrelevant, even if it were true. If what were ultimately true about the world could not give us any more fulfillment to the longing of our hearts than the escapisms listed in the preceding section, then truth would be boring and unimportant. But if a religion turns up whose teaching would give fulfillment, we would then do well to take the time and energy required to investigate the validity of its claim to truth. If such a claim proves true, the search for enduring joy and contentment would be ended, for news is only good news if it is true news.

Following through with such a strategy, then, we will not linger long considering any polytheism—such as existed in the religions of ancient Babylon, or Greece, or Rome, and such as exists today in Hinduism with its 330 million gods. No doubt part of the reason why we seek to overcome finitude is the desire for the greater security thereby afforded, but when we realize that in polytheism, the gods themselves are still finite, and so are constantly vying with one another to maintain their place in the sun, it becomes clear that we could not expect much help from them. The gods in polytheism are striving about as earnestly for fulfillment as are we mortals upon earth. Just as we mortals upon earth try to use other people to make them a means for our fulfillment, so the gods use each other for the same purpose, and surely, they would have no scruples against also using us mortals as mere pawns on their chessboards. Life is difficult enough, with the people around us in the world who are trying to use us, without complicating things further by having the gods of polytheism doing the same thing to us, only more so, because they are vastly wiser and stronger than we mere mortals. Certainly then, if we are trying to find fulfilment, we will not turn to polytheism. To be sure, hundreds of millions of people today are avid, sincere Hindus, and many of them would die for their faith. But this should not impress us, since we have already shown how unreasonable people proceed in the task of satisfying the craving of the heart.

Virtually the same argument would also rule out animism, that religion of so many peoples in which the components of an environment are viewed as being empowered by spirits which must be placated before anyone can have a quantum of happiness. Indeed, there have been, and still are, animistic cultures—those of the Native Americans and the Australian aborigines—which affirm a supreme deity who rules over all. But in animism this deity is always so remote from people in comparison to the spirits that inhabit the trees, mountains, rivers, and oceans that the animist does not look to him for much help. The animist's hands are full trying to humor the spirits so they will continue to let him enjoy life a little bit. We will therefore pass animism by, for life is complicated enough already without having to learn how to placate an endless array of spirits.

Students of comparative religion have pointed out that there is within animism and polytheism always the tendency toward something better, because the human desire for happiness causes us to be dissatisfied with any worldview whose practical explanation for reality never goes beyond a plurality. Says one authority on the subject, "There is also in man's spirit something which insists on asking questions about the world and about human and divine relations with it. There is a search for unity, for a single principle or 'law' which will provide an explanation for all that man sees about him. This philosophical instinct varies a great deal in different people and in different races, but in greater or lesser degree it is nearly always present."[104]

In support of this we see that the great polytheisms of history have often given rise to the greatest philosophies. It was the pantheons of Greece and Rome, with their conflicting explanations of reality and concepts of morality, which gave rise to the attempts to synthesize reality found in such giants as Plato and Lucretius. The same phenomenon appears in Hindu polytheism. With the development of its 330 million gods, there arose the literature of the Upanishads, which embodies the philosophy of Hinduism. In reaction against the extreme pluralism of the pantheon, this philosophy of Hinduism asserts that the one thing explaining the many is a nameless something which lies at the root of both thought and matter. For several millennia, and even to the present, these contradictory views of life have coexisted within Hinduism. But when Buddhism arose in the sixth century BCE, it so vigorously proclaimed an application of the basic concept of Hindu philosophy that it could no longer exist under the aegis of Hinduism and so became a separate religion.

Buddha taught that since the reason for all suffering was desire, the way to abolish suffering was to become absorbed in Nirvana, the nameless essence at the root of all existence. Though one might have to go through several reincarnations to accomplish this goal, yet progress is aided by seeking, through meditation, to renounce all desire and the illusion of individuality, and by following a very high ethical standard.

The history of Buddhism after the death of its founder provides evidence for deciding whether to make further investigation into this system. Later Buddhism abounds with temples and images either of Buddha or his more illustrious followers. How can we explain within Buddhism this development which is contrary to its ideal of the denial of personality and individuality? The answer is that the majority of human beings fail to find satisfaction in a religion whose object and goal is namelessness. We do not intuitively feel that the way to alleviate anxiety is to seek to overcome individuality by becoming one with the whole of reality.

Confucianism, another great philosophical religion, also indicates that it fails to banish anxiety. Living about the same time as Buddha, Confucius had some very wise things to say about living in this present, visible world. But he sidestepped talking about the future or the unseen world by such famous statements as, "We don't know yet how to serve men; how can we know about serving the spirits?" and "We don't know yet about life; how can we know about death?" Confucianism has had a very deep influence on Chinese culture, and yet it is significant that a large percentage of Chinese have

---

[104] T. H. Robinson, *A Short History of Comparative Religions*, 2nd ed. (London: Gerald Duckworth & Co., 1951), pp. 74–75.

supplemented their Confucianism with that later form of Buddhism which worships before the images of either Buddha or his followers.

Apparently, we humans intuitively sense that a religious philosophy is not satisfying which does not point to some being who, as a person, is able to influence human existence. In preference to worshiping a nameless cause or all-pervading essence, we will even revert to a polytheism or an animism. The Taoism of the Chinese philosopher Lao-tse (c. 550 BCE) confirms this conclusion. In this philosophical religion, the one thing which explains all existence is the Tao, a nameless essence which pervades all of the universe. Yet a mute testimony to the inadequacy of this religious philosophy is the fact that Taoist temples in China are little more than the homes of animistic superstition.

There is little difference between a philosophical religion and the various human philosophies to which, as Plato said, people must cling until they find a surer word from God. Perhaps it was for this reason that Plato wanted to make a journey into Persia to consider Zoroastrianism, with its claim to have a sure word from Ahura Mazda, purportedly the creator and ruler of all things.[105] Zoroastrianism is one of the world's four monotheistic religions. By their very nature, such religions give better promise of solving the problem of anxiety than do the various animisms, polytheisms, and philosophical religions, for if we can look to One who is in control of all things, then it is possible to see a reason for all that happens to us. Likewise, since by definition such a One is self-sufficient and in need of nothing, he is therefore free to devote all his attention to accomplishing the very best for his creatures. If from such a being a sure word could be found which declared his loving intentions for humanity, then we might be able to overcome our anxiety. Thus, we must make a more thorough investigation of the World's four monotheisms: Zoroastrianism, Islam, Judaism and Christianity.

Zoroastrianism originated in Persia (modern day Iran) through the teachings of the shepherd, Zarathustra, who seems to have lived in the sixth century before Christ. According to the record, when Zarathustra was thirty, and after ten years of searching for the answers to the deepest questions of existence, an archangel, ten times the size of a person, appeared to him and escorted him into the presence of Ahura Mazda, the supreme being over all the universe. Here Ahura Mazda instructed Zarathustra on how to be his prophet and gave him the message he should proclaim to humanity. For ten years Zarathustra preached without success, but finally he converted a powerful king to believe in Ahura Mazda, and thereafter the religion spread rapidly, though today there are only a few thousand adherents in India.

Zoroastrianism teaches unequivocally that Ahura Mazda is the creator and upholder of the universe and that he is good. But he is viciously opposed by a bad spirit named Angra Mainyu. Despite this fearful battle, however, Zoroastrianism teaches that Ahura Mazda eventually triumphs. Human beings must align themselves either with Ahura Mazda or Angra Mainyu. Soon after death people face judgment as they approach the bridge of the Separator. Here the record of each life is read, and one's merits are balanced against

---

[105] John R. Noss, *Man's Religions* (New York: The Macmillan Company, 1949), p. 460.

one's demerits. If the bad outweighs the good, then the individual must go to the hell in the abyss beneath the bridge. But if the merits prove heavier, then the person may cross the bridge into paradise. At the end of the present world order there will be a resurrection of all who have lived. These will then be subjected to an ordeal by fire: to the evil, this fire constitutes the awful burning of hell, but to the good it will be as soft and healing as milk. Thus, Ahura Mazda brings about the triumph of good over evil.

Islam is a monotheism which was developed about a thousand years later. Its ostensible founder, Mohammed, was a caravanner who travelled all over Arabia and even to lands on its borders. According to his testimony, the truth that there is but one God came to him in a series of visions while on these journeys. Tradition affirms that after he and his few followers became established at the head of a military state at Medina, his teachings spread with extreme rapidity—though not without the use of violence—so that scarcely a hundred years later they had blanketed all of western Asia and northern Africa, and had entered Europe across the straits of Gibraltar.

One of the reasons for the great popularity of Islam is its comparative simplicity. To become a Muslim, one must simply subscribe to the proposition that there is no deity but Allah and that Mohammed is his prophet. The Koran is the final revelation of Allah in literature, and this, with the applications which can be deduced from it, is held to be the supreme authority over all matters of life. Throughout history there have been six greater prophets who have spoken for Allah: Adam, Noah, Abraham, Moses, Jesus and Mohammed. Mohammed is the capstone for all the prophets, and after him no prophet is to arise. For the Muslim, conduct consists of repeating the creed—"There is no god but Allah, and Mohammed is his prophet"—praying five times a day, fasting during the daylight hours of one month each year, giving alms, and at least once during one's life-time making a pilgrimage to Mecca, either in person or through a representative. Certain foods, all intoxicants, and gambling are prohibited. Though many Muslims are monog-amous, four wives are permitted by the Koran.

As in Zoroastrianism, so there is a general resurrection in Islam. But it is after this that the judgment is finally given. The books are opened and people are consigned either to heaven or hell, depending on whether their merits outweigh their demerits. The Koran declares, "For when the trumpet is blown, that day there shall be no kinship anymore between them, neither will they question one another. Then he whose scales are heavy— they are the successful, and he whose scales are light—they have lost their souls, dwell-ing in Gehenna forever" (23:101–103). During this life people should work very hard to insure themselves of forgiveness: "And hasten to forgiveness from your Lord ... Those who spend (benevolently) in ease as well as in straightness, and those who restrain (their) anger and pardon men; and Allah loves the doers of good. And those who when they commit an indecency or do injustice to their souls remember Allah and ask forgiveness for their faults—and who forgives the faults but Allah—and (who) unknowingly persist in what they have done. Their reward is forgiveness from their Lord, and gardens be-neath which rivers flow, wherein they will abide forever" (3:133–136). "Forgiveness with Allah is only for those who do evil in ignorance, then turn (to Allah) soon, so these it is to whom Allah turns (mercifully)" (4:17).

It is conceivable that the person who achieved final forgiveness on the terms of either Zoroastrianism or Islam might find the fulfillment which people crave. But it is difficult to see how any fulfillment could be experienced or enjoyed in this life when ahead lay the terrible test of the judgment, whose outcome could not be known in this life. To face such a test at the end of life, wondering all the time whether we had been good enough to deserve forgiveness—knowing that forgiveness would more likely be given to those who had sinned "unknowingly" and who "persist" in righteousness—would create such anxiety, if not downright despair, that we would have little, if any, of that inward peace and satisfaction of heart essential for loving other people without strings attached. Such anxiety, then, instead of stimulating righteous conduct, would tend to destroy it, thus establishing a vicious circle spiraling downward from anxiety to total despair. Therefore, to take either Zoroastrianism or Islam seriously in this life would preclude not only the possibility of finding fulfillment in this life but also in the life to come.

Next, we consider Judaism, and in this preliminary investigation of it—which must be brief because our time and energy as human beings is so limited—it will be convenient to confine our study to Judaism's primary source, namely, the writings of the Jewish Bible, which Christians label the "Old Testament." Here it is evident that the God of the Old Testament is dealing with people not merely on the basis of whether their quality of life deserves punishment or blessing, but also on a principle of grace in which God removes obstacles to receiving his blessing by pardoning sin. To Abraham, guilty of such sins as the idolatry of moon worship (Joshua 24:2) and lying about his wife (Genesis 13), God nevertheless accounted his faith as righteousness when Abraham simply trusted him (Genesis 15:6). The forgiveness implied in this reckoning can, according to the Old testament, be known here and now, for David remarked, "Blessed is the one whose transgression is forgiven, whose sin is covered. Blessed is the person against whom the Lord does not devise punishment ..." (Psalm 32:1ff.). The blessings imparted on the basis of forgiveness are so great that it is obvious that the problem of anxiety could be completely solved. David declared that God's extravagant kindness and mercy pursued him all the days of his life (Psalm 23:6), and Jeremiah quoted God as saying that he would not turn away from doing good to his people but would rejoice over them to do them good with all his heart and soul (Jeremiah 32:40f.).

If it were true that God, who has all power and wisdom, employs this power and wisdom to do good to those who trust him, it is obvious that we would no longer have any anxiety. Why be concerned about the pain and loss that can result from our finitude if indeed the omnipotent God's whole heart and soul is taken up with doing his people good forever? The peace of mind that such a God brings is indicated in Isaiah 26:3: "You will make everything just right for your committed people because they trust in you."

The Old Testament teaches that the essence of human sin consists in the attempt to overcome finitude so we ourselves can become like the Most High God (Genesis 3:1ff.; Isaiah 14:14; Ezekiel 28:1ff.). According to the Old Testament, we ought not try to find fulfillment by increasing our power in some way that will enable us to contemplate ourselves as more glorious, but rather by worshiping God, who alone is all-glorious. "[God's] delight is not in the strength of the horse, nor his pleasure in the legs of a man, but the Lord takes pleasure in those who fear him, in those who hope in his extravagant kindness" (Psalm 147:10f.). "One thing have I asked of the Lord, that I will seek after; that I may dwell in the house of the Lord all the days of my life, to behold the beauty of the Lord ..." (Psalm 27:4). "Whom have I in heaven but you? And there is nothing upon earth that I desire besides you. My flesh and my heart may fail, but God is the strength of my heart and my portion forever" (Psalm 73:25f.).

How then can Christianity, which distinguishes itself from Judaism by adding the New Testament to the Old, have any superiority? The New Testament, like the Old, teaches that God forgives sin; but in the person and work of Jesus Christ, it shows *how* God, who is righteous, can nevertheless forgive sinners and bestow such ultimate blessings upon them. Then too, in line with its emphasis that the blessings of God, enjoyed by the people of God in all ages, come through Christ's death and resurrection, the New Testament clears up the ambiguity and imprecision of the Old Testament regarding eternal life. "Jesus Christ abolished death and brought immortality and life to light through the gospel" (2 Timothy 1:10). The New Testament sees all of God's promises as having already been guaranteed and vouchsafed to us in Christ (2 Corinthians 1:20). Whereas the Old Testament drops hints about a future resurrection and eternal life (e.g., Isaiah 26:19), it is only in the New Testament that such teaching comes emphatically to light (John 11:25; Philippians 3:20–21).

Accordingly, it is in the New Testament that the blessings of God are offered to all nations, whereas in the Old Testament, while such blessings do occasionally come to non-Jews, the prophets stress a future time when the nations will explicitly receive these blessing. Therefore, Christianity has the slight edge over Judaism in that (1) immortality becomes explicit, (2) how God can be righteous when he forgives becomes explicit, (3) the future blessings of the Old Testament become present, and (4) the people of all nations receive an explicit offer of blessings. Like the Old Testament, the New speaks of how God completely quenches heart thirst (Isaiah 55:1f.; John 4:13f.), but it adds that God will do it forever (Ephesians 2:7). Both the Old and New Testaments speak of how God satisfies the heart with great joy (Psalm 4:7; 1 Peter 1:8). Surely, then, if the Old and New Testaments are true, we can find enduring joy, rustless treasure, contentment's camping ground, and deathless pleasure in the God who revealed himself throughout the redemptive history recorded in the Old and New Testaments, and consummately in the person of Jesus Christ. Here alone, then, of all the claims to truth we will find that which truly answers to the cry of the human heart. If the Bible is true, it is not boring. Therefore, it is reasonable to turn our attention to the question of whether the message of the Bible is true.

Now it should be clear that we are not concerning ourselves with the question of the Bible's truth because of a predisposition to believe it as true—which would then rank our efforts to show that it is true on the same level as the apologetics for every claim to truth. Instead, we are considering whether it is true because an examination of the options narrows our field of inquiry only to the Bible as giving that teaching which could, if true, satisfy our quest for happiness. Note well that we are not saying the Bible is true because it meets our needs; all we are saying is that its claim to truth merits our consideration because it alone would answer to our heart's cry. Its claim to truth will be good news only if it is true news. We must now turn our attention to the question of whether or not the Bible is true.

Chapter Nine—Why the Good News Is True News

What methodology should we follow to determine whether the Bible's understanding of God is true? The Bible claims that God is love, that throughout eternity his extravagant kindness will never depart from those who trust him, that he will raise them from the dead, that he will judge the world in righteousness so that all of earth's wrongs will finally be set right. The Bible claims that God will forgive sin on the basis of faith in what Christ has done. It claims that for the believer, death constitutes no loss but rather the incomparable gain of all that Christ has secured for us. It claims that God will never allow his own to be tested above what they are able to bear, but will always make a way out for them. It claims that God will supply all of the needs of those who trust him, etc., etc. People could find fulfillment for the ultimate longings of their hearts if all this were true, but how can its truth or falsehood be known?

The German philosopher, Ludwig Feuerbach (1804–1872), argued that Christians (or those espousing any religious faith) were simply expressing, in that faith, their inner dispositions and thoughts. "Such as are a man's thoughts and dispositions, such is his god," declared Feuerbach.[106] Thus, for example, "The essence of faith ... is the idea that that which man wishes actually is: he wishes to be immortal, therefore his is immortal; he wishes for the existence of a being who can do everything which is impossible to Nature and reason, therefore such a being exists; he wishes for a world which corresponds to the desires of the heart ... while nevertheless there exists a world the opposite of that subjective one, and hence this [objective] world must pass away ..."[107] For Feuerbach, religion was only the projection of the desires of a person's heart, but he argued that no faith could survive which ever acknowledged this: "Ignorance of [this] is fundamental to the peculiar nature of religion."[108]

But the American philosopher of pragmatism, William James (1842–1910), believed it was possible to acknowledge that religion was primarily "the will to believe" without thereby destroying itself. He argued that, in response to the momentous option offered by a religious claim, skepticism is by no means the more reasonable course of action. Skepticism is primarily interested in avoiding error, but in so doing it risks missing the truth. "If religion be true and the evidence for it be still insufficient," said James, "I do not wish ... to forfeit my sole chance in life of getting upon the winning side—that chance depending, of course, on my willingness to run the risk of acting as if my passional need of taking the world religiously might be prophetic and right."[109] No doubt, then, if James were convinced by the preceding chapter that only the religion of the Bible could give true fulfillment to a person's soul, he would then say that we ought by all means espouse it, yet "we lose the good *if it be true* just as certainly as if we positively

---

[106] Ludwig Feuerbach, *The Essence of Christianity*, Marian Evans (tr.) (London: Kegan Paul, Trench, etc., 1890), p. 12.

[107] *Ibid.*, p. 128.

[108] *Ibid.*, p. 13.

[109] W. James, "The Will to Believe," *The Will to Believe and Other Essays in Popular Philosophy*. Dover ed. (n. p., Dover Publications, 1956), p. 27.

chose to disbelieve."[110] Therefore, with so much possibly to gain by believing and so much certainly to lose by remaining skeptical, the reasonable thing, then is to believe.

James knew that this line of thinking sounded very close to Pascal's famous "wager"— briefly: if the odds that God exists are only infinity to one, we should nevertheless stake all on God's existence, for even if we were wrong, and even if believing in God incurred some finite loss for this life, it would still have been better to hold open the possibility of infinite gain than close the door to it.[111] And, James acknowledged that there would be something artificial about a faith that is the product of the strategy of the gaming table. His purpose in using Pascal's wager in his famous essay, "The Will to Believe," was the negative one of showing the unreasonableness of applying the scientist's wait-and-see skepticism to the momentous option implied in all religious claims to truth. "Unless there be some preexisting tendency to believe ... the option offered to the will by Pascal is not a living option."[112] For James the pragmatist, this preexisting tendency came not from the intellect but from a certain set of values in one's heart. James argued that a specific religious belief and a specific conduct always go hand in hand, and that as one learns, pragmatically, how one pattern of conduct brings more sense of felicity and dignity to life, he would then settle for the religious belief which it presupposed. He himself opted for a pluralistic theism of finite gods—a polytheism!—because he thought that belief in an infinite, omnipotent God made men puppets whose conduct was characterized by the undesirable qualities of fatalism. Thus, in espousing polytheism, James was simply expressing the ultimate desires of his heart. But to face this fact squarely is to destroy one's faith, as Feuerbach pointed out.

Thus, we should never say that the Bible's good news is true news because it is good news. Instead, its truth must be based on something besides our desire for it to be true. There are two ways people have attempted to show the Bible to be true. One was is to argue from its historical origins; the other, to argue from the gift of faith that God gives a person to credit it as true. The greatest exponents of this second way were John Calvin and the Danish philosopher, Soren Kierkegaard. Calvin acknowledged that historical arguments have a certain power to confirm faith and to show up the error of unbelief, but God himself, through the Holy Spirit, must finally persuade the heart. Calvin wrote,

> "It is true that, if we were inclined to argue the point, many things might be adduced which certainly evince, if there be any God in heaven, that he is the Author of the Law, and the Prophecies, and the Gospel. Even though men of learning and deep judgment rise up in opposition, and exert and display all the powers of their minds in this dispute, yet, unless they are wholly lost to all sense of shame, this confession will be extorted from them: the Scripture exhibits the plainest evidences that it is God who speaks in it ... Yet it is acting a preposterous part, to endeavor to produce sound faith in the Scripture by disputations ... Though anyone vindicates the sacred word of God from the aspersions of men, yet this will not fix in their hearts that

---

[110] *Ibid.*, p. 26.
[111] James, *op. cit.*, p. 26.
[112] James, *op. cit.*, p. 6.

assurance which is essential to true piety ... [Profane men] wish and expect [Scripture] to be proved by rational arguments, that Moses and the Prophets spoke by divine inspiration. But I reply, that the testimony of the Spirit is superior to all reason. For as God alone is sufficient witness of himself in his word, so also the word will never gain credit in the hearts of men, till it be confirmed by the internal testimony of the Spirit. It is necessary, therefore, that the same Spirit, who spoke by the mouths of the prophets, should penetrate into our hearts, to convince us that they faithfully delivered the oracles which were divinely entrusted to them." (*Institutes*, I, vii, 4)

Calvin continued:

"[Scripture] obtains the credit which it deserves with us by the testimony of the Holy Spirit. For though [Scripture] conciliate our reverence by its internal majesty, it never seriously affects us till it is confirmed by the Spirit in our hearts. Therefore, being illuminated by him, we now believe the divine original of the Scripture, not our own judgment or that of others, but we esteem the certainty, that we have received it from God's own mouth by the ministry of men, to be superior to that of any human judgment, and equal to that of an intuitive perception of God in it. We seek not arguments or probabilities to support our judgment, but submit our judgments and understandings as to a thing concerning which it is impossible for us to judge ... It is such a persuasion, therefore, as requires no reasons; such a knowledge as is supported by the highest reason, in which, indeed the mind rests with greater security and constancy than in any reasons; it is, finally, such a sentiment as cannot be produced but by a revelation from heaven." (*Institutes*, I, vii 5)

Søren Kierkegaard (1813–1855) likewise emphasized that certainty regarding God's revelation in Christ could come only through a miracle in which God effects faith through a direct work on the soul. Like Calvin, he believed that faith could never be satisfied with only the "probabilities" that can be advanced by arguments and reasonings. He said, for example, "An approximation is essentially incommensurable with an infinite personal interest in an eternal happiness."[113] By this he meant that historical evidence for the truth of the Bible could never lead beyond high probability, or, as he preferred to say it, never beyond an "approximation" of certainty. Since the soul has "an infinite personal interest in an eternal happiness," it can never be satisfied with the approximations, the high probabilities which are all that reasoning, based on empirical data, can yield. To satisfy this "infinite personal interest," Kierkegaard, like Calvin before him, had to have an absolute knowledge regarding the nature of empirical data. Thus, Kierkegaard affirmed that "faith is itself a miracle."[114]

Hence God himself completes the knowing process, but Kierkegaard affirmed, in distinction to Calvin, that the thing known in faith must itself be discontinuous with reason. Such truths affirmed by faith—as that the little baby cooing in the manger is really the

---

[113] S. Kierkegaard, *Concluding Unscientific Postscript*, D. Swanson (tr.) (Princeton: Princeton University Press, 1944), p. 26.
[114] *Ibid.*, p. 53.

God who created the universe—are a paradox which is an offense to reason. Reason can never help faith; if granted any value at all in matters of faith, it succeeds only in destroying faith. Thus, when faith alone is in operation, men not only have complete certainty regarding Jesus as the Son of God, but they embrace this truth not in the academic way of a spectator but with the full passion which answers to man's "infinite personal interest in eternal happiness." Thus, for both Calvin and Kierkegaard, knowledge that the Bible's good news is true news comes not by a person's inherent powers to know, but only by a special power imparted by God himself. In this way, they claimed they avoided the merely high probabilities which human knowing-powers can derive from empirical data, for in their system, it is God who gives absolute certainty.

But while God himself has absolute knowledge of all things, it is a real problem to understand how someone distinct from him can know as he knows. Calvin spoke of having a certainty that the Bible is the word of God as "equal to that of an intuitive perception of God in it" and as being produced by a "sentiment" made possible only by revelation. But when we experience an intuition or sentiment, we are conscious that they are distinct from us, and we deal with them as such. We have to decide whether or not they should be credited. Even though a sentiment or intuition arises from the Holy Spirit in the heart (cf. Romans 8:16, "The Spirit himself bearing witness with our spirit ..."), we still remain separate from it. Therefore, we must "test the spirits to see whether they are of God" (1 John 4:1). As long as we remain a knower distinct from a claim to knowledge, even as inward as that of a sentiment or intuition, we still have to test it and thus decide whether or not to accept it. As long as we remain distinct from the Holy Spirit who dwells in us, we will have to test all sentiments and intuitions rising up in our hearts to see whether or not they stem from the Holy Spirit. To do this we must use criteria. But in applying criteria to test the validities of our sentiments, we are really standing off from them and handling them as we would handle claims to truth coming from the outward empirical world. Thus, in handling our sentiments and intuitions, we can never achieve the absolute certainty of such non-empirical formal knowledge as two plus two equals four; we must be content with high probability and close approximation.

To Kierkegaard's objection that close approximation does not answer perfectly to the soul's infinite interest in an eternal happiness, we need only observe with what complete passion we can react to only highly probable knowledge. We have only approximate certainty that our life is in danger when we see a car bearing down on us while in a cross walk (we might be dreaming), but we leap out of the way with a passion that makes every nerve in our body tingle. We have only approximate certainty that we must submit our income tax return by the April 15 deadline, but we respond so passionately to this knowledge (and the penalties for filing it late or not at all) that we can dredge up energies to go on calculating all night, if necessary. Why then cannot the soul's consuming interest in an eternal happiness be fully satisfied with a high probability, gained from historical, empirical reasoning that the Bible is true? Then too, if faith is based on historical data, we can preach as did the apostles and seek to persuade people by an appeal to data shared in common with them, rather than having to resort to the *tour de force* of saying, in effect, "I am right because I have the Holy Spirit."

But how can we validate every part of the Bible on the basis of historical evidence? It is not possible to apply what the historian calls "control" to every affirmation made in Scripture. In the parlance of the historian, we possess "control" in handling a document purporting to tell what happened when we know enough about the milieu from which it emerged to be able to show the probability of its being true or of its being a product of a writer's fancy or deliberate deception.

This concrete example will help explain just what the term "historical control" means: One of Napoleon's officers, Jean-Baptiste Antoine Marcellin Marbot, wrote in his book *The Memoirs of General Baron de Marbot*, that on the night of 7 May 1809, he crossed the raging torrents of the Danube in order to free some prisoners from the Austrian army camped on the other side. Marbot's boast is subject to historical control because there is much knowledge from many sources about what both Napoleon's army and the Austrian army were doing on or about 7 May 1809. There is also knowledge about what kind of person Marbot was. Napoleon's letters indicate that even on 8 May, the Danube had not yet begun to flood. Records from both armies indicate that the Austrians were not across the river on 7 May. Napoleon's army records also reveal a request for promotion from Marbot, made six weeks later, in which he said nothing at all about performing such a daring exploit—a fact which any officer seeking promotion would most certainly have included. Then too, from various sources the historian knows that Marbot was an inveterate braggart. Thus, there is sufficient knowledge of the milieu of Marbot and the purported evening of 7 May 1809, for the historian to have "control," that is, a basis upon which to conclude that in all probability Marbot, in making this entry in his diary, was simply remaining true to his reputation of being a braggart.

Now it is obvious that for much of the Bible, no such control exists. This is especially true the farther we go back into the biblical narrative. The biblical writers claim that Israel was released from bondage in Egypt and led to the promised land through a most remarkable series of God's mighty acts. Egyptian history, however, provides no corroborating evidence for such an event. Except for what the Bible tells us, we know nothing of the milieu out of which the book of Exodus came. How, on the basis of historical reasoning, then, can we know that the Exodus occurred in the manner and with the interpretation that the Bible ascribes to the event; or that Cain slew Abel; or that Adam and Eve sinned in the Garden of Eden; etc., etc.? To be sure, there are scattered events here and there in the Old Testament for which there is some historical control. The Moabite Stone, discovered in 1868, confirms 2 Kings 3:5, "[Mesha], the king of Moab rebelled against the king of Israel," for example.

There is more control for the New Testament, and a number of events to which it alludes receive confirmation from other sources of knowledge for that time. Writing around 90 CE, Josephus the Jew mentions John the Baptist (*Antiquities*, xviii, 116–119), Jesus (?) (*Antiquities* xviii, 63f.), and James the brother of Jesus (*Antiquities*, xx, 200). The mention in Acts 18:1f. that during the reign of the Emperor Claudius the Jews had to leave Rome is alluded to by the Roman historians Suetonius (*The Deified Claudius*, XXV, 4) and Dio (*Roman History*, LX, 6, 6). There are other such places, but for the most part these are of such an incidental nature that they offer no help whatsoever in answering our question of whether the Bible is true when it claims that God, on the basis of the death and resurrection of Jesus Christ, is able to keep from expressing his anger against us for our sins but rather expresses his love for us with his whole heart and soul, as we trust in him, and will therefore pursue after us to do us good in this life and raise us up so we can enjoy him throughout eternity. **The only way the truth of this claim could be verified is for there to be some event in the Bible for which there is sufficient historical control to confirm it as having happened, and which at the same time could confirm the whole of the redemptive history recorded in the Bible, both in regard to the events comprising this history and the meaning which the biblical writers ascribe to them.**

The Historical Argument for the Truth of the Bible

Paul's Conversion and Commission

Such an event occurs in connection with the great turning point in redemptive history when, according to the Bible, God no longer dealt almost exclusively with the Jewish nation but, through the apostles of Jesus, and particularly Paul, sent the message of redemption to the other nations of the world. There is sufficient historical control to credit the basic elements of this event which are necessary for knowing the truth both of the events and the meaning of the redemptive history that the Bible sets forth. The easiest place to gain access to knowledge of this event is Paul's report of his own conversion experience in Galatians 1:13ff.

Historians are agreed that the apostle Paul wrote Galatians. In the early part of this epistle, Paul's purpose was to convince his readers that he was an apostle and thus had the authority to be Christ's spokesman. Paul had founded the churches in Galatia, but after he had gone to preach elsewhere, certain leaders from Jerusalem, whom it is convenient to call Judaizers, came into Galatia and declared that Paul's teaching was false. They argued that he had received no direct commission from Jesus Christ himself but that, instead, he had been a mere understudy of those who were apostles. Claiming to be true representatives of the apostles, the Judaizers taught that for Gentiles to share in the blessings which God had been promising to the nation of Israel ever since the time of Abraham, they must not merely repent of their sins and trust Christ (as Paul had taught), but must also be circumcised and adhere to the dietary regulations of the Jews. Reports of what these Judaizers were teaching and of how quickly the Galatians were moving away from his teaching (Galatians 1:6) reached Paul. He immediately dispatched a letter to the Galatian churches in which he began by asserting that he was "an apostle—not from men nor through men, but through Jesus Christ and God the Father, who raised him from the dead" (Galatians 1:1).

In the thinking of the early church, the term "apostle" came to be applied to those who had been personally commissioned by the risen Jesus to stand in his stead and preach his message to the world. Those who received this title in the gospels were the ones whom Jesus sent forth to preach his message that "the kingdom of heaven is at hand," and to have authority to perform miracles, even to the extent of raising the dead (Matthew 10:1ff.; cf. Mark 6:7ff., especially v. 30; and Luke 9:10). Despite Jesus' promise that he would not remain in death, these men fled from him when he was arrested, and Peter, the chief apostle, denied him. The gospel records indicate that not one of these had the courage to be around when Jesus was buried (Matthew 27:55ff.). They were in hiding because they feared the Jews (John 20:19). Nevertheless, when Jesus rose from the dead, he appeared to these people and commanded them to be his spokesmen before the whole world (Matthew 28:18–20; Luke 24:44–49; Acts 1:6–8). "The Gospels and the Acts leave no doubt that it was solely through the work of the risen Christ that from the scattered disciples there arose a church full of hope and ready for work. It was also through the risen Christ that the disciples received a renewal of their commission to preach and so carry out their vocation as apostles."[115] Thus, to be an apostle one had (1) to have the risen Christ appear to him and (2) to have been commissioned by him to convey his message to the world.

But it was not merely the twelve who fulfilled these prerequisites. In Romans 16:7 Paul classes Andronicus and Junias as apostles. In Galatians 1:19 he seems also to regard James as an apostle when he says, "I saw none of the other apostles except James the Lord's brother." Luke, in Acts 14:4 and 14 regards Paul and Barnabas as apostles. That a group larger than the twelve were apostles is indicated by 1 Corinthians 15:5ff., where Paul, in listing those to whom Jesus appeared, included not only the twelve but also "five hundred brethren," James, "all the apostles," and then "last of all," Paul said, "as to one untimely born, he appeared to me. For I am the least of the apostles, unfit to be called an apostle, because I persecuted the church of God. But by the grace of God I am what I am, and his grace toward me was not in vain. On the contrary, I worked harder than any of them, though it was not I, but the grace of God which is with me." Hence while the circle of the apostles in the early church was large enough to include not only James but also Andronicus, Junias, Barnabas, and Paul, it does not appear that all to whom Jesus appeared became apostles. It does not seem that all of the five hundred brethren who saw him at one time were apostles any more than the women to whom he appeared. Those to whom Jesus appeared became apostles only if he also commissioned them to preach.

Paul's first step in combating the Judaizers was to persuade his readers that he was an apostle and that the message they had received from him was the message of Jesus Christ himself. Paul said, "If anyone is preaching to you a gospel contrary to that which you received, let him be accursed … Now I want you to know, brothers and sisters, that the gospel I preached is not of human origin. For I did not receive it or learn it from any human source; instead I received it by a revelation of Jesus Christ." (Galatians 1:9, 11–12). Paul made this statement, not as one who was assuming divine prerogatives to himself but as one who could only conclude, from the way God had dealt with him, that he

---

[115] K. H. Renstrof, "apostolos," *Theologisches Wörterbuch zum N. T.* (Stuttgart: W. Kohlhammer, 1933), I, 431.

had been made an apostle, not because of any worth in himself but simply by the grace of God. Indeed, Paul regarded himself as standing before people "on Christ's behalf" (2 Corinthians 5:20), but always as one who was simply "a slave of Jesus Christ." In rebuking the parties at Corinth who were championing him or Apollos or Peter, he replied that their work mattered little in comparison to what God was doing (1 Corinthians 3:6ff.). Paul regarded the message both he and the other apostles preached to be so completely from Jesus Christ that he said, "even if we [himself and the other apostles] or an angel from heaven should preach a gospel contrary to the one we preached to you, let him be condemned to hell!" (Galatians 1:8). Paul was convinced that he had such authority because he was simply an instrument in the hand of Jesus Christ.

Paul traced the source of this profound conviction back to what happened to him on the Damascus road. The appearance of Jesus to him there was, to him, a wholly objective occurrence, which completely changed him from being a persecutor of the church to being a missionary to the Gentiles. And just as the memory of this experience sustained his conviction that Christ had commissioned him as his spokesman upon the earth, so Paul also thought that the contrast of his past life with his present life was so complete that everyone else should be just as persuaded as he that he was an apostle.

Paul therefore did not simply make the claim that his teaching was that of Jesus Christ and let it go at that. Rather, with the conjunction "for" at the outset of Galatians 1:13, he began to rehearse the reasons why everyone should be as persuaded as he that he was an apostle. In Paul's thinking, a person's faith should not rest blindly on his claim to truth, but on the evidences that he was indeed an apostle. Verses 13 and 14 recount Paul's life before his conversion: "For you have heard of my previous way of life in Judaism, how intensely I persecuted the church of God and tried to destroy it. I was advancing in Judaism beyond many Jews of my own age and was extremely zealous for the traditions of my fathers." We notice how every point which Paul made in these verses functioned to support his claim that the message he preached came from Christ and not from himself. By the use of the imperfects ἐδίωκον (I was persecuting), ἐπόρθουν (I was destroying), and προέκοπτον (I was advancing), Paul stressed the dogged continuity and firm adherence of purpose that characterized his life before his conversion.[116] The final participial clause in verse 14, "being extremely zealous for the traditions of my fathers," gives the cause for this unwavering resolve for Judaism and hatred of the Christian church: he was more zealous to maintain the traditions of the fathers than any other Pharisee.

It is not difficult to reconstruct the reason why Paul was so implacably opposed to Christianity. Philippians 3:4–7 is another place where Paul spoke of his pre-conversion past. There he stressed how great was the glorying and sense of satisfaction that he received from bearing all of his Jewish distinctives: "I do not rely on human credentials—though mine too are significant. If someone thinks he has good reasons to put confidence in human credentials, I have more: I was circumcised on the eighth day, from the people

---

[116] H. Schlier, *Der Brief an die galater Kommentar*, von H. A. W. Meyer, 12th ed. (Göttingen: Vandenhoeck & Ruprecht, 1962), *ad. loc.*

of Israel and the tribe of Benjamin, a Hebrew of Hebrews. I lived according to the law as a Pharisee. In my zeal for God I persecuted the church. According to the righteousness stipulated in the law I was blameless. But these assets I have come to regard as liabilities because of Christ." What Paul was through birth, and what he had come to be through his zealous adherence to Pharasaism, gave him a sense of gain and confidence in himself that he believed no one else could match. No doubt Paul was very much like the Jew whom he described in Romans 2:17–20, who relied on having the law (or the temple, cf. Jeremiah 7:4), boasted about his relationship to God, and who, because he regarded himself as instructed out of the law, prided himself on knowing God's will, approving what is excellent, being a light to the blind, a corrector of the foolish, and a teacher of children. There is no way a person can be happier with himself than to be convinced that he is living in such a way that God himself is applauding.

Such a person could view the teaching of the Christians only with horror. From the sermon at Pentecost, it was clear that Peter regarded all Jews as lost, regardless of their religious credentials, until they believed in Christ. Repentance and faith in Christ, Peter had declared, gave one forgiveness of sins and acceptance with God. Paul saw that such teaching completely destroyed his basis for believing that God was applauding his pedigree and religious zeal. If remission of sins came through faith in Christ, what difference did it make, then, whether he was circumcised the eighth day, a Pharisee, and a blameless adherent of the law? More perceptive than many another Jew, Paul could see that the teaching of the Christians was diametrically opposed to the presumably orthodox teachings of the Pharisees, and therefore, out of devotion to God and as a proof of his devotion, Paul took it upon himself to lead a persecution against the church. To see Stephen stoned and to drag other Christians off to prison, far from hurting his conscience, enabled him to exult that he, more than his fellows, was truly devoted to God.

Many have, of course, argued that Paul's conscience must have been hurting when he was persecuting the church, so that his conversion was simply another step in a psychological process which had been developing for some time. For example, C. H. Dodd said, "We may be sure that the principal reason why [Paul] could embrace this grim task [of persecuting the church] was that here were enemies of the Law whom he could smite as he was failing to smite the enemies of the Law in his own breast. … The repressed passions of his nature found a consecrated outlet here: the 'threats and slaughter' which he breathed out promised to cleanse his bosom of much perilous stuff."[117]

According to Paul's own testimony, however, he was conscious only of being completely "blameless" (Philippians 3:6) in his pre-conversion days. In 1 Timothy 1:13 he said that in those days he had acted "ignorantly in unbelief." In 2 Timothy 1:3 he declared, "I have served God with a clear conscience as my ancestors did." Such statements concur with Luke's quotation of what Paul said when he stood before the Sanhedrin: "Brothers, I have lived before God in all good conscience up to this day" (Acts 23:1). To the objection that such statements were merely part of Paul's way of making a good case for himself, it may be replied that Paul must have sincerely thought that his

---

[117] C. H. Dodd, *The Mind of Paul* (Manchester: John Rylands Library, 1934), p. 12.

conscience had been clear before, as well as after, his conversion. Often, what Jesus said to Paul when confronting him on the Damascus road, namely that "it hurts you to kick against the goads" (Acts 26:14), has been regarded as a clear indication that Paul had been suffering pangs of conscience in persecuting the Christians. But this phrase was used by the Greeks to express the futility of striving against fate or against the gods, and its meaning to Paul on the Damascus road was that it was now as futile for him to try any longer to work against Christ as it would be for an ox to kick against the plowman's goad.[118]

Concerning the state of Paul's mind in his pre-conversion days, Schlier says, "Paul's pre-Christian past serves unmistakably as a guarantee that there can be no talk of any kind of receptivity on his part (even an unconscious one!) for the Gospel (with its emphasis on grace) preached by the spokesmen for the Christian community. His inner bent of mind and his way of acting were wholly incompatible with the Christian message."[119] Schlier continues, "Whoever talks about an inner, private preparation in Paul for the Gospel affirms not only that he understands Paul better than Paul himself, but that he wants to force Paul's religious experience, contrary to his own statements, into some kind of a psychological scheme of conversion."[120]

Note. Maurice Goguel thought that it was impossible to postulate that Paul was conscious of any struggle going on in his soul while he persecuted the church. But Goguel argued that in Paul's subliminal self the ethical superiority of the very Christianity he persecuted was working away at Paul so that "a moment came when the activity in the unconscious gained such strength that it ... burst forth in the field of consciousness and became objectified in a vision which the apostle judged to be the direct presence of Christ himself."[121] The only evidence that Goguel can advance to enforce such a hypothesis is the supposedly parallel conversion stories of how Sundar Singh was converted to Protestantism and how Ratisbonne, the Jew, was converted to Roman Catholicism. But in recounting the stories of these men, Goguel includes incidents which certainly seem to involve prior conscious tugs toward the religion finally espoused. Sundar Singh, days before his conversion which is supposed to parallel Paul's, was reading his Bible secretly,[122] and Ratisbonne, days before his conversion, confessed that he felt strange emotions when he entered a Roman Catholic church. One must conclude, then, that Goguel failed to provide any true analogy for the conversion of Paul.

Note. Paul's conversion story is also far different from that of Joseph Smith, the founder of Mormonism. As Joseph Smith was growing up in upper New York state, he became exceedingly troubled at the fact that the Presbyterians, Methodists, and

---

[118] Kirsopp Lake and H. J. Cadbury *The Acts of the Apostles*, vol 4. *The Beginnings of Christianity*, 5 vols. (London: Macmillan, 1920–33), p. 318.
[119] Schlier, *op.cit.*, p. 52.
[120] *Ibid.*
[121] Maurice Goguel, *The Birth of Christianity*. H. Snape (tr.) (London: George Allen & Unwin, 1953), p. 85.
[122] *Ibid.*, p. 77.

Baptists were carrying on such violent theological disputes with one another. He concluded that none of them could be representing the Word of God if all were disagreeing with each other so much. His consuming passion then became finding the true Word of God;[123] therefore, there is no reason to exclude the possibility that his claim to see the angel delivering the Word of God to him was simply a hallucination.

Thus, according to Galatians 1:13–14, Paul's only contact with Christian leaders before his conversion had been as one who persecuted them; therefore, his present preaching of the Gospel could not have originated from that period. In making this point, which is so crucial to his argument that he is an apostle, we should note that Paul makes statements which have historical control in that they echo what was already general knowledge for his readers and others. "You have heard of my former life in Judaism ..." indicates a knowledge of Paul that was so widespread that the Judaizers could not hope to discredit his complete disinclination and hatred of Christianity before he was converted. This knowledge of what Paul was like before conversion must have been widespread, for if Galatians 1:13–14 were something that Paul was now declaring for the first time, it would simply have been his word against the Judaizer's word, and the Judaizers could have refuted it by saying that such a statement was simply one more of Paul's devious ways of trying to pawn himself off as an apostle. Therefore, historical control credits rather than discredits what Paul was saying in Galatians 1:13–14.

In Galatians 1:5ff. Paul's point was to show that at no time after his conversion did he ever become an understudy of any of the apostles—a point which has control that validates it, because surely if the fact had been otherwise, the Judaizers would have known and could have won the day at Galatia immediately. Thus, since Paul's preaching is not the result of any contact with the other apostles, and since there had been no predisposition on his part to espouse Christianity, it follows that Pauls' present occupation of spearheading a Christian mission to the Gentiles is explained by God's appearing to him and commissioning him for this task. Paul's thesis in verse 12 is that he received the Gospel not from men, but only from Jesus Christ, and the only event in his past life that could account for his present activity as a minister to the Gentiles is that God "was pleased to reveal his Son in me that I might preach him among the Gentiles" (Galatians 1:16).

That Paul should have become a Christian when he was single-mindedly opposed to Christianity for reasons already mentioned is difficult enough to account for apart from his own explanation that Jesus met him on the Damascus road. But to explain—from forces already present in Paul's own background—how he who was so zealous for the law and the traditions of the Jews should have become not only a Christian but the one spearheading the Christian mission to the Gentiles confronts us with such a tremendously difficult task that it is hard to see how there could be any takers. Also, his stand for Christ, far from giving him any worldly gain, placed his life in jeopardy almost daily; but people never risk their lives for what they know to be a fraud.

---

[123] History of the Church of Jesus Christ of Latter-Day Saints. Period I. *History of Joseph Smith, the Prophet*, by himself. (Salt Lake City: Desert News, 1902), pp. 3ff.

We do well to reflect on how a Jew of Paul's orthodox stripe shrank back in horror from any thought of sitting down and eating with a Gentile. If Peter, stemming from the general common folk of Israel, argued loud and long with God that he should not be required to eat any of the foods forbidden in Leviticus, which would have kept him from entering the centurion Cornelius' house (Acts 10:9ff.), how much more difficult would it have been for Paul, having received a scribe's thorough education, to have gone into a Gentile's house and be heard saying, "Pass me another helping of pork, please"? Paul, before he was converted, no doubt agreed with other Jews in regarding Gentiles as dogs. In those days there were no humane societies to clear cities of stray dogs, and neither were there any garbage collectors. But the large bands of stray dogs that roamed the cities took care of the garbage problem, devouring whatever was edible. To the Jews, the Gentiles seemed like dogs (cf. Matthew 15:26; Philippians 3:2; Revelation 22:15), because they ate indiscriminately. But after his conversion, Paul sat down to table with the "dogs," and was even more willing to eat with them than was Peter, as we learn from Galatians 2:11–14.

It is no wonder that Acts reports that when Paul returned to Jerusalem, he was such a *persona non grata* that scarcely a week had passed before the whole city was in an uproar (Acts 21:30ff.) and people were saying, "Away with such a fellow from the earth! For he ought not to live!" (Acts 22:22). How could Paul, who was once the chief persecutor of the Christians because their teaching implied a denigration of the Jewish distinctives, now be the one whom the Jews sought to kill chiefly because he declared to the Gentiles that they could have all of the blessings of Abraham simply by faith in Christ, apart from taking on any Jewish distinctives?

No one doubts that Paul did head up the Gentile mission and that a distinctive feature of this mission was that Gentiles were not required to take on any Jewish distinctives. Here, then, is an effect that is established as having occurred in history, but what is its cause? We search in vain for its cause in Paul's having hallucinated, because when people hallucinate (and they often do), they think in directions in which they are already inclined to go. But there was nothing in Paul's background that inclined him to make the Jewish distinctives of secondary importance and put Gentiles on an equal footing with the Jews. The only satisfactory explanation is the one which Paul himself supplies, namely, that the risen Jesus appeared to him on the Damascus road and commissioned him to be his spokesman to the Gentiles. As one reads Paul's epistles, one senses how large a role his consciousness of being commissioned as an apostle to the Gentiles played in carrying out his mission to them.

In Galatians 1:15ff., part of the passage which has been chiefly under consideration, Paul stressed that the underlying force which had driven him since his conversion had been that God revealed his Son in him that he might preach him among the Gentiles. This makes it clear that the cause for Paul's subsequent action of spearheading the Gentile mission was not at all the mere brute fact that Jesus appeared to him on the Damascus road, but that Jesus appeared *and* commissioned him to preach amongst the Gentiles. Likewise, in Ephesians 3:2ff, Paul regards his work amongst the Gentiles as stemming from the fact that he was entrusted with the stewardship of making known the revelation that "through the gospel the Gentiles are fellow heirs, fellow members of the body, and fellow partakers of the promise in Christ Jesus" (Ephesians 3:6). Then he goes on to say, "Of this gospel I was made a minister according to the gift of God's grace which was given me by the working of his power. To me, though I am the very least of all the saints, this grace was given, to preach to the Gentiles the unsearchable riches of Christ ..."

Thus, in Paul's thinking, his having spearheaded the Gentile mission would never have happened had Jesus merely appeared to him on the Damascus road or had he done nothing more than simply turn him away from persecuting the church. To the contrary, Paul regarded his carrying out of the Gentile mission as possible only because Christ had commissioned him to be his spokesman and to be a channel through which God's plans for the Gentiles would be revealed. Therefore, since Paul did head up the Gentile mission, and since his doing such an outlandish thing can be explained only by his having been commissioned as one to receive, from Christ, revelation regarding God's plans for the Gentiles, Paul must have been a channel through whom revelation came from the risen Christ, or in other words, he must have been an apostle.

Such an understanding of Paul is confirmed in the report of his Damascus road experience in Acts 26:13ff. "At midday, O King, I saw on the way a light from heaven, brighter than the sun, shining round me and those who journeyed with me. And when we had all fallen to the ground, I heard a voice saying to me in the Hebrew language, 'Saul, Saul, why do you persecute me? It hurts you to kick against the goads.' And I said, 'Who are you, Lord?' And the Lord said, 'I am Jesus whom you are persecuting. But rise and stand upon your feet; for I have appeared to you for this purpose, to appoint you to serve and bear witness to the things in which you have seen me and to those in which I will appear to you, delivering you from the people and from the Gentiles—to whom I send you ... Wherefore, King Agrippa, I was not disobedient to the heavenly vision, but declared first to those at Damascus, then at Jerusalem and throughout all the country of Judea, and also to the Gentiles, that they should repent and turn to God and perform deeds worthy of their repentance. ... To this day I have had the help that comes from God, and so I stand here testifying both to small and great ..."

From this passage it is plain that it was not Jesus' mere appearance to Paul that sent him to the Gentiles. The mere appearance, to the contrary, had the effect of only smiting Paul down in shame over his having persecuted Jesus, whom he now understood to be Lord. It is the "but stand ..."—note the strong adversative in the ἀλλὰ that begins Acts 26:16— and what follows in which Jesus appoints Paul as a witness both of what he has seen and of what Jesus will reveal to him in the future, that catapults Paul into the Gentile mission. When we consider how unlikely it was that *Paul* should head up a Gentile mission, and yet that this is just what he did, and that the best explanation of why he did it was that the risen Jesus not only appeared to him but commissioned him as his spokesman, then it becomes apparent that Paul was, indeed, an apostle of Jesus Christ, which means that what he taught was the equivalent of what Jesus Christ wanted taught upon the earth.

Implications

The implications that come from having established that Paul was an apostle are far reaching. To begin with, the absolute authority that Paul ascribed to his teaching should not be charged off as the rantings of an eccentric egotist, but should be taken as a sober recognition of the fact that in all of his teaching, none other than Jesus Christ, the Son of God, is speaking. Thus, it is only natural that if anyone preaches a gospel different from Paul's, he will be accursed (Galatians 1:8–9). Likewise, it was only natural that Paul, when talking on the very complex subject of marriage in 1 Corinthians 7, should carefully notify his readers when he is speaking merely from his own opinion and not from Jesus Christ (cf. 1 Corinthians 7:10, 12). It is also natural that Paul should say to the Thessalonians, "I *adjure* [!] you by the Lord that this epistle be read to the whole congregation" (1 Thessalonians 5:27), and "If anyone refuses to obey what we say in this letter, note that person, and have nothing to do with him, that he may be ashamed …" (2 Thessalonians 3:14f.). Nor is it strange that Paul should rule the teachings of some pseudo-apostles as unworthy of consideration (2 Thessalonians 2:2).

Then too, it should not seem strange that Paul talks of himself as teaching through the inspiration of the Holy Spirit. 1 Corinthians 2:6–13 is a classic passage that sets forth the revelatory powers of Paul and other inspired spokesmen in New Testament times. In verse 10 Paul declares that "God has revealed [revelatory truth—cf. vv. 6–9] to us through the Spirit." Then in verse 13 he says, "We speak [these revelatory truths] in words not taught by human wisdom but taught by the Spirit, interpreting [i.e., "bringing together"—συγκρίνω] spiritual truths to those who possess the Spirit." While 2:14ff. goes on to explain what is true of ordinary people, namely that they can welcome revelatory truth if their hearts have been changed by the Holy Spirit, 2:13 makes it clear that Paul, as one of Christ's spokesmen, claimed that even the words he used to utter revelatory truths were taught him by the Holy Spirit.

> Note: In other words, Paul claimed to be "verbally inspired." Verbal inspiration must be distinguished from mechanical dictation. The latter would be analogous to the way a secretary takes down the boss's letter in shorthand, so that the resulting letter bespeaks the boss's style rather than the secretary's. Though Paul claims to teach in words taught by the Holy Spirit, yet his epistles reveal a style that is peculiar in comparison to the writings of other revelatory spokesmen in Scripture. Thus, in verbal inspiration the Holy Spirit uses a man's peculiar ways of speaking and thinking, but in so doing what he speaks and thinks is still exactly what God wants said.

Thus, if such things are true about Paul, then we regard all of his epistles as the very Word of God. The meaning of each of their parts as determined by their intrinsic genres is what God wants us to know. But we notice in 1 Corinthians 2:6–13 that Paul implied that there were others who were also endowed with the capacity to transmit revelatory truths. The "we" who impart revelation in words taught by the Holy Spirit would naturally include Peter, whom Paul mentions as being on a par with him in the immediate context of this passage (1 Corinthians 3:22), as well as in the more remote contexts of this epistle (1 Corinthians 9:5; 15:5, 7). The way Paul talks in 1 Corinthians 9:6 indicates that he also included Barnabas as an apostle—a fact which would be confirmed by Acts 14:4, 14. In Galatians 1:19, it seems that James is classed along with the other apostles, and according to 1 Corinthians 15:7, Christ did appear to James along with Jude. James was also one of Jesus' brothers, and since, in 1 Corinthians 9:5 "the brothers of the Lord" have the rights of apostles, it follows that Jude should also be included in the "we." Since Paul, who was an apostle, regards these as also being revelatory spokesmen, then we should also regard them as such, and credit their writings as the Word of God. This means crediting the gospels of Matthew and John, Paul's epistles, James, the epistles of Peter, the epistles of John, Jude, and Revelation. Thus, on the basis of the controllable event of Paul's heading up the Gentile mission, we can know that twenty-three of the twenty-seven books of the New Testament are the Word of God.

One of the many ideas these books teach regards the Old Testament as the Word of God. Warfield showed that the formulas "God says ..." and "Scripture [Old Testament] says ..." were interchangeable equivalents in the thinking of the New Testament writers.[124] The classic statement for the authority of the Old Testament is 2 Timothy 3:16, where Paul said, "All Scripture is given by inspiration of God." Paul made this statement to Timothy, who was a Greek, and it would therefore be likely that by "Scripture" Timothy would understand the Greek translation of the Old Testament called the Septuagint, or LXX. In the ancient compilations of the LXX that come down to us today, we find a number of other books besides those comprising the thirty-nine books of the Old Testament in our Bibles. Generally speaking, these extra books—such as Tobit, Judith, Wisdom of Solomon, 1 and 2 Maccabees, etc.—fall into the category of what is called the Apocrypha. In attributing inspiration to the "scriptures" was Paul also certifying the inspiration of the Apocrypha? If so, then the Roman Catholic and Greek Orthodox groups are right in having these books in their Bibles, and we Protestants are wrong in leaving them out.

The answer to this question will depend on which books the Jews regarded as canonical in those days. Such books would be what the apostles also regarded as canonical. There is nothing to indicate that the first Christians and the apostles had any interest at all in revising the prevailing Jewish view of what constituted the Old Testament canon. The first Christians were Jews who did not regard themselves as a schism from Judaism but as those who were in the mainstream of ongoing Judaism. For many years the Christian Bible was simply the Jewish Old Testament, and so what the Jews had regarded as canonical would be what Paul declared to be inspired by God.

IV Esdras 14:18–48, written around 117 BCE, speaks of twenty-four books as comprising the canon, and expressly excludes a number of writings which in all probability were the Apocrypha. Likewise, Josephus, writing around 90 CE, declares, "We [Jews] have not an innumerable multitude of books among us [as the Greeks], but only twenty-two books, which contain the record of all the past times; which are justly believed to be

---

[124] Benjamin Warfield, "'It Says'; 'Scripture Says'; 'God Says,'" *The Inspiration and Authority of the Bible*, S. Craig (ed.) (Philadelphia: Presbyterian and Reformed Publishing Co., 1948), pp. 299–348.

divine; and of them five belong to Moses, which contain his laws and the traditions of the origin of mankind until [Moses'] death. ... As to the time from the death of Moses till the reign of Artaxerxes, king of Persia, who reigned after Xerxes, the prophets, who were after Moses, wrote down what was done in their times in thirteen books. The remaining four books contain hymns to God, and precepts for the conduct of human life. It is true that our history has been written down since Artaxerxes very particularly, but has not been esteemed of like authority with the former by our forefathers, because there has not been an exact succession of prophets since that time ..." (*Apion*, I, 8). Traditions coming down through Judaism indicate that Josephus had two less than the writer of IV Esdras because he regarded Ruth as being part of one book with Judges and Lamentations as part of one book with Jeremiah. Thus, the canon, as indicated by these two sources, consisted of the five books of Moses, thirteen books of the prophets (Joshua, Judges-Ruth, Samuel, Kings, Isaiah, Jeremiah-Lamentations, Ezekiel, the Twelve Minor Prophets, Job, Daniel, Esther, Ezra-Nehemiah, and Chronicles), and the four remaining books, which were Psalms, Proverbs, Song of Solomon, and Ecclesiastes. In other words, the Jewish canon was and is the thirty-nine books in our Old Testament.

Both IV Esdras and Josephus indicate that the books of the Apocrypha were not on a par with these canonical books. These books were written after the Jews were conscious that the prophetic tradition had ceased. The cessation of this is referred to, for example, in 1 Maccabees 9:27, "There was great distress in Israel, such as had not been since the time that prophets ceased to appear among them," and in 14:41, "The Jews and their priests decided that Simon should be their leader and high priest forever, until a trustworthy prophet should arise."

Thus, while the Jews revered the writings made after the time of Artaxerxes (and therefore were prone to have them in their versions of the LXX), they did not, however, regard these books as having the authority of those written before Artaxerxes. It is significant that Philo, living in Alexandria in the middle of the first century, knew of the Apocrypha but never quoted them as Scripture in all his many writings. It is also significant that neither Jesus nor the apostles (who would simply reflect the prevailing Jewish view of this matter), though alluding to the Apocrypha a few times, never quoted from it as Scripture. Thus, the evidence is that Paul, in declaring the "Scriptures" to be inspired, meant only the thirty-nine books presently in the Protestant canon.

The Roman Catholic canon, on the other hand, is the result of having received the Old Testament in the form of the LXX whose editions, as we have said, also included a number of apocryphal books. The usage of these books became firmly entrenched in that tradition of western Christendom. But when Jerome wanted a more accurate translation of the Scriptures and went to Palestine to learn Hebrew, he became acutely aware that the Jews had not regarded these apocryphal books as canonical, and he pled with the Roman church to remove them from the canon. But Jerome did not prevail, for there was the fear that people's faith might be upset if parts of the Bible were taken away. A millennium later, the Reformers did expressly declare that the apocrypha, while consisting of edifying religious writings, were of no authority in the church. Then, in reaction to the Reformation, the Roman church at the Council of Trent declared anyone to be anathema who did not regard the Apocrypha as having equal authority with the rest of Scripture. (In so doing, though, the Roman church left out the apocryphal books of I and II Esdras, as well as the Prayer of Manasseh. There is no general agreement on exactly what books constitute the Apocrypha—which is another reason for rejecting its canonicity.) It is significant, however, that the Russian Orthodox church was bold enough to let facts overthrow tradition in that they banished the Apocrypha from their canon in 1839.

So far, then, the thirty-nine books of the Old Testament and twenty-three of the New Testament have been shown to be the Word of God by arguing from the historically controllable fact that Paul was commissioned as an apostle by Jesus Christ. What then of the remaining four books of the New Testament—Mark, Luke, Acts, and Hebrews—which were not written by apostles? Again, we refer to 1 Corinthians 2:6–13 for help in solving this problem. The immediate context of this passage demands that Apollos be included among those in the "we" who are the revelatory spokesmen to whom the Holy Spirit revealed the things of God. Paul places Apollos on the same level with him in 1 Corinthians 3:4f., 21; 4:6. In 1 Corinthians 4:1 Paul says, "This is how one should regard us, as servants of Christ and stewards of the mysteries of God," and then he makes clear that he included Apollos in the "us" of verse 1 when he said in verse 6, "I have applied all this to myself and Apollos for your benefit ..." Thus, Robertson and Plummer in the *International Critical Commentary* on 1 Corinthians 2:6 say, "St. Paul includes others with himself, not only his immediate fellow-workers but the Apostolic body as a whole." Likewise, G. G. Findlay, in commenting in the *Expositor's Greek Testament* on those included in the "we" of 1 Corinthians 2:6ff. says, "Paul uses the plural ["we"] ... of his fellow-preachers generally, including Apollos."

Therefore, even though Apollos was not an apostle but rather one who had been taught by Paul (Acts 18:25ff.), yet by including him in the "we" of 1 Corinthians 2:6ff., Paul is declaring that he and others who worked together with him in preaching the Gospel were also revelatory spokesmen, even though they were not apostles to whom the risen Jesus had appeared. In that Apollos and others could work and teach harmoniously with Paul and the other apostles, it was evident that such people taught things which were in harmony with what an apostle taught. But Paul takes the matter a step farther and declares that such people were just as inspired as he and the other apostles.

In connection with this it is significant that the authors of Mark, Luke, Acts, and Hebrews were people who, as close associates of the apostles, were certainly in harmony with them. As for John Mark, the author of the Gospel of Mark, the evidences indicate that he was closely associated with the apostles. His home in Jerusalem had been a haven for the persecuted apostles (Acts 12:12ff.). And although he could not live up to Paul's standards for missionary discipline (Acts 13:13; 15:38ff.), later on Paul said that Mark was profitable for the ministry (2 Timothy 4:10). Then too, according to the tradition passed on through Papias, Mark wrote his Gospel in close conjunction with Peter (Eusebius, *Ecclesiastical History*, III, 39). As for Luke who wrote Luke-Acts, there is abundant evidence of how closely associated he was with Paul. In Philemon 24, Luke is called a "fellow worker." His close work with Paul is reflected in the "we" passages of Acts 16:10–17; 20:5–21:18; and 27:1–28:16.

As for the writer of Hebrews, we do not know who he was. Very many people in the early church found comfort regarding Paul as its author, but this is manifestly impossible, since the writer of Galatians 1:11–12 would not be found saying that the word "spoken through the Lord, was confirmed unto us by those who heard [Christ]" (Hebrews 2:3). In this statement the writer of Hebrews explicitly links himself with those who had had the word of Christ mediated to them through the apostles, and thus rules himself out from being an apostle. Origen, the great scholar of the early church, was the first to point out that the Greek style of Hebrews is quite different from that of Paul (Eusebius, *Ecclesiastical History*, VI, 25). Origen confessed that "only God knows" who wrote Hebrews, but from the statement of Hebrews 2:3 and also from the way the author talks of being in close company with Timothy, who was in close company with Paul, we see evidence that its writer moved in the sphere of apostolic influence.

Therefore, since the authors of these four books were in close association with the apostles, there is, on the basis of 1 Corinthians 2:6ff., every reason to regard them as just as inspired as the apostles themselves.

According to the apostles' own teaching, there was no way in which they could appoint their own successors who, like them, would be apostles. Those whom they appointed were bishops, not apostles. Paul declared in 1 Corinthians 15:8 that "last of all, as to one untimely born, [Jesus] appeared also to me." In saying this, Paul clearly indicated that he was the last one to be appointed as an apostle. Then too, Jude in the third verse of his brief epistle said that Christians should "contend earnestly for the faith once for all delivered to the saints." Jude made this statement sometime between 80 and 90 CE, when all of the apostles except himself and John had either died or passed out of the picture. A teaching had infiltrated the churches which denied the lordship of Christ and turned people away from a righteous lifestyle. Hence, he felt constrained to write to the churches and exhort them to contend earnestly for the faith *once for all* delivered to the saints. This faith was the teaching which the apostles had set forth, for in verse 17 Jude exhorted his readers to "remember the words which have been spoken before by the apostles of our Lord Jesus Christ." Thus, Paul and Jude concur in declaring that the teaching of the apostles was the message which God had given *once for all* to the churches. The church down through the ages is therefore not to look for any revelation or teaching beyond that which was given by the apostles themselves or by their close associates. Jesus himself made it clear that the teaching of the apostles was to be final and normative for the church. In the prayer recorded in John 17, he said, "Neither do I pray for these alone [the apostles] but for them also which shall believe on me through their word" (v. 20). Thus, the only source for the word of Jesus both during the apostolic age and since is the apostles.

But how were the words of the apostles to be kept available for the church after the apostles died? The apostle Peter faced this problem as he awaited his martyrdom during the reign of Nero in the year 66. His solution was to summarize his teachings into what is now 2 Peter, so that "at every time you may be able, after my decease, to call these things to remembrance" (2 Peter 1:15). In this way, he would keep his teachings from being distorted. Paul was also martyred during the reign of Nero, and it is significant to note that as Peter concludes his last epistle, he mentions the permanent form which Paul's teaching had assumed in his epistles, collections of which were now possessed by many of the churches (2 Peter 3:15). He even goes so far as to class these writings of Paul with the "Scripture."

Hence, Peter makes it clear that the church would continue to be taught down through the centuries only through the *writings* of the apostles. The New Testament is the collection of these writings which stem either from the apostles themselves or from their close associates. Here is the climax of God's revelation that began in the Old Testament, and here is the teaching which has been once for all delivered to the saints.

After the close of the apostolic age, we find a very definite tendency in the church to follow Peter's lead and regard the teachings of the apostles as continuing in the writings which they had left. In 125 CE, Basileides quoted from the New Testament as Scripture (Hippolytus, *The Refutation of All Heresies*, VII, 14). Justin Martyr, writing in 148, mentions how the churches, during their worship services, read from the "memoirs of the apostles and the writings of the prophets" (*The First Apology of Justin*, 46–47). This means that the words of the apostles were deemed to be Scripture as much as those of the Old Testament prophets. Thus, the church follows the opinion of the apostles who considered themselves on a par with the writers of the Old Testament texts (Romans 1:1; Ephesians 2:20; 3:5).

But for some fifty years after the close of the apostolic age, another tendency is also noticeable in the life of the churches. There was a nostalgic longing for the living voice of the apostles that the church had once enjoyed. Thus Papias, writing about 130 CE, told how he had made it a practice to talk with everyone possible who had known the apostles or their close associates, because as he explained: "I suppose that the things out of books did not profit me so much as the utterances of a voice which lives" (Eusebius, *Ecclesiastical History*, III, 39.4). But this living voice did not help Papias very much. Of the few traditions of his which have survived, there is, for example, the obviously legendary and obscene account of the death of Judas Iscariot. Other legendary accounts of the life of Jesus appeared at this time from those who, like Papias, claimed special knowledge of the apostles' teaching through those who remembered them. They depict the infant Jesus as creating live sparrows and killing his companions when they annoyed him. Such nonsense supports Peter's fear that the apostolic teaching would be distorted if its availability to the church were to depend upon the memory of human beings rather than upon the apostles' own writings.

From 150 CE onward, however, so many traditions purporting to stem from the apostles had appeared that the churches began to realize that they had to give up all attempts to get back to the apostolic word through oral tradition and be content to find this only in what the apostles and their close associates had left in writing. Furthermore, the great heretic, Marcion, had arisen and established a canon consisting only of the gospel of Luke and Paul's epistles—all greatly revised. This realization came not through the decision of any church council but through a conclusion reached by various churches independently. They realized that only by shutting themselves up to the apostolic writings could they remain subservient to the apostolic word upon which they had been founded. As Oscar Cullmann puts it, "Among the numerous Christian writings, the books which were to form the future canon forced themselves on the Church by their intrinsic apostolic authority ..."[125] Thus, in owning up to the primacy of the written record of apostolic teaching, the churches were not, as is sometimes claimed, establishing the New Testament, but were simply acknowledging the apostolic authority on which they had been based all along.

> Note: The great majority of the New Testament books were accepted without dispute as apostolic among the churches. But four or five were questioned in some churches: Hebrews, 2 Peter, 2 & 3 John, Revelation. One reason for questioning a book was that it taught something which several churches regarded as giving a footing to heresies rampant in their particular regions, e.g., Hebrews was disputed in some churches because the heretical sect known as the Montanists used Hebrews 6 to ground their teaching of no possibility of a second repentance (cf. 6:4–6). But the majority of churches regarded these books as canonical, and their decision was acknowledged by the Council of Carthage in 397 CE. If, through modern historical research, it should turn out that some books (the Gospel of John or 2 Peter or Ephesians) were not the immediate products of John or Peter or Paul, their authority nevertheless remains so long as they stem from the historical milieu of the apostles.

When the churches realized that they could know the teachings of the apostles only through the writings which they had left, they experienced a change. Men like Irenaeus and Tertullian, who wrote after 150 CE, reveal a better understanding of salvation as dependent solely upon the grace of God than do those who wrote before 150, when the churches were still longing to return to the apostles via a living voice. These later writers were closer to the apostles than the earlier ones, because they realized that their only source of knowledge of the apostolic teachings was the apostolic writings.

Today we live many centuries after Tertullian and Irenaeus, but we also are able to remove all distance between us and the apostles' teaching by focusing our attention on the New Testament as the climax of God's revelation and the only source for the Word of God. Though removed by two millennia from the conclusion of God's revelation to humanity, we will nevertheless be close to the apostolic teaching to the extent that we are willing to set aside our own preconceived notions of what the Bible means and simply let it speak for itself. Thus, we will come to know the faith once for all delivered to the saints; and, more importantly, we will have that knowledge which will make us wise unto salvation.

---

[125] O. Cullmann, "The Tradition," *The Early Church*, A. Higgins (ed.) (Philadelphia: Westminster Press, 1956), p. 91

Words having once been committed to writing do not change, and since the faith once for all delivered to the saints has been committed to writing by the original spokesmen for that faith, it follows that we have immediate access to it through their writings. The value of having such a book has been well stated by John Wesley: "I am a creature of a day. I am a spirit come from God; and returning to God. I want to know one thing: the way to heaven. God himself has condescended to teach me the way. He hath written it down in a book. O give me that book! At any price give me the book of God! Let me be a man of one book."[126]

Thus, on the basis of the historically controllable event of Paul's apostolicity as demanded by his having spearheaded the Gentile mission, we know that the biblical writers reliably interpret the events of the Bible's redemptive history. Since what the Bible teaches is true, its good news, which alone could satisfy the craving of the heart for happiness, is true news. Therefore, we accept the Bible's teachings with joy and know that we are not, in so doing, simply projecting our deepest desires (Feuerbach) or betting on being on the winning side (Pascal, William James). Our faith rests on the sufficiency of the evidence. E. J. Carnell puts it this way: "In no instance do the Scriptures encourage the penitent to believe that by a subjective 'leap' of faith he may atone for a deficiency in the objective authority. On the contrary, cordial trust in Jesus Christ is always grounded in reasonable evidences."[127]

An objection to saying that faith is not a leap but a "resting in the evidences" is that such a stance counters the biblical antithesis between faith and sight (John 20:29; 2 Corinthians 5:7; 1 Peter 1:8). In reply to this objection, Wolfhart Pannenberg's observation is pertinent that while faith does rest on knowledge of what is true, the element of trust and commitment is not thereby eliminated, because part of what faith knows concerns what is true in the future.[128] Thus, for example, we believe, that is, rest on the evidences, that God's Word is true when it says that we shall rise from the dead and live throughout the eternal future in bliss with God. But all that is around us in the world, apart from our knowledge that the Bible is the Word of God, seems utterly to belie this promise of God's word. But in faith we rest on the sufficiency of the evidence that what the Bible says is true, even though so much of experience seems to say that death has the last word. Therefore, we do walk by faith, not by sight.

Can We Have Historical Knowledge of a Supernatural Event?

Many historians claim that the historical method is not capable of giving knowledge that a supernatural event happened. In fact, they argue that even to admit the possibility of the supernatural destroys all possibility of any historical knowledge. If they are right,

---

[126] Quoted from the preface to Wesley's "Sermons on Several Occasions," L. Tyerman, *The Life and Times of Wesley.* 5th ed.; 3 vols. (London: Hodder and Stoughton, 1880), I, 531f.
[127] E. J. Carnell, *A Philosophy of the Christian Religion* (Grand Rapids: Eerdmans, 1952), p. 449.
[128] W. Pannenberg, "Dogmatische Thesen zur Lehre von der Offenbarung," *Offenbarung als Geschichte*, W. Pannenberg (ed.) (Göttingen: Vandenhoeck & Ruprecht, 1963), p. 101.

then of course the foregoing argument for the truth of Scripture on the basis of Paul's having spearheaded the Gentile mission is destroyed. Others, even historians who have theological interest, assert that the pursuit of historical knowledge is really justified only when the historian excludes the possibility that *miracles* could have occurred at certain points in history.[129]

The Question of Presuppositions

Rudolf Bultmann has often expressed the following conviction:

> The historical method includes the presupposition that history is a unity in the sense of a closed continuum of effects in which individual events are connected by the succession of cause and effect ... Even a free decision does not happen without a cause, without a motive; and the task of the historian is to come to know the motives of actions. All decisions and all deeds have their causes and consequences; and the historical method presupposes that it is possible in principle to exhibit these and their connection and thus to understand the whole historical process as a closed unity. This closedness means that the continuum of historical happenings cannot be rent by the interference of supernatural transcendent powers and that therefore there is no 'miracle' in this sense of the word. Such a miracle would be an event whose cause did not lie within history.[130]

James Robinson joins Bultmann in this assertion, even though Robinson is more interested than Bultmann in making the findings of the historical method pertinent to faith. He has said, "The possibility of miracles must be excluded from positivistic historiography not because of certain dogmatic presuppositions but because of the demands of the historical method itself."[131]

Just what are these *demands* which are supposed to make it necessary to exclude the possibility of the supernatural in pursuing the *historical* method?

In the book entitled *The Historian's Craft*, written by the late French historian Marc Bloch, we find representative reasoning for why so many historians have insisted that they must exclude the possibility of miracles. Bloch cites the example of a certain Marbot [also mentioned above], an officer in Napoleon's army, who in his *Memoirs* relates how on the night of May 7, 1809, he crossed the raging torrents of the Danube, then in full flood, to free some French prisoners from the Austrians. But other evidences indicate that the old braggart Marbot was simply acting in character when he penned this portion of his book. For one thing, a petition drawn up by Marbot himself on June 30, 1809,

---

[129] The following material was originally a paper delivered before the Theological Fellowship of the Southwestern Baptist Theological Seminary, Fort Worth, TX, 12 January 1967. It was later published as "The Fundamental Presupposition of the Historical Method," *Theological Zeitschrift*, 24 January 1968.

[130] R. Bultmann, "Exegesis Without Presuppositions?", *Existence and Faith*, S. M. Ogden (tr.) (1961), pp. 291f.

[131] J. Robinson, *Kerygma and Historischer Jesus* (1960), p. 14n.

contains no mention of his supposed exploit of the preceding month. There was no conceivable reason why Marbot would have kept silent about such an exploit when he drew up this petition, for to relate all that was in his favor would surely be his desire and would be expected by his superiors. What, then, should the historian do? Should he credit the *Memoirs*, or should he declare that Marbot had simply lost another bout with truth when he penned this incident?

According to Bloch, the fundamental precept which enables the historian to know that Marbot was most surely lying is that "the universe and society possess sufficient uniformity to exclude the possibility of overly pronounced deviations."[132] "We have been able to clear our picture of the universe of so many fictitious marvels," he declares, because "we are doubtless primarily indebted to the gradual evolution of the idea of a natural order governed by immutable laws."[133] As Bloch applies this presupposition of the regularity of the world to the question of whether or not to credit Marbot, he notes that everything is happening with regularity if one understands that Marbot's story of freeing the French is a lie. In writing this tale, Marbot was simply continuing to be the braggart he always was, and the very motive which led him to brag in his Memoirs, namely, his desire for approval from others, would also have led him to refrain, when seeking his promotion, from lying before those who would have had an immediate check on the veracity of his tale. In an orderly world, a cause consisting of Marbot's being a braggart, would lead to the effects that, on the one hand, he would not lie before those who already knew the truth, and, on the other hand, that he would lie to the readers of his *Memoirs* who would not take the trouble to check out his story.

Bloch argues that the world, however, becomes an exceedingly disorderly place if we try to insist that Marbot was telling the truth, for then, despite the fact that Marbot is a braggart, he becomes modest at a time when it was fitting and to his interest to tell of his worth. If Marbot is telling the truth, then his behavior is an overly pronounced deviation. If Marbot's behavior can deviate to the extent of acting contrary to his motives and circumstances, then we live in a world where there is spontaneity, that is where causes do not necessarily lead to commensurate effects. In such a world it would not be possible to test whether the report of what happened was valid. Only in a world where we can feel confident that there are no overly pronounced deviations can we be assured that by following the historical method we gain knowledge of the past.

If Marc Bloch's reasoning is correct, how can the Christian, who believes that Jesus rose from the dead (a confessedly overly pronounced deviation), still be an historian?

Going back to both Bultmann's and Bloch's statements of the basic presupposition on which the historical method operates, we notice that this *presupposition* has *two parts*. First, there is the insistence, to use the words of Bultmann, that "individual events are connected by the succession of cause and effect." Second, there is also the insistence

---

[132] M. Bloch, *The Historian's Craft*, P. Putnam (tr.) from *Apologie pour l'histoire, ou métier d'historien* (1954), p. 115.
[133] *Ibid.*, p. 135.

that the succession of cause and effect is closed. "This closedness," declares Bultmann, "means that the continuum of historical happenings cannot be rent by the interference of supernatural transcendent powers." We should note how *completely separate* these two parts are. The second assertion, that the world is a closed continuum of causes and effects, is by no means a logically necessary corollary from the first assertion, that for every effect there is an efficient cause. The statement that every effect has an entirely adequate cause says nothing at all about whether the source of this cause is transcendent or immanent. Therefore, the second assertion, which denies that effects can have a transcendent cause, stands wholly by itself and could be discarded without modifying the first statement in any way. Thus, if it could be shown that the gaining of historical and scientific information depends only in the first assertion, that every effect must have a sufficient cause, then it would still be possible for a Christian to be an historian and a scientist ("A firm belief is generated in the experimental scientist's mind that the production of any natural phenomenon depends on the value of a surveyable finite number of causes."[134]).

Marc Bloch, we remember, discredited Marbot's story on the basis of the presupposition that "overly pronounced deviations do not occur in nature or society." But an analysis of the Marbot problem reveals that all one needs to presuppose in order to conclude that Marbot was lying is that every effect must have a sufficient prior cause. The truthfulness of Marbot's story is to be rejected, because if he were telling the truth, the effect, consisting of his penning the incident in his *Memoirs,* could not lie in a cause that would also have kept him quiet about the story when coming up for promotion. But if he were telling a lie, then the motive which led him to write the incident in his *Memoirs* would also have kept him quiet before his superiors. The historian can therefore accept the hypothesis that Marbot was lying since this hypothesis maintains the bond between cause and effect. Indeed, then the historical method does depend very heavily on the hypothesis that effects are connected to causes by an indissoluble bond. Does it also depend on closing the door to all thought of miracles?

Perhaps the best way to answer this question is to imagine how historical reasoning would fare if it were possible that through a miracle the braggart Marbot became so humble that when he was up for promotion, he demurred from mentioning anything about this remarkable exploit. Then indeed there would be sufficient cause to explain why he remained silent before his superiors. But, notably, there would still be no cause for telling of his exploit in his *Memoirs*. If, through a miracle, he became so humble as not to tell of his exploit before his superiors, then it would be difficult to explain why he then turned around and wrote his *Memoirs*. But since he did write his *Memoirs*, the historian could still exclude the possibility of his having been made humble by a miracle, simply by holding to the indissoluble bond between cause and effect. Since a miracle is not sufficient to account for both his silence before his superiors and his writing the *Memoirs*, the historian must exclude the possibility of a miracle.

---

[134] A. Pap, "Has Science Metaphysical Presupposition?" Herbet Feigh and Mary Brodbeck (eds), *Readings in the Philosophy of Science* (1953), p. 30.

But someone may object that we would not know whether Marbot was lying or not if it were possible that two miracles had occurred: one to make him humble before he came up for promotion and another to change him back to being a braggart before he penned his *Memoirs*. To be sure, if such a thing were to have happened, then it would not be possible to know whether merely natural forces were operating and Marbot was lying, or whether these two miracles had occurred so that Marbot was telling the truth. If for every event which can be explained as stemming from natural causes there is just as much possibility that it stemmed from a supernatural cause, then indeed, all possibility of gaining historical and scientific knowledge vanishes. Does this mean, then, that to keep the historical method intact, we must go along with Bultmann and shut the door of our thinking to the possibility of miracles?

Shutting the Door to Miracles?

It would seem that the best way to maintain the validity of the knowing process is not to close the door in our thinking to any possibility of miracles, but simply to say that where there is knowledge of natural causes which in themselves are perfectly adequate to explain a phenomenon, we should understand this phenomenon as stemming from these causes and not from a miracle. Only when all the immanent causes antecedent to an effect would, of themselves, produce an effect that is opposite to that which occurred should we assign a miracle as the cause. Thus, we would exclude the possibility that Marbot was telling the truth because two miracles had happened and simply say that the causes already existent are sufficient to explain what happened, and therefore, that he was lying.

The Marbot incident, therefore, provides an instance where historical reasoning can conclude that no miracle occurred.

But the *case of Paul's* spearheading the Gentile mission provides an instance where, it would seem, historical reasoning must conclude that a miracle occurred. Before his conversion, Paul was more zealous for his religion than any other Jews (Galatians 1:13–14). He was very proud of his rigid adherence to the details of the Mosaic law, and thus he was totally opposed to any thought of proffering God's covenant blessings to the Gentiles unless they were willing to assume the Jewish distinctives of circumcision and the dietary laws. There was nothing in Paul that would encourage him to preach a Gospel of grace to the Gentiles. So opposed was he to anything like this that he gave himself wholly to the task of persecuting the Christian Church, because it seemed to him that their emphasis that salvation of the Jew could come only by repentance and faith in Christ tended to divest the Jewish distinctives of any basis on which one could boast before God. Paul makes it clear that before his Damascus Road experience he was in no wise tending gradually toward the Christian point of view; rather according to Galatians 1:14, he was advancing (προέκοπτον, imperfect tense) in Judaism. All of Paul's motivation before his conversion was so taken up with Judaism that as Heinrich Schlier has said:

Paul's pre-Christian past is itself a guarantee for the fact that there can be no talk of any kind of a reception of the Gospel (even an unconscious receptiveness on his part to the Gospel) with its principle of grace from any Christian spokesman. His inner bent of mind and his way of acting were wholly incompatible with the Christian message.[135]

To catch a glimpse of how contrary Paul's Gentile mission was to Jewish thinking, we have only to remember how, later on, the Jews tried to kill him when he had become very successful in leading this mission (Acts 22–26). How then did Paul ever come to lead this mission when he was originally like the Jews in wanting to kill anyone preaching the gospel of grace?

Since we look in vain for any causes in Paul to explain how he who had once persecuted the Church could now preach the gospel of grace to the Gentiles, we are forced to understand that a miracle took place in which, as Paul relates, the risen Jesus appeared to him on the Damascus Road and commissioned him to head up this mission. Not to be willing to go along with Paul's explanation for this change is to run the risk of allowing an effect to exist (the Gentile mission) without a commensurate cause to explain it, and this would nullify the very presupposition which is so essential for gaining all scientific and historical knowledge. To avoid doing this, then, we credit the miracle of the appearance of the risen Jesus to Paul on the Damascus Road to explain how he could spearhead the Gentile mission.[136]

Hence, I argue that to maintain the validity of the pursuit of historical knowledge there is no need to close the door of our thinking to any possibility of miracles, but only to *keep it closed* so long as there are perfectly adequate *natural causes* to explain a phenomenon. But *when this fails*, then we must *open the door* to the possibility of a miracle, or else destroy all possibility of knowing anything. All that is necessary for keeping the historical method intact is the indissoluble bond between cause and effect. This bond is honored both by closing the door to the possibility of a miracle so long as there are sufficient immanent causes to explain an effect, and then by opening the door when there are no such causes.

The Integrity of the Historical Method

The lengths to which David Hume was willing to go in *denying* that *miracles* can occur is an illustration of how such an insistence threatens to *destroy* the bond between *cause and effect*, and thus the very cornerstone of the historical method. Hume declared that "no testimony for any kind of miracle has ever amounted to a probability, much less to a proof."[137] So unwilling was he to admit the possibility of miracles that he said that if

---

[135] H. Schlier, *Der Brief an die Galater* (1962), p. 52.
[136] For a more detailed presentation of this argument, see my *Easter Faith and History* (1965), chapters 7 & 8. [republished as *Resurrection Faith* (2016).]
[137] D. Hume, *An Enquiry Concerning Human Understanding* (ed. LaSalle, IL: Open Court, 1949), pp. 133f.

Queen Elizabeth I appeared in public a month after she had died and claimed that she had risen from the dead, he would still insist that no miracle had taken place. He would deny that she rose from the dead even though he would have to say that the good queen, for no conceivable motive, had deliberately deceived her people in allowing them to believe that she had died, and even though he would have to credit the virtual impossibility that all the chamberlains, courtiers, and ladies in waiting that surrounded her would not have let the secret out somehow.

> All this might astonish me, but I would still reply that the knavery and folly of men are such common phenomena that I should rather believe the most extraordinary events to arise from their concurrence, than to admit of so signal a violation of the laws of nature [as a resurrection from the dead].[138]

To go to such lengths to keep the door shut against the possibility of miracles virtually succeeds in saying that effects can occur without prior causes. According to Hume, human beings in their knavery and folly are constantly able to act so contrary to any conceivable motive that there is no limit, apparently, to what any given person can do in any given situation, and as a result, "the most extraordinary events" are to be credited before one agrees that a miracle has happened. To apply what Hume said to the case of Marbot's *Memoirs*, it would have been perfectly possible for Marbot to have done this remarkable exploit and yet have remained silent about it when coming up for promotion, for his "knavery and folly" would have been sufficient to keep him quiet before his superiors and yet allow him to pen his memoirs. If Hume is right, then Marbot, or anyone else for that matter, can act in contempt of motives and circumstances. But to grant this is to give up all possibility of gaining historical knowledge.

Therefore, we conclude that shutting the door on the possibility of miracles does not safeguard, but rather jeopardizes, the *integrity* of the historical method. An insistence that miracles cannot happen can force us to understand effects as happening spontaneously without prior causes. This, it would seem, would make the historical method completely unworkable.

The only way, then, to safeguard the pursuit of knowledge is to honor the indissoluble bond between cause and effect by shutting the door to miracles so long as natural causes for an effect exist, and then opening it when they do not exist. On this basis a Christian can believe that Jesus rose from the dead and still be an historian or scientist.

While the chief purpose of this chapter is to take issue with those who believe they must deny miracles in order to maintain the integrity of the historical method, I would point out that it also takes issue with that view of history in which miracles happen as a result of the fact that the personal God is at the center of existence of this world. According to this view, the most essential aspect of this world (whether nature or history) is the *God who acts in freedom* and is therefore not at all bound to the rigorous law of cause and effect. Two leading representatives of this view would be H. Richard Niebuhr and Wolf-

---

[138] *Ibid.*, p. 135.

hart Pannenberg.[139] Both of these men emphasize that the essential thing about history is its *contingency* rather than the connection by which every effect is related to a prior cause. My objection against this view of history is that if the phenomena within the world itself can emerge of themselves, as it were, because the freely acting God informs all of history, then one could never be sure that any phenomenon actually occurring in history would produce its commensurate effect upon its surroundings. These surroundings might at that given moment act contingently instead of in accord with cause and effect, and if this is indeed the way the world operates, one can never test a claimed cause by reference to relevant effects. It would seem, then, that with this view of history all *knowledge* would be *impossible*. Even the simplest knowledge—such as that one faces a tree because he sees it through his eyes—would become problematic. For, how could one be sure that the cause-effect sequence by which the nerve impulses from the retina to the brain were acting according to cause-effect, if the chief thing about the world (including one's optic nerve) is contingency?

In the system which I am advancing, the world is so constructed that every *cause* (whether immanent or transcendent) *must* produce a commensurate *effect* in the world, because the world itself does not behave contingently but only in accordance with the law of cause and effect.

A Historical Faith for Non-Historians

Another serious objection that arises from the way the good news is known to be true news is that scarcely anyone comes to believe the Bible by following a pathway of historical reasoning. To go this route requires understanding how to apply the historical method and research to the historical origins of the faith. But if genuine faith really comes only in this way, then very few people could be held responsible to follow Jesus in the obedience of faith.

We have, however, remarked that the apostles did follow this methodology in principle. In the sermon at Pentecost, Peter did work upward from the common ground shared with his hearers to the conclusion that Jesus was Lord and Christ. Then too, Paul in his defense before Agrippa II (Acts 26) used this courtroom situation as an opportunity to try to convert King Agrippa, procurator Festus, and the whole audience gathered there (see verse 29 where Paul says, "I would to God that not only you but also all who hear me this day might become such as I am—except for these chains."), and his method was simply to argue from things which were not "done in a corner" (26:26), and on the basis of the Scriptures which Agrippa II, as a Jew, would accept (cf. vv. 22f.). But there are other places in Scripture where people become converted through means which seem quite different from such an approach. We read for example, in Acts 11:23ff. that when Barnabas came to Antioch "and saw the grace of God, he was glad; and he exhorted them all to remain faithful to the Lord with steadfast purpose; for he was a good man,

---

[139] H. R. Niebuhr, *Resurrection and Historical Reason* (1957); W. Pannenberg, *Heilsgeschehen und Geschichte: Kerygma und Dogma* 5 (1959), pp. 218–237, 259–288; id., *Dogmatische Thesen sur Lehre von der Offenbarung: Offenbarung als Geschichte (1963), pp. 91–114.*

full of the Holy Spirit and of faith. And a large company was added to the Lord." It seems that the writer's purpose is to say that a decisive factor for the large number of converts that was made was that Barnabas was full of the Holy Spirit and of faith.

There are other places where the existence of a person like Barnabas becomes sufficient reason for people to become converted. The Psalmist declared, "I waited patiently for the Lord; he inclined to me and heard my cry. He drew me up from the desolate pit, out of the miry bog, and set my feet upon a rock, making my steps secure. He put a new song in my mouth, even praise to our God. Many will see and fear and put their trust in the Lord" (Psalm 40:1–3). To be happy in God and praising him is like being full of the Holy Spirit and of faith, and so this passage in Psalm 40 teaches that such a quality of life persuades people to believe God. In Psalm 51:12 the same concept emerges: "Let me again experience the joy of your deliverance! Sustain me by giving me the desire to obey! Then I will teach transgressors your ways and sinners will turn to you."

Likewise, in 1 Thessalonians 1:5ff. we read, "Our gospel came to you not only in word, but also with power and with a holy spirit and with full conviction, just as [καθώς = restatement] you know what kind of men we proved to be among you for your sake [2:1–12 details the kind of life Paul, Silvanus, and Timothy lived as they presented the gospel—it has that Barnabas ring.]. And you became imitators of us and of the Lord, for you received the word in much affliction, with joy inspired by the Holy Spirit; so that you became an example to all the believers in Macedonia and Achaia. For not only has the word of the Lord sounded forth from you in Macedonia and Achaia, but your faith in God has gone forth everywhere, so that we need not say anything." This passage shows that the kind of lives the apostles lived in the presence of the Thessalonians caused their message to be heard not only in words but also in conviction. Then when the Thessalonians became the same kind of people, their lives were such a testimony that the gospel would go on being preached effectively, even if the apostles remained silent.

There are also examples of the same sort of thing from more recent times. The great missionary-explorer in Africa, Henry M. Stanley, relates that as he was journeying through Uganda, he came upon a young prince name Mtesa. "I have witnessed," said Stanley in his diary, which he quotes, "with astonishment such order and law as is obtainable in semi-civilized countries. All this is the result of a poor Muslim's labor; his name is Muley bin Salim. He it was who first began teaching here the doctrines of Islam. False and contemptible as these doctrines are, they are preferable to the ruthless instincts of a savage despot, whom Speke and Grant left wallowing in the blood of women [Speke and Grant, earlier explorers, had seen Mtesa and his people before he was converted to Islam], and I honour the memory of Muley bin Salim—Muslim and slave-trader though he be—the poor priest who has wrought this happy change. With a strong desire to improve still more the character of Mtesa, I shall begin building on the foundation stones laid by Muley bin Salim, I shall destroy [Mtesa's] belief in Islam, and teach the doctrines of Jesus of Nazareth.[140]

Then Stanley continued the story after this diary entry: "Since the 5th of April, I had enjoyed ten interviews with Mtesa, and during all I had taken occasion to introduce topics which would lead up to the subject of Christianity. Nothing occurred in my presence, but I contrived to turn it towards effecting that which had become an object to me, viz., his conversion … I simply drew for him the image of the Son of God humbling himself for the good of all mankind, white and black, and told him how, while he was in man's disguise, he was seized and crucified by wicked people who scorned his divinity, and yet out of his great love for them, while yet suffering on the cross, he asked his great Father to forgive them. I showed him the difference in character between him whom men love and adore, and Mohammed, whom the Arabs revere; how Jesus endeavoured to teach mankind that we should love all men, excepting none, while Mohamed taught his followers that the slaying of the pagan and the unbeliever was an act that merited Paradise. I left it to Mtesa and his chiefs to decide which was the worthier character."[141]

During another visit to Mtesa, Stanley made a book for him which was a rough and abridged translation of the Bible "embracing all the principal events from the Creation to the Crucifixion of Christ. St. Luke's Gospel was translated entire, as giving a more complete history of the Savior's life."[142] When this was complete, Mtesa said before all his court "'Now God be thanked, a white man, "Stamlee," has come to Uganda with a book older than the Koran of Mohammed, and Stamlee says that Mohammed was a liar, and much of his book taken from this … I find that this book is a great deal better than the book of Mohammed … Now I want you, my chiefs and soldiers, to tell me what we shall do. Shall we believe in Jesus and Moses, or in Mohammed?' Chambarango replied, 'Let us take that which is best.' Katekiro said, 'We know not which is the best. The Arabs say their book is the best, and the white men say their book is the best. How then can we know which speaks the truth?' … Mtesa said, 'Chambarango says, "Let us take that which is best." True, I want that which is the best, and I want the true book; but Katekiro asks, "How are we to know which is true?" and I will answer him. Listen to me: The Arabs and the white men behave exactly as they are taught by their books, do they not? [Christians are not immune to hypocrisy, however. As early as 400 CE John Chrysostom complained: "even now, there is nothing else that causes the heathen to stumble, except that there is no love ... Their own doctrines they have long condemned, and in like manner they admire ours, but they are hindered by our mode of life."[143] So, it's a good thing not too many white men had passed that way yet.] The Arabs come here for ivory and slaves, and we have seen that they do not always speak the truth, and that they buy men of their own colour, and treat them badly, putting them in chains and beating them. The white men, when offered slaves, refuse them saying, "Shall we make

---

[140] Henry M. Stanley, *Through the Dark Continent*, 2 vols. (New York: Harper & Brothers, 1879), I, 193f.
[141] *Ibid.*, p. 202.
[142] *Ibid.*, p. 324.
[143] John Chrysostom, "Homily 72 on the Gospel of John."

our brothers slaves? No; we are all sons of God." I have not heard a white man tell a lie yet. Speke came here, behaved well, and went his way home with his brother Grant. They bought no slaves, and the time they were in Uganda they were very good. Stamlee came here, and he would take no slaves ... What Arab would have refused slaves like these white men? Though we deal in slaves, it is no reason why it should not be bad; and when I think that the Arabs and the white men do as they are taught, I say that the white men are greatly superior to the Arabs, and I think therefore that their book must be a better book than Mohammed's, and of all that Stamlee has read from his book, I see nothing too hard for me to believe ... I have listened to it all well pleased, and now I ask you, shall we accept this book or Mohammed's book as our guide?' To which question, no doubt seeing the evident bent of Mtesa's own mind, they all replied, 'We will take the white man's book;' and at hearing their answer a manifest glow of pleasure lighted up the Emperor's face. In this manner Mtesa renounced Islam, and professed himself a convert to the Christian faith, and he now announced his determination to adhere to his new religion, to build a church, and to do all in his power to promote the propagation of Christian sentiments among his people, and to conform to the best of his ability to the holy *precepts* contained in the Bible ... 'Stamlee,' said Mtesa to me, as we parted ... 'say to the white people that I am like a man sitting in darkness and born blind, and that all I ask is that I may be taught how to see, and I shall continue a Christian while I live.'"[144] Thus the superior standard of life found not only in the Bible but in Christians was the decisive factor which turned this African emperor and his subjects from Islam to Christ.

David Wilkerson, minister to teenagers in Manhattan, related a story of the conversion of a certain "Elaine" which makes the same point. After being contacted by Linda, one of Wilkerson's workers, Elaine, who was a heavy drinker and dissolute, began coming to the "Gang Church" meetings that were held every Wednesday night. She became converted and had a complete change of heart. She explained why it was she turned to Christ: "I've finally got it figured out, Reverend Wilkerson. Christ's love is a love with no strings attached."[145] Coming into contact with Wilkerson's work, Elaine was confronted by a love strikingly different from any love that she had known up to this time. What she had known had been a love in which people sought her as a means to their ends, but in the context of the Christian community, she found a spirit of love "which does not seek its own" (1 Corinthians 13:5).

People in the world are incapable of producing such love. Unable, apart from the knowledge of God in Christ, to fill the "God-shaped vacuum" of their hearts, they are constantly concerned to gratify themselves at the expense of others. Thus, they find it impossible to have a truly disinterested benevolence for others— "disinterested" not in the sense of being unconcerned for others, but in the sense of having no ulterior motives for gratifying themselves by what they do for others. It is quite possible for such people to give their whole lives over to philanthropy, but philanthropy is one of the best ways

---

[144] *Ibid.*, p. 323ff.

[145] David Wilkerson, *The Cross and the Switchblade* (Westwood, NJ: Fleming H. Revell, 1964), p. 135.

to satisfy the ego. It is also possible for such people to be very jolly, but doubtless each of us has experienced the difference between the atmosphere of joy produced by a Dean Martin and that produced by a David Wilkerson or a Billy Graham. The carnival-spirit joy of Dean Martin does not strike one as genuinely going out to people as a love without strings attached, while even the most hardened atheists have acknowledged Billy Graham's genuinely disinterested love. The joy of the latter comes from having a full heart; for a heart that is filled has its interests met and thus is free to flow out in concern for others "without strings attached." When people hear Billy Graham preach, they sense a love that they know cannot come from resources already available in this world. Without being explicitly conscious of the reasoning process involved, they know that since the world cannot produce such love, it must therefore come from being in fellowship with God, and what Billy preaches from Scripture is thus credited. The following letter, which came in to my father [radio evangelist Charles Fuller] in October, 1962, was typical of so many that he received: "In Proverbs we read, 'My son.' I can imagine the speaker's voice was like yours—filled with God's love and concern for all mankind everywhere, not willing that any should perish but rather that they should look to Jesus and live."

The Bible, as well as godly people, creates an atmosphere of disinterested love, as Stanley's story of Mtesa makes evident. Books carry with them a spirit as much as people do. What a difference between the spirit prevailing in the writings of Scripture and in the life of Francis Chichester. To read the Bible is to be confronted by the attitude of the God who is so sufficient in himself that he rejoices over people only to do them good; to read Francis Chichester is to be confronted with the spirit of a fussy, vain man who went to fantastic lengths to be able to say, "I sailed around the world alone twice as fast as anyone before me," and "I would feel an intense depression every time I achieved a great ambition."[146] Thus it is that people often pick up the Gideon Bible placed in hotel rooms and, reading it, are confronted by its atmosphere of love and are thus convinced that it is indeed the Word of God. Even little children can become acutely aware of the atmosphere of love that originates only from God.

The perceptive person will see that the argument in a Barnabas is the same as the core of the argument for Paul's being an apostle. Before his conversion, Paul's joy in life came from the sense of superiority which he as a Jew felt that he had over the Gentiles. Such joy could not reach out in love for others, because it depended on his sense of superiority over others. "Lord, I thank you that I am not like other men ..." But this source of joy, which was gain to Paul before conversion, became worthless in comparison to the knowledge of Christ. "But whatever gain I had, I counted as loss for the sake of Christ my Lord" (Philippians 3:7f.). Thus, when Paul found a truly satisfying source of joy in knowing Christ, there was no longer any need to try to find joy in reliance on the Jewish distinctives and trying to outdo his fellows in religious zeal. Now his joy was in Christ, and this satisfied him so completely that he was able to become "as a Gentile in order to win a Gentile." He was able to say "I seek not what is yours but you" (2

---

[146] Francis Chichester, *The Lonely Sea and Sky* (New York: Ballantine Books, 1964), p. 175.

Corinthians 12:14), and in seeking others his only purpose was to make Christ known to them, for only then would their hearts become truly satisfied.

The love of Paul could not stem from the forces at work in his motivation and background, nor can the love of a Barnabas-like person be reproduced by recourse to any resource already available in this world. Yet the love of Paul in heading up the Gentile mission did exist, and Barnabas types, having love without strings attached, exist today. Since such effects must have commensurate causes, and since the cause cannot be found immanently, the cause, as Paul and the Barnabas types declare, is in the God of the Bible. It is plain that the evidence presented by Paul which leads to his being an apostle and so to the Bible as the Word of God is, at root, the same kind of evidence that exists in the Barnabas types, who account for most of our own conversions, or in the atmosphere of love that the Bible creates. Therefore, faith rests on the evidence—even in the case of the many believers who are not historians.

Chapter Ten—Pitfalls in Interpretation

Having determined that the Bible's message is both desirable and valid, and assuming a reasonable method for coming to an understanding of the various texts of Scripture, it would seem that the two basic parts of the hermeneutical task are now finished and that nothing more needs to be said about how to interpret Scripture. The history of biblical interpretation has shown, however, that crediting the Bible as the Word of God has sometimes caused people to leap to conclusions about the Bible which have led to a distortion of its intended message. In this chapter we will consider how to avoid some of the pitfalls that could confront the interpreter who credits the Bible's claim to be the Word of God.

The Role of the Holy Spirit in Biblical Interpretation

Origen (185–254 CE) set forth a complete hermeneutic (probably the first in Christianity) in his *De Principiis*, IV. In the first part, he argued for the completely divine inspiration of Scripture by appealing to such evidences as the superior esteem in which Moses, as a law giver, was held by Jews and Christians in comparison with the law givers of other nations; the fulfillment of Old Testament prophecies in Christ; and the remarkable growth of the church in the Roman empire. But Origen reasoned that since the Bible is inspired by God, its meaning is not immediately evident from its words, but instead is hidden and secret and made known only to those who had reached spiritual maturity.

> These particulars, then, being briefly stated regarding the inspiration of the sacred Scriptures by the Holy Spirit, it seems necessary to explain this point also, viz., how certain persons, by not reading them correctly, have given themselves over to erroneous opinions, in as much as the procedure to be followed, in order to attain an understanding of the holy writings is unknown to many … (IV, 8).

> Now the reason of the erroneous apprehension of all these points … is no other than this, that holy Scripture is not understood by them according to its spiritual but according to its literal meaning (IV, 9).

> Let us do our utmost endeavor, by abandoning the language of the elements of Christ, which are but the first beginnings of wisdom, to go on to perfection, in order that the wisdom which is given to the perfect may be given to us also (IV, 7).

In support of this, Origen quoted 1 Corinthians 2:6ff.: "Now we do speak wisdom among the mature ... we speak the wisdom of God, hidden in a mystery ..." But according to our earlier analysis of this passage, Paul, up until 1 Corinthians 2:14, is speaking only of revelatory spokesmen, not ordinary Christians. The ordinary Christian, who hears the message of God, is then addressed from 2:14–3:4.

It is well known how Origen, despite his firm belief in the inspiration of the Scriptures, opened the door to their distortion by seeking deeper meanings which he arrived at by allegorizing certain portions which he, because of his basic commitment to Platonism, regarded as unbecoming of God. His way of interpreting the Scripture dominated the church until the time of the Reformation. Martin Luther said, "St. Jerome and St. Origen, God forgive them, were the cause that allegories were held in such esteem. But Origen altogether is not worth one word of Christ. Now I have shaken off all these follies, and my best art is to deliver the Scripture in the simple sense …"[147] While Luther's teaching and example made an impact of succeeding generations of interpreters, we still encounter quite a bit of Origenistic interpretation today, even by those who, no less than Origen, insist on the divine inspiration of Scripture. For example, C. H. Mackintosh, a Plymouth Brethren writer of the 19th century, said of interpreting the details of the construction of the Tabernacle, "Nature can do nothing here. Reason is blind … The most gigantic intellect, instead of being able to interpret the sacred symbols, appears like a bat in the sunshine, blindly dashing itself against the objects which it is utterly unable to discern. We must compel reason and imagination to stand without … God the Holy Spirit is the One who can … expound to our souls the true meaning of all that meets our view … The one who furnished beauteous symbols [of the Tabernacle] can alone interpret them."[148]

We too have argued that the Scriptures are inspired by God, and according to the Bible the Holy Spirit does play an essential role in the interpretation of Scripture. 1 Corinthians 2:14 says, "The natural person does not *receive* the things of the Spirit of God, for they are foolishness to him; neither can he know them because they are spiritually discerned." But does this text mean that, apart from the Holy Spirit, the words of Scripture are incapable of conveying even a cognition of what God is saying in his word? If this were so, then this verse would mean that the Holy Spirit would have to add something to the text that was not already there in order to make it comprehensible. But if the Holy Spirit does this, how could we refute allegorizing carried on by one who claimed, as Origen claimed, that he had the illumination of the Holy Spirit? Or how could we discriminate between differing interpretations of a text advanced by several people, each of whom claimed to be illumined by the Holy Spirit?

In this passage, the Greek word for "receive" is not λαμβάνω, which focuses attention merely on the physical acquisition of an object; it is δέχομαι, which stresses *the manner* in which we acquire something. Thus, the point of this verse is that the natural person will not *welcome* God's Word. That person's having cognition of what the Bible says is not denied in this verse, for the natural person can understand what it is saying well enough to be able to say that it is foolishness. Just as Festus must have had cognition of what Paul said in Acts 26:4–23 in order to say, in verse 24, "Paul, you are mad." Ernst Haenchen declares: "Festus must surely have had a surprisingly good understanding of what Paul had been saying, in order to have been able thus to deny the teaching of the

---

[147] *The Table Talk of Martin Luther*, W. Hazlitt (tr.) 2nd ed. (Philadelphia: Lutheran Board of Publication, 1868), p. 399.
[148] C. H. Mackintosh, *Notes on Exodus* (New York: Loizeaux Bros., n.d.), p. 275.

resurrection."[149] So, natural people declare the Bible to be foolishness when they grasp what it is saying.

Thus, apart from the Holy Spirit we can understand what the Bible is saying, but we will not welcome what we understand, for it will seem foolish to us. We cannot know it in the sense of its having any value for our own lives because, as natural people, we lack the ability, provided by the Holy Spirit, to discern how the teachings of the Scripture answer so well to the needs of our lives.

Edwin A. Burtt, a humanist, provides an example of one who, not espousing the Christian world view, nevertheless has such excellent cognition of it that he can condense it and state it much better than many Christians.[150] He summarizes the conservative Protestant point of view with such fairness that it is hard to see how any evangelical Christian would balk at ratifying it.

Thus, the Holy Spirit's work is not to add anything to the historical and grammatical data by which alone all communications, including the Bible, are to be understood. Rather, his work is to overcome our preference to try to find happiness by glorying in our accomplishments in overcoming finitude. His work is to make us own up to the obviously reasonable fact that we can never even begin to overcome finitude sufficiently to be anywhere near glorious enough to find happiness in delighting in ourselves. His work is to cause us to accept the obvious fact that all that we have has come to us as a gift, so that even if we do outdo others in overcoming finitude at some point (lift heavier weights, get better grades, be more popular, have better looks, be more shrewd in playing the stock market, create new approaches and new devices for doing things, etc., etc.), yet the very ability to overcome finitude a little more at some point is nothing but a gift from God for which we can take no credit at all. The Holy Spirit makes us admit to the inescapable truth, supported by facts and logic, of 1 Corinthians 4:7: "What have you that you did not receive? And, if you received it, why do you boast as if it were not a gift?" We cannot even boast in how hard we have worked to accomplish things, for the opportunity to work, and the energy and discipline it requires, were themselves wholly something we received from outside ourselves. "It is God who gives you power to get wealth" (Deuteronomy 8:18; cf. 1 Corinthians 15:10). Even the determination by which some of us work harder than others is not something we can crank up by ourselves but is, rather, the reflex of motives, and ultimately motives always exist prior to choice, so that they are something that are given. It is this aspect of the biblical world view which we, apart from the Holy Spirit, hate and will not acknowledge, even though it is manifestly and irrefutably reasonable. "For every one who does evil hates the light, and does not come to the light, lest his deeds should be exposed" (John 3:20).

Other aspects of the biblical world view are also repulsive to us without the Holy Spirit because they counter our desire to glory in what we are. Human beings, who seem to be spring-loaded to glory in themselves, do not take kindly to the biblical teaching that

---

[149] Ernst Haenchen, *Die Apostelgeschichte* (Göttingen: Vandenhoeck & Ruprecht, 1959).
[150] E. A. Burtt, *Types of Religious Philosophy* (New York: Harper & Row, 1939), pp. 158–160.

when we are slaves of sin, we are unable to do anything to please God. The teaching of the cross is also offensive because it implies that our condition before God is so serious that nothing less than the crucifixion of the Son of God avails to remedy our plight. Neither do we like the idea that we are saved by faith, not by works, lest any should boast—because boasting is just what we desire. Doing as the psalmist who found happiness only in beholding the beauty of the Lord (Psalm 27:4) is the exact opposite of what we want. If we were writing that psalm, we would say, "One thing have I desired, that will I seek after, that all my days I may be able to behold how glorious I am in having overcome finitude." Natural human beings also hate the biblical teaching that the supreme value is the glory of God. We do not like to think that God created us for his own glory, even though in so doing God was giving us the ultimate benefit of glorifying him through enjoying him forever with the same enjoyment that God has in glorying in himself. Thus, when the Bible teaches that God punishes people eternally for scorning his glory by trying to establish their own, we count it as foolishness, because surely (to our way of thinking) it is not the glory of God but what benefits us that is the supreme good. Though it is manifestly reasonable that the ultimate value is that God's glory be maintained at all costs and that any injury people inflict upon it be repaired, either by punishing us eternally or by having Christ die for us on the cross, yet, as 1 Corinthians 2:14 declares, we cannot make such teaching our own but rather regard it as foolishness, because we are so completely in love with our various world views constructed around the premise that we will be happy only as we glory in ourselves.

Such world views are pitifully unreasonable, for surely such finite, limited, little creatures, who are a mere vapor that appears for only a season and to whom everything we are or have is given—such little ants can never succeed in finding anything in ourselves in which to glory which answers the cry coming up from the God-shaped vacuum of our hearts. The widespread murmuring heard from all kinds of people bears this out. Nevertheless, there are some few of us who do succeed in convincing ourselves, unreasonably, that we have full happiness—as Paul did before his conversion. But even the majority who murmur, will persist in holding our irrational world view until we are regenerated by the Holy Spirit. "Neither will they be convinced even if one should rise from the dead" (Luke 16:31). But if such people are like Edwin Burtt and handle Scripture without being under any obligation to regard the Bible as true, they can nevertheless represent its teachings without distortion.

But those whose position in life demands that they regard the Bible as true in some way will not be able, apart from the Holy Spirit, to avoid distorting the meaning. An example of this may be found in Ernest DeWitt Burton, the late President and Professor of New Testament Interpretation at the University of Chicago, who wrote the classical commentary on Galatians in the *International Critical Commentary Series*. For the twenty-four years prior to its publication in 1921, Burton worked meticulously on the textual and historical data of Galatians. So thorough was this work that the late J. Gresham Machen termed it "perhaps the most elaborate New Testament exegetical work that has appeared within the past thirty or forty years."[151] Machen commended Burton for the great exegetical skill which led him to many conclusions which accord entirely with evangelicalism and are thus implicitly contrary to the liberalism which he espoused.

But it is interesting to note how Burton handled Galatians 3:13, the most notable passage in Galatians on Christ's vicarious death: "Christ redeemed us from the curse of the law, being made a curse for us ..." In accordance with good exegetical procedure, Burton understood the curse from which Christ redeems people to be the curse of the law spoken of in verse 10, which is a quotation from Deuteronomy 27:26, "Cursed be anyone who does not confirm the words of this law by doing them."

According to Burton, however, this curse of the law is not something which God imposes on people for their failure to conform to his will. Rather, it is humanity's own erroneous idea that God's policy is simply to bless people when they are good and punish them when they are bad. "It is necessary to distinguish between the verdicts of the law and the judgments of God, and to recognize that the [verdicts of the law] are, for Paul, not judgments of God which reflect God's attitude now or at any time or under any circumstances ..."[152] Thus, when Christ died on the cross, Burton thinks that the law's curse was imposed on him in that *people* supposed such suffering to be, *ipso facto*, the proof of his sinfulness.

In imputing sinfulness to one who was so obviously righteous, however, the law's "verdict is manifestly false and monstrous."[153] The crucifixion, therefore, manifested the untrustworthiness of the law, and in so doing it redeemed humanity from the law's curse, which led him to think that all blessing comes from being righteous and all suffering from being evil. Since God permitted such a miscarriage of justice in the crucifixion of Christ, it is evident that God does not act toward people on the basis of a consideration of their moral qualities. Rather, he acts toward them in love, even though they are sinners. "In the fact that Christ the righteous died the death of the cross it is evident that the government of God is not one of legalism but of love ..."[154] Hence, rather than being the place where Christ suffered God's wrath against people because of their sins, the cross is the place where it becomes evident that God blesses people apart from their moral qualities and apart from any necessity for making an expiation for their sins.

Burton's interpretation is valid if, indeed, it represents Paul's mind in writing Galatians. The crux of the whole problem lies in what Paul meant by the "curse" which was upon Christ during his crucifixion. In this passage the antithesis of the curse is the blessing (vv. 8, 9, 14). It is evident that in Paul's mind this blessing is something which God himself imparts, for according to verse 8, it is God who imparts the blessing of justification to those who exercise faith. If God be the author of the blessing, then we must

---

[151] *Princeton Theological Review*, XX (January, 1921), p. 142.
[152] Ernest DeWitt Burton, *The Epistle to the Galatians* (Edinburgh: T. & T. Clark, 1921), p. 165.
[153] *Ibid.*, p. 173.
[154] *Ibid.*, p. 174.

understand Paul to mean that God is also the author of the curse, unless from the immediate context there is evidence to the contrary. No such evidence exists. Therefore, the data leads to the conclusion that Paul understood the curse upon Christ to be imposed by God himself.

Additional confirmation for this conclusion comes from Deuteronomy 27:26, which Paul quotes in Galatians 3:10: "Cursed be anyone who does not confirm the words of this law by doing them." In Deuteronomy 28:20, which falls within a portion that resumes the theme of the curse for disobeying the law found in Deuteronomy 27:11–26, the author explicitly states that God himself is the author of the curse: "*The Lord* will send upon you the curse …" Therefore, the curse for disobeying the law is, according to Deuteronomy 27 and 28, something which comes from God himself. Since, when Paul quotes from Deuteronomy 27:26, he does not assign a different meaning to the curse, the evidence indicates that he means the same thing as does Deuteronomy. According to Paul's thinking, then the curse of the law from which Christ redeems people is God's judgment upon them for their sins, and when Paul said that Christ redeems people by becoming a curse himself, he meant that Christ vicariously bore the guilt of our sins when he died on the cross.

Thus, in interpreting Galatians 3:6–14, Burton has not been docile to the data. Instead of letting the Bible speak for itself, he has interpreted the words to mean that sin is something less than that which arouses God's wrath. His interpretation is less offensive to human pride, but his exegetical skill should have led him to different conclusions.

If Burton had not considered himself to be personally committed to Christianity, and had not desired to regard the Bible as an authority, he could have dealt dispassionately and fairly in setting forth biblical Christianity, just as Edwin Burtt did. However, since Burton did not believe biblical Christianity, even though he was a professed Christian, he was under great necessity to remain committed to the Bible, and he could do this only by finding scholarly ways to sidestep the crucial biblical doctrines.

Thus, if we interpret the Bible like Burtt, within a vocation that makes no demands that we regard its teachings as true in some way (like being a professor of religion in a university who teaches Pauline thought as something to be known but not necessarily true), then we do not need the Holy Spirit to enable us to learn what it is saying. All we would need is to be a good exegete, skilled in the art of grasping what another person intended to say. This is why many commentaries written by non-Christians are better than those by professed Christians. But the moment we are under any necessity from our chosen vocation or from our profession that the Bible is authoritative, then accurate interpretation of the Scripture will not be forthcoming, no matter how good an exegete we might be. We must be indwelt by the Holy Spirit through having been born again. We must also be filled with the Spirit so that we set our affection on God rather than on the things of this world. The delight we thus enjoy in God gives us every incentive to go along with all the biblical passages that teach that humanity's chief end is to glorify God by enjoying him forever.

Thus, delighting in this basic biblical premise that the supreme value is God's glory, we would not balk at its teachings of human sin, of Christ's vicarious atonement, of justification by faith, or of the eternal separation between the wicked and the just. Neither would we balk at the biblical teaching of the necessity to die to our love of self-glory and the praise of the world needed to enforce this love. A. H. Francke, one of the founders (along with Spener) of the Pietistic Revival that arose in Germany during the eighteenth century and resulted in a great impetus in missionary effort abroad as well as relieving social injustice and need at home (establishing orphanages for foundlings, etc.), said, "To the extent that you are crucified to the world, you will be able to grasp what the holy Scriptures are saying."[155]

But when the love of the world gains supremacy in the heart, this will clash with what the Bible wants to say. The only way to relieve this clash is either to repent and turn to God or to find some way to feel justified in distorting the biblical message so it will harmonize with a love for the world. Thus one who would be a minister of the Word must be willing to do two things: (1) spare no effort in becoming skilled in exegesis, and (2) spend time at least daily in seeking the face of God and letting God speak through Scripture, putting his finger on the places where one is more interested in delighting in one's own glory than in simply knowing and loving (delighting in the value of) God. Like the apostles, the minister's priority must be to engage in "prayer and the ministry of the Word" (Acts 6:4). The minister who does this will engage in the exegesis of Scripture without any desire to distort its meaning, for this person's intention will be to learn exactly what the Bible is saying, having made the effort to become a skilled exegete who could be confident to be thinking God's thoughts after him.

In this way, then, the Holy Spirit is absolutely essential for biblical interpretation. Understanding the Holy spirit's essentiality in this way blocks us from the pitfall of Origen and many others like him. When we understand that the Holy Spirit's function is to make us reasonable enough to love what the prophets and apostles taught, we as interpreters will never try to support our interpretations, Origen-like, by declaring that they arise from the deep, hidden knowledge that the Holy Spirit has given us. Rather, we will support our interpretations simply by an appeal to the grammatico-historical data.

Neither will the interpreter who thus understands the Holy Spirit's function in interpretation ever let Christian experience become the norm for construing Scripture. The interpreter who obeys the Holy Spirit does enjoy a personal, mystical knowledge of Christ (Philippians 3:10). This does constitute a personal revelation, for John 14:21 teaches that Jesus *manifests himself* to the obedient believer. But the Scriptures command us to test the spirits to discern if they are of God (1 John 4:1), and the objective, propositional Word of God in the Bible is the only way to test the validity of an inward spiritual experience. No matter how exciting or attractive such an experience may be, it must correlate with the results of a careful exegesis of Scripture before it can be regarded as right. True Christian experience greatly aids biblical interpretation because it provides us with

---

[155] Quoted by Gerhard Peschke, "Zur Hermeneutik A. H. Franckes," *Theologische Literaturzeitung*, 89, 2 (February, 1964), p. 103.

an immediate knowledge of what the Bible is talking about in words, and so, just as having been to Jerusalem helps us understand more readily a travel guide for the city, so experience of what the Bible is talking about helps us understand the Bible. But we must ever be careful not to become so enamored of our Christian experience that we start to read the Bible in light of it. We must ever discipline ourselves to see reality the way the prophets and apostles saw it and then measure our experience by their teaching.

Note: To understand the Holy Spirit's work in biblical interpretation as consisting in causing people to admit to the truth conveyed by the grammatico-historical data of Scripture gives no encouragement to understanding the Holy Spirit as imparting new data. The theory of the "internal testimony of the Spirit," however, can give such encouragement. If genuine faith does not rest merely on the empirical data, which give approximate certainty, but also on what the Holy Spirit *adds*, so that we gain absolute certainty, then we could also say that understanding what a passage means depends not only on the grammatico-historical data but also on something the Holy Spirit adds over and above this data. Robert M. Grant believes that Calvin's doctrine of the internal testimony of the Holy Spirit "opened the way for subjectivism even while he tried to exclude it."[156] Indeed, Calvin succeeded very well in excluding subjectivism in his actual exegesis, for though he no doubt made mistakes in exegesis, he never appealed to anything but the grammatico-historical data in his commentaries. But in the case of Karl Barth, it seems that this doctrine of Calvin's gave him encouragement to be much less tied to the text. Barth applauded Calvin for basing faith only on the internal testimony of the Holy Spirit. To David F. Strauss' charge that this doctrine of the internal testimony was the Achilles heel of Protestantism because it is self-contained and has no sufficient credentials to validate it, Barth replied, "At [Protestantism's] weakest point, where it can only acknowledge and confess, it has all its indestructible strength."[157]

In Barth's system, "revelation remains identical with Jesus Christ."[158] Thus, the Bible itself can never be equated with revelation, according to Barth. "When we have to do with the Bible, we have to do primarily ... with the witness which as such is not itself revelation but only—and this is the limitation—the witness to it."[159] This basic principle in Barth, that revelation remains identical with Jesus Christ, seems to be the generating principle for all the new interpretations of Scripture with which his *Church Dogmatics* abounds. For example, in his doctrine of election, he makes the "hermeneutical decision" not to depart one step from the Word of God which calls us and exhausts our knowledge of God, for this "Word of God," that is, Jesus Christ—not the Bible—must control the entire interpretational process.[160] Thus, in

---

[156] Robert M. Grant, *A Short History of the Interpretation of the Bible*, rev. ed. (London: Adam and Charles Black, 1965), p. 107.

[157] Karl Barth, *Church Dogmatics*. G. Thompson (tr.) (Edinburgh: T. & T. Clark), I/1, p. 536f.

[158] Karl Barth, *Church Dogmatics*. G. Bromiley (tr.) (Edinburgh: T. & T. Clark, 1956), I/2, p. 118.

[159] *Ibid.*, p. 463.

[160] Karl Barth, *Church Dogmatics*. G Bromiley (tr.) (Edinburgh: T. & T. Clark, 1957), II/2, p. 152.

the doctrine of election we cannot look away from Jesus Christ but must rather see him as both the electing God and the one who, by having become reprobate for humanity, shows them that now only God's blessings are to be enjoyed. Hence as the church concerns itself simply with proclaiming the Gospel, it will not wonder whether there will be a final universalism or whether some will finally not have believed, for such questions are a turning aside from Christ, the Word of God, to abstractions.[161] Because Barth makes all to depend on what Christ is, and not just on what the Bible says, he can avoid the many passages in Scripture which teach that many will be lost (e.g., Matthew 7:14, "those who find the way to life are few"). Thus, the doctrine of the internal testimony of the Holy Spirit gives Barth encouragement to set the Bible aside.

A Canon Within a Canon

According to the preceding chapter, all the revelatory spokesmen in the Bible are on a par with one another. All the apostles who have left us writings, whether Peter or John or Paul, and even their close associates, whether the writer of Hebrews, Mark or Luke, have the same authority as Moses, the prophets, and other writers of the Old Testament. However, such a view has not always been held throughout the history of the church. Martin Luther performed a great service to the church by freeing exegesis from the allegorizing of Origen and by stressing a return to the grammatico-historical sense of Scripture. He was not careful, however, to let this be the only sense for determining the meaning of the texts. Luther called the intrinsic genre of Scripture its "rule of faith,"[162] and the following statements show the sovereign power that it wielded in his interpretation of the Bible: "It is the attribute of Holy Scripture that it interprets itself by passages and places which belong together, and can only be understood by the rule of faith."[163] "Some passages in Scripture are obscure, but in these you find nothing but what is found elsewhere in clear and plain passages."[164] "Every word should be allowed to stand in its natural meaning, and that should not be abandoned unless faith forces us to it."[165]

For Luther, this rule of faith was Jesus Christ and the truth of justification by faith alone, which had made such an impact on his life when he discovered it in Scripture. "In the whole of scripture," he wrote, "there is nothing but Christ, either in plain words or involved words." Scripture contains "nothing but Christ and the Christian faith."[166] "But

---

[161] *Ibid.*, p. 418.
[162] Also known as the "analogy of faith." For a more detailed analysis of this concept, see the appendix to this book.
[163] Quoted by Charles A. Briggs, *Biblical Study* (New York: Charles Scribners' Sons, 1884), p. 332.
[164] Quoted by J. Theodore Mueller, "Luther and the Bible," *Inspiration and Interpretation*, John F. Walvoord (ed.) (GrandRapids: Eerdmans, 1957), p. 111.
[165] Briggs, *op. cit.*, p. 332.
[166] Quoted by A. Skivington Wood. *Luther's Principles of Biblical Interpretation* (London: Tyndale Press, 1960), p. 33.

if any adversaries urge scripture contrary to Christ, we will urge Christ against Scripture."[167]

On the basis of this rule of faith, some books of the canon fared better than others. In his preface to the New Testament, written in 1522, Luther said:

> From all of these books, you can, in a flash, correctly discriminate between all of them and distinguish which are the best. John's gospel and St Paul's epistles (especially the one to the Romans) and St. Peter's first epistle contain the true kernel and marrow among all the books, for in these you do not find Christ's deeds and miracles described very much, but you find emphasized in a most masterful way how faith in Christ overcomes sin, death, and hell, and gives life, justification, and blessing—which is the true nature of the Gospel. If I should have to choose between the deeds or the preaching of Christ, I would prefer to leave the deeds go, for these don't help me; but his words are the words of life … Therefore, John's gospel is the only gospel which is delicately sensitive to what is the essence of the Gospel, and is to be widely preferred to the other three and placed on a higher level. Likewise, the epistles of St. Paul and St. Peter are to take precedence over the three gospels of Matthew, Mark and Luke. To sum it all up—St. John's gospel, and his first epistle, St. Paul's epistles (especially those to the Romans, to the Galatians, and to the Ephesians) and St. Peter's first epistle—these are the books which show you Christ and teach everything which is needful and blessed for you to know, even if you don't see, or even hear, any other book … Wherefore St. James' epistle is a true epistle of straw compared with them, for it contains nothing of an evangelical nature."[168]

In his preface to the Epistle to the Hebrews, which along with James, Jude, and Revelation, he placed at the end of his New Testament, Luther said, "Up till now we have had the truly genuine books of the New Testament. The four that follow have in other times been regarded otherwise … [Then he quotes Hebrews 2:3 to show that it could not have been written by Paul or an apostle.] Moreover, Hebrews has the difficult problem that in 6:4–6 and 10:26 it denies and refuses repentance to the sinner after baptism, and in 12:17 says Esau sought repentance but couldn't find it,[169] which is against all the gospels and the epistles of St. Paul.[170]

Concerning James, he said:

> Although the Epistle of St. James was rejected by the early Fathers, yet I hold it in high esteem, because it does not give any human teaching but rather urges God's

---

[167] Quoted by F. W. Farrar. *History of Interpretation*, reprint ed. (Grand Rapids: Baker Book House, 1961), p. 334.

[168] Quoted by Eduard Reuss, *History of the Canon of the Holy Scriptures in the Christian Church*. D. Hunger (tr.) (Edinburgh: R. W. Hunter, 1891), pp. 322, 329.

[169] Luther asserted this because he misconstrued what Esau sought. The pronoun αὐτήν refers to the blessing, not to repentance.

[170] Quoted by Reuss, *op. cit.*, pp. 325ff., and from W. G. Kümmel, *Das Neue Testament. Geschichte der Erforschung seiner Probleme*. (Munich: Kalr Alber, 1958), p. 17

law very strongly ... [But] I do not regard it as apostolic because, first of all, against St. Paul and the other Scripture, it flatly grants justification on the basis of works and says, 'Abraham was justified by his works, since he offered up his son.' But St. Paul ... taught the opposite, that Abraham was justified purely on the basis of his faith and proves this with Genesis 15:6 written before he offered up his son ... Secondly, [I reject its apostolicity] because it professes to teach Christian people, but it says nothing about the death, resurrection, and spirit of Christ. It names Christ only once, but rather than teaching anything about him, it talks only of mere faith in God. Now the office of a true apostle is to preach Christ's death, resurrection, and intercessory office ... All genuinely holy books agree in that they preach and urge Christ. And this is the genuine touchstone by which to discriminate against all books: when one sees whether they urge Christ or not, since all Scripture testifies of Christ (Romans 3:21ff.) and since Paul wants to know nothing except Christ (1 Corinthians 2:2). That which does not teach Christ is not apostolic, even if Paul or Peter are teaching; on the contrary, that which preaches Christ is apostolic, even if it should come from Judas, Annas, Pilate or Herod. But this James does nothing but urge people to the law and to its works, and he inconsistently mixes one thing into another ... He terms the law as a law of freedom (1:25), whereas Paul termed it a law of bondage, of wrath, of death, and of sin ..."

No one can deny that the Epistle of St. Jude is a summary or copy from St. Peter's other epistle, so that its words are almost the same. He also speaks from the apostles as one who is their disciple living a long time after them (v. 17). He also quotes words and events, that do not appear anywhere in the Old Testament—which was what incited the early Fathers to throw this book out of the basic canon ...

With regard to the book of the Revelation of John, I permit each man's own judgment to prevail. I don't want anyone to be bound by my arrogance or opinion. I say what I feel: my problem with this book is not only that I regard it as neither apostolic nor prophetic. More to the point is the fact that the apostles do not occupy themselves with visions ... For a necessary aspect of the apostolic office is to speak of Christ clearly and without figures."[171]

The circularity of this argument which distinguishes that which is truly apostolic is only too obvious. Instead of first determining who are revelatory spokesmen and letting them speak what they will, Luther decided in advance how an apostle should speak, and then let those books which speak in that way enjoy an apostolic standing. But how does he establish that an apostle should only speak in the certain way he describes? "Luther's theology," says Eduard Reuss, "while fully extolling the Word of God and its inspiration, always placed the spirit above the letter, the Gospel above its organs, and showed that it received the truth for its own sake and not because of any external guarantees."[172] Luther, then, is an example of another pitfall into which we could fall because of a conviction that the Bible is inspired. Because Luther was convinced that the Bible was

---

[171] Quoted by Kümmel, op.cit., pp. 17ff.
[172] Reuss, op.cit., p. 329.

inspired by the Holy Spirit, he felt impelled to allow his understanding of the Holy Spirit to determine "the rule of faith" by which a canon within the canon should be established.

To be sure, Luther based his harsh view of Hebrews, James, Jude, and Revelation in part on the fact that in the early church these were among the disputed books—the antilegomena—because there was some question whether they originated from an apostle. But he failed to see that the early church finally placed these books on a par with the undisputed books—the homologoumena—because it was convinced that these books, in distinction from all other Christian books which came later, gave a decisive witness to the teaching of the apostolic age. As Floyd Filson puts it, "The Church was dealing with essential facts when it stated this view [that the canon was to consist only of books of apostolic origin] ... It sensed the fact that the event of Christ and the witness of the Apostolic Age were decisive. Writings that were to be authoritative for the Church had to give the witness of that crucial period. They had to come from apostles or from those who could give witness of the Apostolic Age. This is in fact what the canon gives us ..." [173] Similarly, Oscar Cullman observed: "Among the numerous Christian writings the books which were to form the future canon forced themselves on the Church by their intrinsic apostolic authority."[174]

Once we understand that the writings of the apostolic age, which stem from the apostles and their close associates, constitute the faith once for all delivered to the saints, then it is obviously a pitfall to single out a certain line of teaching and emphasis within these writings and give them more weight. We should remember that since Paul said, "*We* [including other apostles and close associates] speak revelatory truths," he put all revelatory spokesmen on an equal level. So, we do well not to set some above others. Calvin provides the model we should follow. After studying his view of the canon, Warfield concluded that "Calvin's attitude towards the canon was thus somewhat more conservative than, say, Luther's. He knew of no such distinction as that between the Canonical and Deutero-Canonical [Hebrews, James, Jude, and Revelation] Books ... The so-called 'Antilegomena' of the New Testament he accepted without exception."[175] Calvin saw no contradiction between James and Paul on justification by faith. In the preface to his commentary on James, Calvin said, "What seems in the second chapter to be inconsistent with the doctrine of free justification, we shall easily explain in its own place." Luther, however, persisted to the end in saying that the contradiction was irreconcilable. Jesting about the trouble Melanchthon had taken to bring the statements of Paul and James into agreement, Luther said, "Faith justifies; faith does not justify. I shall put my doctor's bonnet on the man who will make that rhyme, and I wish to pass for a madman."[176]

---

[173] Floyd Filson, *Which Books Belong in the Bible?* (Philadelphia: The Westminster Press, 1957), p. 124.

[174] Cullman, *op.cit.*, p. 91.

[175] Benjamin Warfield, "Calvin's Doctrine of the Knowledge of God," *Calvin and Warfield*, S. Craige (ed.) (Philadelphia: Presbyterian and Reformed Publishing Co., 1956), p. 49.

[176] Quoted by Reuss, *op. cit.*, p. 334.

Note: Edward J. Carnell came close, in my opinion, to Luther when he summarized his whole hermeneutic in these two propositions: "First, the whole of Scripture is inspired, secondly, some parts of Scripture are subject to illumination of other parts."[177] From these two propositions followed five rules: 1. The New Testament interprets the Old Testament. 2. The epistles interpret the gospels. 3. Systematic passages interpret the incidental. 4. Universal passages interpret the local. 5. Didactic passages interpret the symbolic. In applying rule #2, Carnell remarked, "When Jesus told the rich young ruler to sell his possessions (Mark 10:17–22), or when he depicted scenes from the Final Judgment (Matthew 25:31–36), he implied that sinners are justified by works. This seems to conflict with Paul's teaching that sinners are justified by faith (Romans 4:16–25). But the conflict exists in the cultic mind, for it was never Jesus' intention to develop a systematic theology."[178] In applying rule #3, he said, "There are only two places in Scripture where justification is treated in a systematic, didactic form. These are Romans and Galatians ... [This] means that justification is *implied* in some places, while in others it is *systematically developed* ... John develops the plan of salvation; so does the book of Hebrews. But only Romans and Galatians make a didactic effort to connect the blessings of the covenant with the gift of God's Son. Therefore, if the church teaches anything that offends the system of Romans and Galatians, it is cultic."[179]

Note: The *Scofield Reference Bible*, and the Dispensationalism for which it has been the champion for many decades, also has much in it that echoes Luther's preference of Paul over the synoptic gospels and over Hebrews and James. Scofield, in commenting on the Sermon on the Mount, said, "In its primary application, [it] gives neither the privilege nor the duty of the Church. These are found in the epistles. Under the law of the kingdom, no one may hope for forgiveness who has not first forgiven (Matthew 6:12, 14–15). Under grace the Christian is exhorted to forgive because he is already forgiven (Ephesians 4:30–32)."[180] When he introduced Hebrews, James, etc., he wrote, "The Jewish-Christian writings deal with the elementary and foundational things of the Gospel, while to Paul were given the revelations concerning the Church, her place in the counsels of God, and the calling and hope of the believers as vitally united to Christ in the one body. The other characteristic difference is that while Paul has in view the body of true believers, who are therefore assuredly saved, the Jewish-Christian writers view the Church as a professing body in which, during this age, the wheat and the tares are mingled. Their writings, therefore, abound in warnings calculated to arouse and alarm the mere professor ... The

---

[177] Edward J. Carnell, *The Case for Orthodox Theology* (Philadelphia: Westminster Press, 1959), p. 53.

[178] *Ibid.*, pp. 57f.

[179] *Ibid.*, pp. 58.f

[180] *The Schofield Reference Bible*, C. I. Schofield (ed.) new and improved edition. (New York: Oxford University Press, 1909), p. 1000.

two Epistles of Peter, however, are less Jewish and more truly catholic than the other Jewish-Christian writings."[181]

The Old Testament did not fare much better with Luther. Rather than being content simply to free it from the Apocrypha and go back to the canon of the synagogue, "Luther's exegesis was skillful in discovering the evangelical elements in the documents of the Old Covenant, and he did not hesitate to acknowledge his disappointments in this respect when his sagacity was deceived, and at once to draw from this fact conclusions similar to those he had uttered regarding [Hebrews, James, Jude, and Revelation]."[182] In his preface to the translation of the Old Testament of 1523, he said, "Here (in the Old Testament) shalt thou find the swaddling-clothes and the manger in which Christ lies. Poor and of little value are the swaddling clothes, but dear is Christ, the treasure, that lies in them."[183]

Reuss gives the following collection of Luther's statements on various books of the Old Testament: Ecclesiastes "rides in simple sandals, as I used to do when I was still in the convent." "As to the second book of Maccabees, and that of Esther, I dislike them so much that I wish they did not exist; for they are too Jewish and have many bad pagan elements." "The books of Kings are a hundred thousand steps in advance of those of Chronicles, and they also deserve more credit. Still they are only a calendar of the Jews, containing a list of their kings and of their kind of government." "Job ... is like the subject of a drama with a dialogue in the style of Terence's comedies and for the purpose of glorifying resignation." "Moses and the prophets preached; but we do not there hear God himself. For Moses received only the law of angels and has only a subordinate mission. People are not urged to good works by preaching the law. When God himself speaks to men, they hear nothing but grace and mercy. The intermediate organs—angels, Moses, emperor, or burgomaster—can only command; we ought certainly to obey them; but only since God spoke by the Son and the Holy Spirit, do we hear the parental voice, the voice of love and grace."[184] Luther, in this last statement, is dangerously close to Marcion, who taught that the Creator-god of the Old Testament is essentially different from the New Testament's loving God, whose Son is Jesus.

There is much scriptural data which would flatly deny this idea that one does not hear God speaking in Moses and the prophets. When the prophets repeatedly said, "Hear the word of the Lord," and then went on to quote God, it is evident that their intention was to repeat what God had said. And once we grant that they were verbally inspired, we acknowledge that their intended meaning was true, and then it is not possible, as Luther, to set them below the statements of John, Paul, and Peter. It is plain that the New Testament's revelatory spokesmen regarded the earlier spokesmen of the Old Testament to be speaking God's word just as much as they were. One evidence for this would be Paul's statement in 2 Timothy 3:16f. that all Scripture is inspired by God and is profit-

---

[181] *Ibid.*, p. 1289.
[182] Reuss, *op. cit.*, pp. 329f.
[183] Quoted by Farrar, *op. cit.*, pp. 333f.
[184] Reuss, *op. cit.*, pp. 330ff.

163

able for doctrine, reproof, correction, and instruction in righteousness. Another is War-field's conclusion that "God says," "Scripture says," or "it says" are synonymous in the usage of the New Testament writers.[185] That Paul saw all parts of the Old Testament on an equal footing with what he himself was teaching is confirmed by Romans 3:10–18, a mélange of quotations taken from Psalms, Proverbs, Lamentations, and Isaiah, which he cites as bearing equal weight in supporting his own teaching in verse 9 that "both Jews and Greeks are all under sin."

The New Testament's Use of Old Testament Texts

But to speak of the way the New Testament writers quoted from the Old Testament is to raise the problem that the New Testament writers often applied an Old Testament quotation in a way not warranted by a grammatico-historical interpretation of it. Psalms 68:18 reads, "You ascended on high, leading a host of captives in your train and receiving gifts among men," and the context indicates that the psalmist here is extolling God's mighty work of the Exodus, in which the people of God, as they left Egypt, were able to despoil the Egyptians. But Paul applies this verse in Ephesians 4:8 to the ascension of Christ, and even reshapes its wording so that it can function as a proof text for Jesus' having dispensed spiritual gifts to various members of his church for its edification: "Therefore it says, 'When he ascended on high he led a host of captives, and he gave gifts to men.'" Thus, Calvin in his commentary on this passage remarked:

> To accommodate it to his argument Paul has twisted this quotation somewhat from its true meaning ... The whole psalm is in the nature of an *epinicion* [victory song], which David sings to God on account of the victories granted to him; but, taking occasion from the things wrought through his [David's] hand, he mentions in passing the wonderful things that the Lord has done for his people ... But although Paul saw that David was hymning his triumph for all the victories which God had wrought for the salvation of his Church, he very properly accommodated this verse about the ascension of God [i.e., ascension in God's lifting up his arm in past victories] to the person of Christ. The greatest triumph God ever won was when Christ—after subduing sin, conquering death, and putting Satan to flight—rose majestically to heaven, that he might exercise his glorious reign over the Church. So far there is no ground for the objection that Paul has twisted this quotation from the meaning of David ... There is rather more difficulty in what follows. For where the psalm says that God has received gifts, Paul reverses it to '*gave*,' and thus seems to translate it into the opposite meaning ... Paul purposely changed the word, and did not take it out of the psalm, but adapted an expression of his own to the present occasion. Having quoted from the psalm a few words on Christ's ascension, he adds in his own language 'and gave gifts,' to draw a comparison between the major and the minor. Paul wants to show that this ascension of God in the person of Christ was far greater than in the ancient triumphs of the Church; because it is more excellent for a

---

[185] Warfield, *op. cit.*, pp. 299–348.

conqueror to dispense all his bounty freely to all, than to gather spoils from the vanquished.

The value of Calvin's exposition of Ephesians 4:8 lies in his understanding that the basic theme unfolded by the Bible's revelatory spokesmen, as they appear successively in redemptive history, is the salvation which God effects for his people through redemptive history on the basis of what Christ did in his death and resurrection. Consequently, a later revelatory spokesman, like Paul, whose function is to fill the gaps in the picture of what God accomplished in Christ, can look back to a triumph of God for his people recorded by an earlier spokesman and cite it as a proof for what occurs as a result of the Christ event. Since we know that what the biblical writers taught is true, we know that there is a real connection between the victory wrought by God for his people in the Exodus, in the time of David, and in the ascension of Christ. In each instance it is the same God working redemptively for his people in order to accomplish his one great purpose in history, which is to fill the earth with the knowledge of his glory (Numbers 14:21; Habakkuk 2:14). Since what God is doing is all of a piece, it follows that evidence for what he has done at a recent point in redemptive history can be gleaned by citing what he did at a prior time. If God received gifts from his enemies, in order to dispense them for the benefits of his people in the times of the Exodus and of David, then surely, in the great Christ-event, which is the foundation for all of God's redemptive work in history, there would be, as Paul has asserted, a giving of gifts to his people. Thus Psalms 68:18, even though Paul changed its wording, constitutes an argument for the fact that Christ has given spiritual gifts to his church.

Psalms 68:18 can thus be used as a proof for a later event in redemptive history because there is a typological connection between earlier and later events. A '*type*' is some aspect of redemptive history which points ahead and bears an analogy to a later event in redemptive history (called an '*antitype*'). Three elements are essential to a type: 1. There is an analogy between the type and its antitype. 2. There is a definite predictive element in the type. And 3. The correspondence between type and antitype is less than one to one.[186] Thus, between God's despoiling of the Egyptians at the Exodus and the ascension of Christ there are a number of analogous elements: God's triumphing over his enemies, God's saving his people, and God's giving them gifts. The Exodus has a predictive element because the whole of redemptive history as it unfolds from Genesis onwards is filled with anticipation of the great things that God is working to accomplish. In Genesis 3:20–24 God provided a way to cover Adam and Eve's nakedness and allowed them to go cultivate the land so humanity would still be around to experience all that God would do for it. When Noah is born, his father gave him a name which expressed the relief from the curse that God would eventually bring to pass (Genesis 5:29; cf. 8:21). Genesis 12:1ff. fairly glows with the great things God will do through Abraham's seed. In Numbers 14:21 God promises that all the earth will someday be filled with his glory.

---

[186] Milton S. Terry, *Principles of Biblical Hermeneutics*, reprint ed. (Grand Rapids: Baker Book House, n.d.), pp. 334ff., 493ff.

Consequently, when a triumph such as the Exodus occurs, it is predictive in its grammatico-historical sense, because it partakes of the anticipation and hope that comes out everywhere in the Pentateuch and throughout the Old Testament. But just because a type anticipates the increasingly great things which God is going to do, it must be inferior to its future antitype. Thus, as Calvin pointed out, Paul, in realizing that what had happened in Christ's triumph was far greater than the triumph of the Exodus, deliberately reworded Psalms 68:18 so that the superiority of the antitype might be made clear. In so handling the words of an earlier revelatory spokesman, Paul was not making himself superior to that spokesman and thus twisting his words arbitrarily to serve his own ends. Rather, what Paul did in Ephesians 4:8 constitutes, on the one hand, an acknowledgement of the validity of what David and Moses had said, but, on the other hand, it also constitutes an acknowledgement of the fact that he, Paul, is a revelatory spokesman who also has something to contribute. But more than that, it acknowledges that both Paul and David are speaking in concert and each is making his contribution to the one message that God has progressively revealed in Scripture.

This understanding of the typological phenomena of Scripture helps clear up many difficulties. For example, it is not necessary to agree with Bultmann that "this method [of allegorizing] was taken over by Hellenistic Jewry and applied to the Old Testament. Where Philo used the method of allegorizing to derive from their reading of the Old Testament timeless truths of theology, cosmology, anthropology, and ethics, the New Testament uses it to find Messianic prophecies. In every case it is clear that what is already known [from New Testament times] is derived from reading of the [Old Testament] texts. But people want to find it in the old texts so that it can count as an authoritative truth."[187] And again, "It is clear that in all these cases the writers of the New Testament do not gain new knowledge from the Old Testament texts, but read from or into them what they already know. If one follows their intention [!] one is obliged to say that the Old Testament becomes clear as prophecy as a result of fulfillment."[188]

Thus, for example, Bultmann argues that "Isaiah 7:14 can only be used in the LXX as a prophecy of the Virgin Birth [in Matthew 1:23] because in it the Hebrew עַלְמָה (young woman) is translated παρθένος [virgin]."[189] But his argument is valid only if Matthew did intend to quote Isaiah 7:14 as a prophecy (in which there would be one to one correspondence between prophecy and fulfillment) and not as a type. The immediate context of Isaiah 7:14 makes it clear that the sign in which a young woman would conceive and bear a son named Immanuel would be accomplished within Ahaz' remaining span of life. By the time that child reached maturity he would eat curds and wild honey, since the land would have been desolated by the king of Assyria. Thus, this prophecy was fulfilled within the next few years, but Matthew can quote the happening as a type of the sign that Joseph would be given when Jesus was born of a virgin. The sign given Ahaz was designed to teach him not to be afraid of Rezin, king of Syria, or on Pekah, ruler of

[187] R. Bultmann, "Prophecy and Fulfillment," *Essays on Old Testament Hermeneutics*, C. Westermann (ed.) (Richmond: John Knox Press, 1963), p. 51.
[188] *Ibid.*, p. 54.
[189] *Ibid.*, p. 53.

the northern kingdom, but to trust in God (Isaiah 7:4), for Assyria, a far greater scourge than Rezin or Pekah, was actually threatening (Isiah 7:17). For Ahaz to have believed God would have meant deliverance for Israel; in the same way the angel's word to Joseph, because he did believe it, meant deliverance for Jesus whom Mary had conceived by the Holy spirit, and thus for the people of God.

Under this interpretation there is no difficulty when Isaiah speaks only of a young woman while Matthew speaks of a virgin, for a type predicts what is future with less than one to one correspondence between prediction and fulfillment. As Machen put it,

> One may hold that in the passage some immediate birth of a child is in view, but that that event is to be taken as a foreshadowing of a greater event that was to come … Grammatico-historical exegesis does not demand the exclusion of all typology from the exalted language of the Old Testament prophets; the question whether all typology is to be excluded is a question which is to be settled, not by the mechanical application of modern exegetical methodology, but only by patient and sympathetic research … The result [of such research], we think, will be that in the dealings of God with his covenant people will be found a profound and supernatural promise of greater things to come. So, in our passage, the prophet, when he placed before the rebellious Ahaz that strange picture of the mother and the child, was not merely promising deliverance to Judah in the period before a child then born should know how to refuse the evil and choose the good, but also … was looking forward … to the day when the true Immanuel … should lie as a little babe in a virgin's arms.[190]

To understand that New Testament writers often thought of an event in their times as an antitype fulfilling a type consisting of some aspect of a redemptive event in Old Testament times refutes perhaps the chief argument used to affirm that later revelatory spokesmen set aside the grammatico-historical meaning of earlier revelatory spokesmen. It shows, instead, how much later spokesmen respected the unity of the truth to which both they and the earlier spokesmen were joint contributors. Among the many difficult passages which this principle clears up is Matthew 2:15, which regarded the reference in Hosea 11:1 to God's calling his covenantal son, Israel, out of Egypt during the Exodus as predictive of God's calling his own Son, Jesus, back from Egypt when his life was no longer endangered by Herod. As R. V. G. Tasker said in commenting on Matthew's usage of Hosea 11:1, "The evangelist's quotation is not the kind of quotation that a modern Christian would think of making; but to the evangelist there was a real analogy between the history of Israel and the experience of him who was 'the fulness of Israel;' and it is just the realization of this truth that differentiates more recent biblical scholarship from the point of view displayed by Burkitt [who regarded such things as did Bultmann, *supra*]."[191]

---

[190] J. Gresham Machen, *The Virgin Birth of Christ* (New York: Harper & Row, 1930), pp. 292f.
[191] R. V. G. Tasker, *The Old Testament in the New Testament* (Philadelphia: Westminster Press, 1947), pp. 20f.

This understanding of an antitype's fulfillment cuts the ground out from underneath Origen's argument in his *De Principiis*, IV, 13, that if Paul could rebuke the Judaizers for not sensing in the Ishmael-Isaac, Hagar-Sarah narrative of Genesis the "allegory" he brought out of it, then surely he, Origen, was justified in doing as Paul and departing from the literal meaning of a biblical passage and delving for its deeper, allegorical meaning. Origen was right, of course, if by "allegory" he meant the same thing that Paul meant by it. An allegory is an interpretation of one thing in terms of another. But the basic question an allegory must answer is whether the "other" terms by which the original is represented are a necessary implication of the original. The basic philosophy controlling Origen's thought was Platonism,[192] and this constituted the other terms by which he represented the Old Testament. But any analogy between the Old Testament and Platonism is purely accidental, and the world view of the Old Testament, far from having Platonism as a necessary inference, is something quite the opposite. But Pauline thinking easily falls within the scope of the Old Testament's intrinsic genre.

The Old Testament narrative of Isaac-Ishmael, Sarah-Hagar speaks in terms of the purely human effort of the flesh on the one hand and of the "promise" and "the Spirit," which point to what God does, on the other hand, in spite of human efforts. Ishmael and Hagar do constitute Abraham's attempt to fulfill God's promises to him by his own paltry efforts, whereas Isaac represents what God does in contempt of human ability. Paul is very much at home in such a world view, so he can cite Genesis and put it in terms of his own vocabulary without, Origen-like, imposing an extrinsic genre on it. Thus, Paul can cite the Genesis narrative, and even though he restates it in his own terms, it stands as a support for what he is saying against the Judaizers at Galatia.

Indeed, Paul terms his restatement an "allegory." But "what's in a name?" so long as what this name stands for is a perfectly legitimate handling of an earlier revelatory spokesman's word. As Paul Jewett says in his very helpful article on this subject, "Now, if it be granted that an error in patristic ... allegorizing arises not from the method as such, but from a failure to establish the organic relationship between the original text and that in terms of which the text is interpreted, then it follows that allegorical or typical interpretations of the Old Testament must, if valid, rest on a genuine analogy between its original meaning and that in terms of which one is interpreting it. To put it theologically, such interpretation presupposes the unity and continuity of biblical revelation."[193]

Thus, Paul's "allegory" in Galatians 4:21–31 constitutes another instance in which a later writer expresses that he speaks in close concert with an earlier revelatory spokesman. Instead of setting the Old Testament aside, as did Origen, Paul respects Moses so much that he speaks only in his terms, so that Moses can be a support for what Paul himself is saying. Hence Paul's "allegory" is one more example of where Paul and the other New Testament writers call upon the Old Testament to speak for itself and thus help them say more fully what they themselves are saying. This use of the Old Testament

---

[192] R. P. C. Hanson, *Allegory and Event* (London: SCM Press, 1959), p. 361.

[193] Paul K. Jewett, "Concerning the Allegorical Interpretation of Scripture," *Westminster Theological Journal*, XVII, 1 (November, 1954), p. 13.

indicates that the later biblical writers never intended to set aside earlier revelation, but, by letting it speak for itself, employed it to support their own statements which, because they come at a point farther along in progressive revelation, have a fullness of meaning compressed into them which was not possible in earlier revelation.

H. H. Rowley[194] understood Jesus' statements in Matthew 5:21, 28 and so on through to the end of Matthew 5, to mean that "our Lord not merely continued to validate for his followers much that is in the Old Testament, he claimed that much was superseded in the New Covenant." If this is so, however, then what Jesus said in 5:21 *et passim* is in direct contradiction with his statement in 5:17, "Do not think that I have come to abolish the Law or the Prophets; I have not come to abolish them ..." Thus, David Daube[195] argues from Rabbinic parallels that the formula "I say unto you" was used to refute false interpretations but not a primary text itself. Daube further insists that some of the things which Jesus is replacing in Matthew 5:21ff. are not even found in the law, and so must reflect a Pharisaic interpretation that had sprung up.[196] Nowhere does the law say, for example, "Hate your enemy" (Matthew 5:43). Thus, in commanding us not to hate, Jesus is refuting the Pharisaic understanding that hatred was justified, but not the Old Testament itself, which has several texts that command us to love our enemies (Leviticus 19:17–18; cf. Exodus 23:4; Job 31:29ff.; Proverbs 25:21–22). Indeed, Jesus set aside the Old Testament commands regarding unclean foods (Mark 7:19), but this marks only a change in the particular terms by which God dispenses the outworking of his single redemptive purpose which commences the move "in the fulness of time" to take the Gospel from the confines of Judaism and send it forth to every nation, kindred, tribe, and tongue.

The point, then, of these last two sections is that all that the Bible teaches, except where (as in Mark 7:19) an earlier revelation is superseded by a later one, is to be allowed to have its say, and then when *each part* has spoken its piece, it is, as it were, to be put in the pot and stirred well so that the interpreter may have the whole counsel of God. To have, as Luther, a rule of faith by which some passages are suppressed in favor of others, can only lead to a distortion and truncation of God's counsel. To set forth the perspicuity of Scripture, as Luther, in which the clear passages control the meaning of the more difficult ones, is wholly arbitrary and makes it possible for the Bible, instead of being the rule of faith to which the Church conforms, to become a nose of wax which can be made to say whatever the Church, comprised as it is by people who have not yet become sinless, wants it to say so that it can use the Bible to justify what it wishes to go on doing. The intended meanings of most of the Bible are perspicuous (clear) to those who are willing to take the pains to achieve a certain level of exegetical skill. But it is courting disaster to talk of an "analogy of faith" or a "rule of faith" by which the Bible should be interpreted. To believe in plenary (i.e., full) inspiration is to regard all parts of the Bible

---

[194] H. H. Rowley, *The Unity of the Bible*, Living Age edition (Cleveland: Meridian Books, 1957), p. 97.
[195] David Daube, *The New Testament and Rabbinic Judaism* (London: Athlone Press, 1956), p. 56.
[196] *Ibid.*, p. 60.

as equally inspired, and this means letting each part have its say and then evaluating this scriptural teaching to see how it coheres with the rest of what the Bible says.

Non-Revelatory Statements and Implications

A salient emphasis of the previous chapter, and also of the preceding sections, is that all the sixty-six books of the Protestant canon are the verbally inspired Word of God. The basic step in coming to this conclusion was the argument from certain historical data concerning Paul's leadership of the Gentile mission. From this historical data, accessible to everyone, comes the certification of the revelatory teachings of the Bible, teachings which human beings cannot find out by themselves.

However, not all of the statements of the sixty-six books, which are verbally inspired, concern such revelatory matters. In Scripture there are statements, or aspects of statements, about matters which fall within the range of what we can know by ourselves. That Emmaus was about seven miles from Jerusalem (Luke 24:13), that the emperor Claudius commanded all of the Jews to leave Rome (Acts 18:2), that "all streams run to the sea, but the sea is not full" (Ecclesiastes 1:7), that "the ants are a people not strong, yet they provide their food in the summer" (Proverbs 30:25), are examples of biblical propositions that we can know the truth of without revelation. But such statements are quite incidental to the central purpose of Scripture, which is to teach revelatory matters we could never know by ourselves. Examples of revelatory statements are that "to depart and be with Christ is far better" (Philippians 1:23), that "whoever believes in Christ shall not perish but have everlasting life" (John 3:16), and that "to those who love God, he works all things for good" (Romans 8:28).

Paul regarded himself as a member of the group of people whom God singled out to be revelatory spokesmen (cf. the "we" of 1 Corinthians 2:6ff.). Thus, "'things that no eye has seen, or ear heard, or mind imagined, are the things God has prepared for those who love him.' God has revealed these to us by the Spirit ... And we speak about these things ..." (1 Corinthians 2:9f., 13). We know the New Testament writers certainly did not deprecate the Old Testament spokesmen but regarded them as speaking in concert with them. For this reason, then, Paul was able to say to Timothy that the Old Testament scriptures, because they are inspired by God and profitable for teaching, for reproof, for correction, for training in righteousness, were therefore able to "make [people] wise unto salvation through faith in Jesus Christ."

Jesus believed that both he and the Old Testament spoke revelatory truth, for he said, "You err in that you do not know the Scriptures or the power of God" (Matthew 22:29). Jesus made this statement in connection with the teaching of the future resurrection from the dead—a subject which we can know only through revelation. Since Jesus said people would err by not knowing Scripture, then it follows that he, like Paul, regarded the Scripture's teachings as inerrant and therefore "able to make people wise to salvation." We have already considered the Bible's claim to set forth revelatory truths and have determined that this claim is valid. Consequently, the Bible is free from any error, since its writers did live up to their intentions of being revelatory spokesmen.

But in the history of interpretation there have been many who have argued that if *all* of Scripture is verbally inspired of God, then the Bible is inerrant not only in its revelatory teachings but also in any and all incidental statements, or aspect of statements, that have to do with such non-revelatory matters as geology, meteorology, cosmology, botany, astronomy, geography, etc. For example, the Lutheran theologian Quenstedt, writing in the immediate post-Reformation era, said, "The canonical Holy Scriptures in the original text are the infallible truth and are free from every error; in other words, in the canonical sacred Scripture there is found no lie, no falsity, no error, not even the least, whether in subject matter, or expressions, but in all things and all the details that are handed down in them, they are most certainly true, whether they pertain to doctrines or morals, to history or chronology, topography or nomenclature. No ignorance, no thoughtlessness, no forgetfulness, no lapse of memory can, or dare, be ascribed to the amanuenses of the Holy Ghost in their penning of the sacred writings."[197]

The same sort of claim has been made in more recent days. Arguing from the fact that God verbally inspired the entire Scriptures, Edward J. Young said, "The Bible in its statements is not contrary to fact."[198] He also said, "If we assert that the autographs of Scripture contain error, we are saying that God is guilty of having told us something that is not true. It may be a matter which we ourselves would call minor, but in this case a minor error is no less an error than a major one. A person who continues to make so-called trifling mistakes is not one whom we can trust ... If God has communicated wrong information even in so-called unimportant matters, he is not a trustworthy God."[199] Arguing in the same vein, Gleason Archer said, "Whatever Scripture asserts to have been historically true, regardless of the intermediate source of the information, must be understood as trustworthy and reliable. I make no essential difference whether the source was written or oral ...; in either case the Holy Spirit eliminated mistakes and insured the inscripturation only of truth ... There is no need to resort to a theory of mistakes copied out in the original autographs, and to do so endangers the authoritativeness of Scripture as a whole."[200]

Since the Bible's importance consists precisely in the tremendous revelatory teachings that it conveys, it might seem quite innocuous to insist that its non-revelatory statements and inferences are likewise inerrant. In fact, these men argue that such inerrancy strengthens the authoritativeness of the teaching of the Bible, because if it is accurate even in trifles, then it is surely accurate in its momentous statements. But the problem is that while the Bible is amazingly accurate in so many of its allusions to matters that can

---

[197] Quoted by J. Theodore Mueller, "Luther and the Bible," *Inspiration and Interpretation*. John F. Walvoord (ed.) (Grand Rapids: Eerdmans, 1957), p. 96.

[198] Edward J. Young, *Thy Word Is Truth* (Grand Rapids: Eerdmans, 1957), p. 136.

[199] *Ibid.*, pp. 165f.

[200] Gleason L. Archer, *Survey of Old Testament Introduction* (Chicago: Moody Press, 1964), p. 17, note.

be checked out by independent research, those holding such a view are forced into the pitfall of affirming all biblical statements, despite what independent research into these matters would say.

For example, Edward Young could not find any plausible way to harmonize the apparent discrepancy in the chronology of Abraham's life between Genesis 11:26–12:4 and Acts 7:1–4. According to Acts 7:1–4, while Abraham was still in Ur of the Chaldees, God appeared to him and commanded him to leave his family and go to another land that God would show him. His father, Terah, went with him as far as Haran, where they settled. Only after Terah died did Abraham go on to Canaan. But according to Genesis 11:26–12:4, Terah was the one who moved Abraham to Haran where Abraham received the vision; he subsequently left his father to go to Canaan, some seventy years before his father died.

Young cannot see his way clear to solve this problem by recourse to the several solutions that commentators have proposed. He cannot replace the Masoretic text at Genesis 11:32 with the reading of the Samaritan Pentateuch, which makes Abraham's departure coincide with Terah's death, because Young was convinced of the authority of the Masoretic text. Sometimes the suggestion is made that Genesis 11:26 mentions Abraham first among the three sons whom Terah sired from age seventy onwards, not because he was born first, but because he was the most prominent. Actually, so the suggestion goes, Abraham could have been the youngest son. If Terah was 130 when he sired Abraham, then Abraham's departure from Haran at age seventy-five would coincide with Terah's death at age two hundred five. But Young rejects this as absurd because it would be impossible to understand how Abraham found it difficult to have a child at age ninety if his own father had sired him at age one hundred thirty. Neither should the death of Terah, which according to Acts 7:4 occurred when Abraham left Haran, be understood as Terah's spiritual death or his death so far as Abraham was concerned, for this would be a gratuitous understanding of the verb "to die" in this context. Like Archer, Young cannot say that Luke simply reported Stephen's use, before the Sanhedrin, of the reading of the Samaritan Pentateuch, for when Stephen gave his speech he was an inspired person— "full of the Holy Spirit" (Acts 7:55);[201] and it is impossible to presume that inspiration would not expunge such an error. "It would certainly be the part of presumption," declared Young, "to assert that at this point there was positive error in Scripture. Far wiser is the course of candid acknowledgment that, with our present limited knowledge, the answer to this particular difficulty is not known to us."[202] Thus, Young is not willing to consider the explanation of Stephen's Abrahamic chronology as deriving from a version of the Septuagint that is still extant in the Samaritan Pentateuch. F. F. Bruce indicates that it was likely that Stephen was well-versed in this text, because there are other parts of his speech in Acts 7 which parallel the usage of the Samaritan Pentateuch.[203]

---

[201] Young, *op. cit.*, p. 177.

[202] *Ibid.*, p. 179.

[203] F. F. Bruce, *The Acts of the Apostles* (London: Tyndale Press, 1951), p. 162, note.

An historian, unfettered by the necessity to uphold Young's doctrine of inerrancy, would immediately declare that it was highly probable that Stephen's peculiar chronology in Acts 7:1–4 stemmed from both his and his hearers' having been nurtured in a text that is today extant in the Samaritan Pentateuch. But Edward Young, historical scholar that he was, could not follow this highly probably pathway of historical reasoning. In the face of this discrepancy all that he could say was that "the answer to this particular difficulty is not known to us."[204] But to be unwilling to let historical data supply a highly probable solution is to reject historical data in the interest of theological dogma. By refusing the data provided by the Samaritan Pentateuch, Young would be forced to say that the parallels between Stephen and the Samaritan Pentateuch were merely coincidental, or, in other words, he would be forced to discount a cause commensurate with the effect found in Stephen's speech. To do this places all historical knowledge in jeopardy, and makes it unnecessary to insist on a grammatico-historical interpretation of Scripture.

To adhere to such reasoning thus implies a basic distrust in the historical method, and to be consistent, would prevent us from ever appealing to archaeology, etc., in support of the Bible, as is so popular in evangelical circles. But more important, such unwillingness to follow out the historical method means that we cannot ground the Christian faith in history, as we have done in this work. We would have to say that while the Bible is true, its truth is not amenable to historical methodology. This is, in fact, what Young did, for he strongly insisted that the truth of Scripture was validated not by any historical argument but by the internal testimony of the Holy Spirit. He said, "[The Christian] is convinced ... that the Bible is the Word of God, because God has told him so. Thus, we come to the blessed doctrine of the internal testimony of the Holy Spirit. The Christian is persuaded and assured of both the infallible truth and the divine authority of the Bible by this inward work of the Holy Spirit within his heart, who opens his mind to perceive the true nature of Scripture and who applies the Word with force and conviction that men may experience the truth that the Bible is from God."[205]

Young is even quite willing to admit that this reduces him to reasoning in a circle: "If God has actually created us, it follows that all we know we must receive from him. He must tell us what we are to believe about anything ... We need not be frightened by the charge that to accept the Scriptures as the infallible Word of God requires us to reason in a circle ... If God is the Creator and man a creature, there is no way in which man can set himself up as a judge of what God has revealed."[206] But such unwillingness to submit the Bible to the criteria of historical reasoning jeopardizes the strong scriptural emphasis that God, in revealing himself to humanity, entered into the very stuff of history—that the "Word became flesh (John 1:14). If the revelation of God did thus become so completely a part of this world and its history, why then cannot this revelation always remain

---

[204] Young, *op. cit.*, p. 179.

[205] *Ibid.*, p. 34.

[206] *Ibid.*, pp. 192f.

subject to historical methodology, the only means we have for knowing what happened in the past?

While it appears that what Young and many other evangelicals have done seems to undergird the Bible as the Word of God, yet as they follow the implications of an insistence on inerrancy not only in revelatory matters but also in incidental, non-revelatory matters, it becomes apparent that in so doing, they fall into the pit of forcing the Bible to say something contrary to its intrinsic genre. The Bible intends to say that God, in revealing himself, has entered fully into the stuff of history, but the inescapable implication from their interpretation is that this revelation has not really become a part of the stuff of history, or, in other words, that the Word did not really become flesh. This would be a reversion to the ancient heresy of Docetism, which taught that Jesus only appeared to be a man, but that, in fact, he was not really flesh.

But what of Young's argument that if even a trifle of Scripture is less than fully true, then a shadow of suspicion is cast over even its most momentous teachings? The answer is that the contexts of Matthew 22:29 and 2 Timothy 3:15ff. make it obvious that these passages affirm the truth of the revelatory teachings of the Bible. Being verbally inspired, the biblical writers were enabled to set forth the message of Scripture so accurately that those reading them think God's thoughts after him. Being verbally inspired, they were also directed to take non-revelatory cultural matters, and without changing them, use them to enhance the communication of revelatory truths to the original hearers or readers.

For example, if, as would seem likely, Stephen and his hearers had been raised on a text that renders Genesis 11:31 as the Samaritan Pentateuch does, then Stephen was helped to communicate revelation by being directed to use this version. Nothing revelatory hinges upon the exact chronology of Abraham's early life, so it was reasonable for Stephen to use this version as a vehicle for trying to persuade the Sanhedrin of the revelatory truth that throughout Israel's history God had been constantly wooing her to repent but that Israel had always resisted the Holy Spirit (Acts 7 *passim*, esp. v. 51). The communication of this revelatory truth would have been hindered had the Holy Spirit directed Stephen to use the more accurate text, for its strange sound would have diverted his hearers' attention *away* from the revelatory point that God was inspiring him to make. Thus, God's inspiration enabled Stephen both to utter, inerrantly, the revelatory truths of his speech and also, for pedagogical purposes, to make best use of the cultural, non-revelatory contents of his speech.

Another example of this is Jesus' allusion to the mustard seed as the smallest of the seeds (Matthew 13:31; 17:20). Botanists know of seeds even smaller than the mustard seed.[207] In the culture of the people to whom he was speaking, however, the mustard seed represented the smallest seed, for it was regarded as the smallest thing which the eye could see.[208] Thus, the culture of the hearers provided Jesus with an illustration that aided the

---

[207] Claus-Hunno Hunziger, "σίναπι," *Theologisches Wörterbuch zum Neuen Testament*, VI. 288.
[208] Strack-Billerbeck, *Kommentar zum Neuen Testament*, I, 699.

communication of the revelatory truths that a very little faith could remove mountains, and that the kingdom of God, though very small then, would eventually become very large. Though there certainly were smaller seeds, Jesus used this facet of the culture of the people to whom he was speaking as a vehicle for conveying the cargo of revelatory truth. Had Jesus spoken of the seed which was indeed the smallest, he would have been scientifically more accurate, but his hearers would have been so confused trying to understand what he was talking about that they would have concerned themselves more with the illustration than with the revelatory truths it was illustrating. Therefore, the doctrine of the inerrancy of Scripture, far from affirming that the Holy Spirit corrects non-revelatory, cultural references, demands instead that they be left unchanged. As Ramm has said, "No objection can be brought against the inerrancy of the Bible because it is a culturally conditioned revelation. The Bible uses the terms and expressions of the times of its writers. Any revelation must be so accommodated to the human mind ... When the religious liberal renounces much of the Bible because it is culturally conditioned, he fails to understand that inspiration used cultural terms and expressions to convey an infallible revelation."[209]

Note: This was the way Calvin, who often spoke of the Bible as being dictated by God, commented on Hebrews 11:21, which follows the Septuagint reading of Genesis 47:31, "Jacob worshiped, leaning upon the top of his staff," when the Hebrew reads, "Jacob bowed himself upon the bed's head." Calvin realized that the translators of the Septuagint had mistaken the Hebrew מִטָּה (bed) for מַטֶּה (staff). But he justified the writer of Hebrews for following the Septuagint, saying, "The Apostle [sic] hesitated not to apply to his purpose what was commonly received: he was indeed writing to the Jews; but they who were dispersed into various countries had changed their own language for the Greek. And we know that the Apostles were not so scrupulous in this respect, as not to accommodate themselves to the unlearned, who had as yet need of milk ... But, in reality, the difference is but little; for the main thing was that Jacob worshiped."

Note: We misinterpret Scripture if we try to harmonize with science and history aspects of biblical statements whose purpose is only to facilitate the communication of revelatory truth. For example, the time span of Genesis 5 has a very essential revelatory aspect in that it emphasizes that events before and after it happened in history. But the exact number of years is not essential to the author's intention to be a revelatory spokesman. No doubt he, along with his original readers, thought that the number of years indicated in chapter 5 was the length of time that transpired between the Fall and the Flood, just as he and they probably thought that the sun and stars moved across the heaven of a stationary earth. Since such matters, however, are non-revelatory, they lie outside the boundary of the biblical writers' intention, and are therefore irrelevant to the question of biblical inerrancy. A book is inerrant only against the criterion of its writer's intention. Interpretation is not

---

[209] Bernard Ramm, *Protestant Biblical Interpretation*, 2nd ed. (Boston: W. A. Wilde Co., 1956), p. 192.

concerned with everything that was in an author's mind, but only with the meaning which he necessarily implied by what he intended to say. Consequently, the biblical writers are to be judged only on the basis of the revelatory teachings they intended to communicate. In all that the biblical writers thus intended to teach they are inerrant.

Thus, since the Bible declares that its purpose is to impart revelation, we honor its intrinsic genre and run no risk of distorting its message as we credit its revelatory teachings and regard its non-revelatory statements and implications as a reflection of the culture of the writer and his original readers. Such an approach is perfectly willing to let biblical statements in the non-revelatory areas of science and history be fully tested against what we can find out ourselves about such matters. Knowing that verbal inspiration kept the biblical writers free from all error in revelatory matters, we are not afraid that what we can learn about history or science ourselves may jeopardize the validity of what the Bible teaches.

To be sure, God revealed himself in the events of redemptive history, and if a highly probable historical conclusion were reached that even one of these events did not happen, it would destroy the truth of Scripture just as much as if historical reasoning should show that Jesus did not rise from the dead. With Warfield we are therefore content to let the Bible always be subject to historical investigation without a theological *a priori*. Warfield said, "We do not adopt the doctrine of the plenary inspiration of Scripture … on *a priori* or general grounds of whatever kind. We adopt it specifically because it is taught as truth by Christ and his apostles, in the scriptural record of their teaching, and the evidence for its truth is, therefore … precisely that evidence in weight and amount, which vindicates for us the trustworthiness of Christ and his apostles as teachers of doctrine. Of course, this evidence is not in the strict logical sense 'demonstrative;' it is probable evidence. It therefore leaves open the metaphysical possibility of its being mistaken."[210]

Since the truth of the Bible, as well as what may be learned about science and history, comes from empirical investigation, the Christian, therefore, is perfectly able to credit the teaching of the Bible and be a scientist or a historian at the same time. It is the Bible which provides the overall matrix into which we fit historical and scientific knowledge. The Bible has much to say about God as the creator and sustainer of this world and the one who rules in the affairs of its history. The Bible also tells about the nature, the inner motivation, of us human beings who live in the world. But this world, its history, and the nature of humanity are areas in which science also gleans knowledge. Science, however, confesses that it cannot answer the ultimate questions about humanity, the world, and history.

---

[210] Benjamin B. Warfield, "The Real Problem of Inspiration," *The Inspiration and Authority of Scripture*. S. Craig (ed.) (Philadelphia: Presbyterian and Reformed Publishing Company, 1948), p. 218.

While science can analyze matter, it can only speculate about its ultimate origin. While historiography can gain knowledge of the past, it can only speculate about the ultimate significance of any event in history. While it can describe the patterns into which human behavior tends to fall in different sets of circumstances, it can only speculate about why human beings differentiate themselves so radically from the animals that they can develop sufficient anxiety about the purpose and meaning of life to commit suicide. But the Bible provides the answers to these ultimate questions and lays out, as it were, the great framework on which a worldview can be built. Science and history contribute a part of the mortar and brick that completes the remainder of the building comprising the unity of truth.

Since the Bible's non-revelatory statements and implications do not have the same function as its revelatory propositions, the Christian need not have a two-compartment structure for knowledge: one for scientific and historical truth, and one for biblical truth. It is the Christian's privilege to construct a worldview from Scripture into which we can fit all other knowledge. But we Christians must constantly work to find the place, in the biblical worldview, where the teaching of each passage of Scripture fits. We all have more or less of a worldview into which we fit what we know. If we Christians do not go farther than learning what the various passages in the Bible intended to teach, if we do not let the various teachings of the Bible cohere, as they must if they comprise God's revelation, then the worldview which we already have and which has not been constructed on the basis of what God has said—that world view will then exercise a decisive and final control over our thought and life, and all emphasis on the Bible as the final authority becomes mere talk.

Therefore, the biblical interpreter must not be content simply to do the task of biblical theology, which is to understand the thought structure of each biblical writer. Our task is complete only when we take these thought structures and allow them to form the worldview of a systematic theology. To regard these as paradoxical would, of course, preclude such an effort. But why should we assume so quickly that the basic themes of Scripture are a paradox? Will we not be more likely to gain truth by working on apparent paradoxes to see if they do not finally cohere than by throwing up our hands and saying, "It's a paradox; let's go to lunch"? But as we construct a *biblical* worldview, a perspective emerges within which the teaching of each passage can be viewed. If the biblical worldview is not there, whatever worldview we already have will ultimately and decisively control, to our detriment, the results of biblical exegesis and all the effort of hermeneutics. Therefore, when we embark on the hermeneutical task, we should be willing to see it through to completion, that is, to the constructing of a system of theology.[211]

---

[211] See my *The Unity of the Bible: Unfolding God's Plan for Humanity* [Zondervan 2010] for my attempt to fulfill the hermeneutical task.

Appendix A: Biblical Theology and the Analogy of Faith

Every theology regarding itself as Christian seems to affirm that it was in agreement with the Bible. There may be another authority alongside the Bible, as in Roman Catholicism, which regards church tradition as a separate source of authority; or among the Latter-Day Saints, who regard the Book of Mormon as a source of authority. But since these groups do not regard these two sources as clashing with each other, they would always affirm that their theologies are biblical.

However, the term "biblical theology" first appeared among the followers of the Reformation, among those who espoused the principle of *sola scriptura*. This principle affirmed that since the Church was founded upon the teachings of the prophets and apostles, the authority for its teaching and practice must be derived from the Bible alone. To support the legitimacy of a claim to know what the prophets and apostles taught, the reformers made several radical departures from the way theologians had interpreted the Bible in preceding centuries.

For one thing, they rejected the medieval practice of finding in a biblical passage a fourfold sense: the literal, the allegorical, the moral, and the anagogical (or mystical, ultimate) sense. At the end of his life, Luther summarized this hermeneutical principle in these words:

> [The Holy Spirit's] words cannot have more than one, and that the very simplest, sense, which we call the literal, ordinary, natural sense ... We are not ... to say that the Scriptures or the Word of God have more than one meaning ... We are not to introduce any ... metaphorical, figurative sayings into any text of Scripture, unless the particulars of the words compel us to do so ... For if anyone at all were to have power to depart from the pure, simple words and to make inferences and figures of speech wherever he wished ... [then] no one could reach any certain conclusions about ... any article of faith.[212]

Studying the Bible in the original Greek and Hebrew languages was another way the reformers earned the right to make claims about what the Bible taught. Both Luther and Calvin strove to master the language conventions of biblical Hebrew and Greek so they could more readily grasp the meaning the biblical writers attached to their own terms, and be less apt to impute current meaning back into those ancient words. But they also wanted their conclusions about the Bible's meanings to be made available to as many people as possible; so, they stressed the need for translating the Bible into contemporary language. The more people could read the Bible for themselves, the more the Bible itself (*sola scriptura*!) would directly teach individual Christians, and consequently there could be a priesthood of all believers.

---

[212] Quoted by W. G. Kümmel, *The New Testament: The History of the Investigation of Its Problems* (Nashville/New York: Abingdon, 1972), p; 22–23.

The reformers also realized that theologians had kept the Bible from speaking for itself because they were so prone to construe its statements in terms of medieval scholasticism, which drew so heavily upon the philosophy of Aristotle. Luther said, "This defunct pagan [Aristotle] has attained supremacy [in the universities]; [he has] impeded, and almost suppressed, the Scripture of the living God. When I think of this lamentable state of affairs, I cannot avoid believing that the Evil One introduced the study of Aristotle."[213] And in arguing against the Roman Catholic view of transubstantiation, Calvin said, "The doctrine which we have put forward has been drawn from the pure Word of God, and rests upon its authority ... Not Aristotle, but the Holy Spirit teaches that the body of Christ from the time of his resurrection was finite, and is contained in heaven even to the Last Day."[214]

Seeking in these ways to let the Bible speak for itself, the reformers demonstrated how much of the principle of *sola scriptura* they had grasped. Ebeling has remarked, "Reformation theology is the first attempt in the entire history of theology to take seriously the demand for a theology based on scripture alone. Only among the followers of the Reformation could the concept 'biblical theology' have been coined at all."[215]

"The Analogy of Faith" by Luther and Calvin

But the reformers also emphasized a hermeneutical principle that is commonly called "the analogy of faith." This principle was used when the time came to combine what two or more biblical writers said about some article of faith, such as the law (Moses and Paul) or justification (Genesis, Paul, and James). In general, the analogy-of-faith principle of hermeneutics affirms that the norm for interpreting other parts of the Bible is certain passages in the Pauline epistles, which supposedly set forth biblical teachings with the greatest clarity and precision.

In stating this principle Luther said, "It is the attribute of Holy Scripture that it interprets itself by passages and places which belong together, and can only be understood by a rule of faith."[216] A century later the Westminster Confession (I, ix) used similar language to enunciate this hermeneutical principle: "The infallible rule of interpretation of Scripture is the Scripture itself, and therefore when there is a question about the true and full sense of any Scripture (which is not manifold but one), it must be searched and known by other places that speak more clearly."

On the surface, the statement that "Scripture interprets itself" seems to be another pillar upholding the principle of *sola scriptura*. But Luther's additional statement that "passages ... can only be understood by a rule of faith" raises the question of how anyone

---

[213] M. Luther, "An Appeal to the Ruling Class," *Martin Luther; Selections from His Writings*, ed. J. Dillenberger (Garden City, New York: Doubleday, 1961), pp. 470–471.
[214] J. Calvin, *Institutes of the Christian Religion*, IV, 17, 26. LCC (26 vols.; ed. J. McNeil; (Philadelphia: Westminster, 1960) p. 21, 1393.
[215] G. Ebeling, "The Meaning of 'Biblical Theology'," *Word and Faith* (London: SCM, 1963), p. 82.
[216] Quoted by C. Briggs, *Biblical Study* (New York: Scribners, 1884), p. 332.

acquires the authority for knowing just what that rule is. As we consider how Luther and Calvin elaborated on this principle of the analogy of faith, it becomes clear that, in the final analysis, individual theologians themselves establish this all-important norm for interpreting the rest of Scripture based on their own subjective preferences. Consequently, the analogy-of-faith principle does not undergird but undermines the *sola scriptura* principle.

In elaborating this principle in another place Luther said, "Every word [of Scripture] should be allowed to stand in its natural meaning, and that should not be abandoned *unless faith forces us to it*."[217] Luther's readiness to let faith force him to suppress the natural meaning of a text becomes evident from the famous statement he made in his disputation thesis, *De Fide*, 11 September 1535. In this he affirmed, "Scripture is to be understood not contrary to, but in accordance with Christ. Therefore, Scripture is to be referred to him, or else we do not have what represents Scripture … If adversaries urge Scripture against Christ, we will urge Christ against Scripture." Likewise, "If it is to be a question of whether Christ or the Law is to be dismissed, we say, Law is to be dismissed, not Christ."[218]

Commenting on Luther's statements, Ebeling says:

> Luther was no biblicist … No biblicist speaks like that … [Luther] had not thoroughly thought [the hermeneutical problem] through from the methodological point of view and therefore the methodology of theology in general remained obscure in decisive questions of fundamental importance. It was not made clear what the principle of *sola scriptura* means for the procedure of theology as a whole.[219]

For Luther there really were places where Christ should be urged against Scripture. In his thinking, the term "Christ" often represented the whole of his understanding of justification by faith. Luther was convinced that what James said about justification could not be reconciled with Paul's teaching on that subject. In the conclusion to an introduction to Hebrews, James, Jude, and Revelation, Luther said, "Many sweat hard at reconciling James and Paul … but unsuccessfully. 'Faith justifies' [Paul] stands in flat contradiction to 'Faith does not justify' [James 2:24]. If anyone can harmonize these sayings, I'll put my doctor's cap on him and let him call me a fool."[220] Consequently, Luther put James and these other books, each of which, in his view, had objectionable features, at the end of his New Testament of September, 1522. In his introduction to James itself, Luther said, "[This book] cannot be defended against [its] applying to works the sayings of Moses in Genesis 15, which speaks only of Abraham's faith, and not of his works, as St. Paul shows in Romans 4 … Therefore, I cannot put him among the chief books."[221]

---

[217] Briggs, *op. cit.*, (italics added), p. 332.
[218] Taken from the Latin given by Ebeling, *op. cit.*, p. 82.
[219] Ebeling, *op. cit.*, p. 82.
[220] Quoted by Kümmel, *op. cit.*, p. 26.
[221] *Ibid.*, pp. 24–25.

In another place Luther singled out the books of the New Testament which did properly, in his view, "urge Christ."

> To sum it all up ... St. John's gospel [not the synoptics!], and his first epistle, St. Paul's epistles—especially those to the Romans, Galatians, and Ephesians—and St. Peter's first epistle; these books which show you Christ and teach everything which is needful and blessed for you to know even if you don't see or even hear any other book ... Wherefore St. James' epistle is a true epistle of straw compared with them, for it contains nothing of an evangelical nature.[222]

The foregoing statements indicate what Luther meant by his assertion, "Scripture interprets itself by passages and places which belong together, and [Scripture as a whole] can only be understood by a rule of faith."[223] They give concrete examples of how the analogy, or rule, of faith justified singling out certain parts of Scripture as the norm by which other parts of the canon were to be judged. Surely, Luther's submission to the Bible, implied in his rejection of the fourfold meaning, scholasticism, and church tradition, enabled him to learn and transmit many scriptural teachings that have greatly profited the Church. But when he set up his understanding of justification by faith as the basis for suppressing such books as the synoptic gospels, Hebrews, and James, he then made it impossible for these books to deepen or improve his understanding of this doctrine. He also made it harder for these books to inform him on other subjects which they taught. So, his use of the analogy of faith undercut the *sola scriptura* principle not only for himself but for all those who have followed his hermeneutical lead ever since.

Matthaeus Flacius (a Lutheran theologian) confirmed this conclusion about the analogy of faith in his *Key to the Scriptures* (1567), the first hermeneutics book to emerge from the Reformation. According to Flacius:

> Every understanding and exposition of Scripture is to be in agreement with the faith. Such [agreement] is, so to speak, the norm or limit of a sound faith, that we may not be thrust over the fence into the abyss by anything, either by a storm from without or by an attack from within (Romans 12:6). For everything that is said concerning Scripture, or on the basis of Scripture, must be in agreement with all that the catechism declares or that is taught by the articles of faith.[224]

---

[222] Quoted by E. Reuss, *History of the Canon of the Holy Scriptures in the Christian Church* (Edinburgh: Hunter, 1891), pp. 322, 329.

[223] *Supra*, note 5.

[224] Quoted by Kümmel, *op. cit.*, p. 30. We note Flacius' reference to Romans 12:6, where Paul exhorts his readers that if they have the gift of prophecy, they should exercise this gift "according to the 'analogy' of faith" (κατὰ τὴν ἀναλογίαν [which all major English language translations render as 'proportion'] τῆς πίστεως). Paul's point is that all Christians should exercise their spiritual gifts in accordance with the appropriate confidence, or inclination, that they have by virtue of God's empowering any particular gift (cf. 1 Corinthians 12:4–6). So, it is clear that "faith" in this passage does not represent some objective body of truth. But this is the sense in which Flacius construed this passage, as did Origen, who, as nearly as I can determine, was the

This statement of Flacius shows how Luther's use of the analogy-of-faith principle had made church tradition, fixed in creeds and catechisms, the key for the interpretation of Scripture. Even though this tradition was now of a Protestant rather than of a Roman Catholic variety, the barrier which it erected against letting biblical exegesis improve or correct that tradition was exceedingly hard to surmount.

John Calvin followed the same hermeneutical procedure as Luther. In his "Prefatory address to King Francis," designed to gain a recommendation for his *Institutes of the Christian Religion*, Calvin appealed to Romans 12:6 and its phrase, "according to the analogy of faith," as his best argument for why his teaching should be regarded as true, he wrote:

> When Paul wished all prophecy to be made to accord with the analogy of faith [Romans 12:6], he set forth a very clear rule to test all interpretation of Scripture. Now, if our interpretation be measured by this rule of faith, victory is in our hands. For what is more consonant with faith than to recognize that we are ... weak, to be sustained by [Christ]? To take away from us all occasion for glorying, that he alone may stand forth gloriously and we glory in him?[225]

There are, to be sure, many passages where Scripture teaches that "no human being should boast in the presence of God," but "let him who boasts, boast in the Lord" (1 Corinthians 1:29, 31). Those who are committed to *sola scriptura* want their understanding of such passages as well as those setting forth all other biblical teachings, to be deepened and corrected by a careful exegesis of all of them.

But *sola scriptura* was threatened when Calvin, like Luther, made the Gospel of John the "key" for understanding the synoptic gospels. Concerning the Gospel of John Calvin said, "The doctrine which points out to us the power and fruit of Christ's coming appears far more clearly in [John] than in [Matthew, Mark or Luke] ... For this reason, I am accustomed to say that this gospel is the key to open the door to the understanding of the others."[226] The problem, however, is that those who are convinced that John's teaching is the key for understanding the other gospels will devote more energy to learning what John teaches than they will to learning what one of the other gospels teaches. This in itself would be contrary to *sola scriptura*, which requires us to be equally docile to all of Scripture.

Calvin also required Exodus through Deuteronomy to be understood in terms of Paul's supposed view of the law. Indeed, Calvin concluded, just from an exegesis of the Pentateuch itself, that "the *same* [italics added] covenant, of which Abraham had been the minister and keeper, was repeated to his descendants by the instrumentality of Moses."

first person to use the words, "according to the analogy of faith," to urge people to conform their language and thinking about a passage of Scripture to an *a priori* understanding of what God's Word must be like (*De Principiis*, IV, 26).
[225] Calvin, *Institutes*, 20. 12–13.
[226] J. Calvin, *The Gospel According to John, 1–10*, Calvin's Commentaries, eds. D and T. Torrance (Grand Rapids: Eerdmans, 1959), p. 6.

But then when he considered what he thought Paul said about the Mosaic law, he said, "Paul opposes [the Mosaic law] to the promise given to Abraham, because as [Paul] is treating of the peculiar office, power and end of the law, he separates it from the promises of grace [that are found in Abraham and Moses] …[227]

Thus, according to Calvin, we could not properly grasp the message of Exodus through Deuteronomy simply by studying these books. We must first know about the antithesis Paul drew between Abraham, on the one hand, and parts of Moses, on the other, before our study of Exodus through Deuteronomy would produce accurate results. For Calvin, unless readers knew that the promises in these books constantly shift back and forth between conditional and unconditional ones, they would be led astray in their study of them—although, Calvin never demonstrated the existence of any unconditional promise in the Pentateuch. So, Calvin concluded the introduction to his harmony of Exodus through Deuteronomy by saying, "I have thought it advisable to say this much by way of preface, for the purpose of directing my readers to the proper *object* [italics added] of the history …"[228]

A major emphasis of his system is that the gospel calling for faith comprises *un*conditional promises, whereas law appears in every conditional promise.[229] But there are numerous passages in Scripture where such blessings as eternal life, and inheriting the Kingdom of God, are given because of the good works that people have done. According to Matthew 25:34–36, 46, the blessed will inherit the Kingdom of God, and eternal life, because they have done such things for "Jesus' brethren" as feeding them when they were hungry. Likewise, Paul commands, "Whatever your task, work heartily, as serving the Lord and not men, knowing that from the Lord you will receive the inheritance as your reward" (Colossians 3:23–24). In his *Institutes* (III, 18, 2), Calvin interpreted these two passages by calling in statements from such remote contexts as Ephesians 1:5–6, 18 and Galatians 4:7. According to Calvin, these affirm that "the Kingdom of Heaven is not servants' wages but sons' inheritance, which only they who have been adopted as sons by the Lord shall enjoy, and that for no other reason than this adoption." So "even in these very passages [Matthew 25:34–46 and Colossians 3:23–24] where the Holy Spirit promises everlasting glory as a reward for works, [yet] by expressly terming it an 'inheritance' he is showing that it comes to us from another source [than works]."[230]

Here is a concrete example of how analogy-of-faith hermeneutics worked in Calvin's thinking. He has to construe Matthew 25 and Colossians 3 in terms of other passages drawn from such distant contexts as Ephesians 1 and Galatians 4. These he selects because they accord well with his understanding of the analogy of faith, that only God, and not men, should be glorified. Then he applies these remote-context passages to the ones in Matthew and Colossians, whose own terminology does not affirm so clearly that God

---

[227] J. Calvin, *Commentaries on the Four Last Books of Moses*, 4 vols (Grand Rapids: Eerdmans, 1950), vol 1, p. 314.
[228] Calvin, *op. cit.*, p. 316.
[229] Calvin, *Institutes*, III, 2, 29.
[230] *Ibid.* 20, 822.

alone is glorified in human salvation. They even say, on Calvin's own admission, that "the Holy Spirit [!] promises everlasting glory as a reward for works." But this statement of theirs must be suppressed and replaced by the passages from Ephesians and Galatians, so that the passages in Matthew 25 and Colossians 3 will make it clear that the *inheritance* spoke of there "comes to us from another source [than works]."

[Note: To the objection that we must remain with analogy-of-faith hermeneutics or else we will let passages like Matthew 25 and Colossians 3 lead us right back to Rome and salvation by works, my answer is twofold. First, we must determine, regardless of consequences, what the intended meaning of each of the biblical writers is. We must let each one speak for himself and avoid construing him by recourse to what another writer said. Otherwise there is no escape from subjectivism in biblical interpretation. That is, since the Bible itself does not point to certain parts as the norm to which other parts must conform, we would be free to set up any analogy of faith that we choose, so long as we can adduce a handful of verses, preferably from the New Testament, to support it.

Second, when we cannot quickly escape from passages running counter to our theological presuppositions by an analogy-of-faith procedure, then we are driven to hear out a biblical writer with an intensity that is not otherwise possible. I am convinced that the whole problem of faith and works, which analogy-of-faith hermeneutics is most often employed to solve, evaporates as we probe more deeply into biblical theology. A good starting point for solving this problem is an understanding of what Paul meant by a "work of faith" (1 Thessalonians 1:3; 2 Thessalonians 1:11). Works that are generated by faith preclude the possibility of any boasting and give all glory to God, yet these works are so vital to a saving faith that those lacking them are not saved. On this line of reasoning Colossians 3:23–24, Matthew 25, and many other passages could speak for themselves without having to be muzzled by an "analogy of faith."]

So long as the exegesis of biblical passages is conducted by such analogy-of-faith hermeneutics, it would be difficult for systematic theology to be nourished and corrected by exegetical considerations from the biblical text. But this was the course which the reformers left for theologians to steer. While the reformers themselves introduced into biblical exegesis many practices which greatly furthered the cause of *sola scriptura*, yet because they did not grasp how their analogy-of-faith principle clashed with *sola scriptura*, they gave a strong impetus for Reformation theology to revert to a scholasticism not unlike the medieval sort against which they had rebelled. Thus, Ebeling argues,

This lack of clarity became apparent in the degree to which Reformation theology, like medieval scholasticism, also developed into a scholastic system. What was the relation of the systematic method here [in the post-Reformation] to the exegetical method? Ultimately, it was the same as in medieval scholasticism. There, too, exegesis of holy Scripture went on not only within systematic theology but also separately alongside of it, yet so that the possibility of a tension between exegesis and systematic theology was *a priori* excluded. Exegesis was enclosed within the frontiers fixed by systematic theology.[231]

There was one big difference, however. The post-Reformation era could not completely forget the several strong impulses which the reformers had given toward *sola scriptura*. So, the more post-Reformation theology became scholastic, the more it clashed with these latent *sola scriptura* impulses. Consequently, it was inevitable that a methodology would arise which (whatever its name) would seek that full conformity with *sola scriptura* that systematic theology, with its analogy-of-faith principle, could not achieve.

The Rise of Biblical Theology

A century after the Reformation the term "biblical theology" first appeared. At the outset the term signified a corrective which certain precursors of Pietism felt Protestant Orthodoxy sorely needed. Philip Spener, one of the founders of Pietism, remarked in his *Pia Desideria* (1675) how two court chaplains in the parliament at Regensburg had complained some years earlier that "scholastic theology," expelled by Luther through the front door, had now come in at the back door to suppress "biblical theology."[232] In his later writings Spener drew an antithesis between "biblical theology" and "scholastic theology." But in making this contrast Spener was not trying to discard systematics in favor of another theological method. He merely wanted to encourage theological students to spend less time mastering philosophical subtleties and more time learning the "simple" teachings of Christ and the apostles. As a result of Spener's plea a number of books appeared that assembled proof texts from all over the Bible to substantiate the affirmations of systematic theology.[233]

It was a century later that Johann Gabler used the term "biblical theology" to designate a method for ascertaining Christian teaching which should supersede systematic theology. In his inaugural address as a professor at Altdorf in 1787, he drew a sharp distinction between biblical and systematic theology. "Biblical theology," he said, "always remains the same since its arguments are historical."[234] What was "historical" had an unvarying quality about it, since "what the sacred writers thought about divine things" was something fixed in the past and represented to us today by an unchanging text of Scripture. Dogmatic theology, on the other hand, "is subjected along with other human disciplines to manifold change." "It teaches what every theologian through use of his reason philosophizes about divine things in accordance with his understanding, with the circumstances of the time, the age, the place, the school [to which he belongs] ..."

---

[231] Ebeling, *op. cit.*, pp. 82–83.

[232] *Ibid.*, pp. 83–84.

[233] F. C. Baur, *Vorlesungen über neutestamentliche Theologie*, 1864 (reprinted Darmstadt: Wissenschaftliche Buchgesellschaft, 1973), p. 3 provides a list of books.

[234] This and subsequent quotations from Gabler are taken from Kümmel, *History of Interpretation of N.T. Problems*, 98–100.

"Therefore," Gabler argued, "we are careful to distinguish the divine from the human and to undertake a separation between biblical and dogmatic theology."

Thus, biblical theology should be pursued in order to grasp exactly how each of the biblical writers thought. To do this, Gabler recommended a three-step approach. First, interpreters must direct every effort to understand "what each of [the biblical writers] thought concerning divine things ... only from their writings." A vital requisite for this is to learn "the time and place" where any single literary unit was composed. Second,

> We must carefully assemble all ideas of the several writers and arrange them in their proper sequence: those of the patriarchs, those of Moses, David, Solomon, those of the prophets—each of the prophets for that matter ... And as we proceed, we are for many reasons not to despise the Apocrypha. In similar fashion, from the epochs of the new form of doctrine, [we must carefully assemble and arrange in proper sequence] the ideas of Paul, Peter, John and James. After accomplishing these two steps, the interpreter's third step is ... to investigate which ideas are of importance to the permanent form of Christian doctrine and consequently apply to us, and which were spoken only for the people of a given age or were intended for a given form of instruction ... Who, I ask, would relate the Mosaic regulations, long since done away with by Christ, to our time, and who would insist on the validity for our time of Paul's exhortations that women should veil themselves in the sacred assembly? The ideas of the Mosaic form of instruction, which are confirmed neither by Jesus and his apostles *nor by reason itself* [italics added], can therefore be of no dogmatic value. We must zealously examine ... what we must regard as belonging to the abiding doctrine of salvation; what in the words of the apostles is truly divine and what is fortuitous and purely human ... Then the consequence is in fact a 'biblical theology' ... And when such solid foundations of 'biblical theology' ... have been laid after the manner we have described ... we shall have no wish to follow uncertain ideas set forth by a dogmatic theology that is conditioned by our own ideas.

Gabler implies, in his first two steps, that we should study each biblical spokesperson with equal diligence. But then in his third step he draws a distinction between "the permanent form of Christian doctrine" and "ideas ... for people of a given age." Later revelation (that of Jesus and the apostles) as well as "reason" were the criteria he used to make this distinction. The problem with Gabler, and with all biblical theology for the next century, was that the criteria for carrying out the third step, and especially "reason," were so amenable to the prevailing philosophy of a given age that in teaching produced by biblical theology, the prophets, Christ, and the apostles sound very similar to the current modes of thinking.

An example of this is Bernhard Weiss' *Biblical Theology* (1868), which argued that the Kingdom of God proclaimed by Jesus existed to the degree that the disciples surrounding Jesus made progress in living up to his ethical principles. Weiss said that "the dominion of God begins to be fulfilled when a company of disciples gather around Jesus, in whose midst is the Kingdom of God."[235] Although Weiss conceded that "Jesus nowhere directly designates the fellowship of his adherents as the Kingdom of God," yet on the basis of verses like Matthew 21:31, "tax collectors and harlots precede you [Pharisees] into the Kingdom of God," he confidently affirmed that "in [the disciples'] fellowship [the kingdom] begins to be realized … [Its] success depends on the condition of men's hearts."[236] It was the Kingdom of God understood in these terms which "must spread over the whole nation, like the mustard seed which grows from small beginnings to a disproportionate greatness."[237]

Such an understanding of the Kingdom of God, however, was saying scarcely anything different from ethical idealism, the prevailing philosophy of that time. And this understanding was a virtual duplication of the theology of Albrecht Ritschl, who stressed that the kingdom which Jesus founded was a community committed to the practice and furtherance of his ethical ideals.

We recall how Gabler had confidently predicted that as his three-step program for a biblical theology was carried out, the result would be ideas that belonged to the permanent form of Christian doctrine. These would replace the teachings of dogmatic theology, which have no permanence in that they are always conditioned by the thinking of their own times. But when a person has deeply committed to biblical authority as Bernhard Weiss practiced biblical theology and came up with an understanding about the Kingdom of God that accorded so well with the prevailing philosophy and theology, it seemed that biblical theology was as vulnerable to the influence of current thinking as was dogmatic theology. The ideal of *sola scriptura* would be achieved only when the exegetical method left the interpreter with no alternative but to let the text speak for itself in its own terms.

The Impact of *Religionsgeschichte*

About the middle of the 19th century, certain biblical scholars became aware of many parallels between Jesus' language in the gospels and the Jewish apocalyptic literature. The use of such writings as an aid for understanding what Jesus meant in his frequent references to "the Kingdom of God" would be an example of one application of the exegetical procedure of *religionsgeschichte*, or "The History-of-Religions School."

In 1892 Johannes Weiss included this procedure in his exegetical method, in which, as he put it, "we attempt once more to identify the original historical meaning which Jesus connected with the words 'Kingdom of God,' and … we do it with special care lest we import modern, or at any rate alien, ideas into Jesus' thought-world."[238]

---

[235] B. Weiss, *Biblical Theology of the New Testament*, 2 vols.; 3rd ed. (Edinburgh: T & T Clark, 1882), 1, 67.
[236] *Ibid.*, p. 68.
[237] *Ibid.*, p. 69.
[238] J. Weiss, *Jesus' Proclamation of the Kingdom of God*, Lives of Jesus Series, L. Keck ed. (Philadelphia: Fortress Press, 1971) p. 60.

J. Weiss noted his father's concession that Jesus did not equate the Kingdom of God with his disciples.[239] Indeed, Jesus said, in Matthew 12:25–28, that the kingdom had already come, but the meaning in this passage is that the kingdom is present in that Jesus had power to cast out demons and to dismantle Satan's realm. So, while Jesus was on earth, the Kingdom of God was invisible and only indirectly evident through Jesus' miracle-working power. But according to Luke 17:20–24, what is now invisible will come, *in the future*, with the highest visibility when Jesus returns as the "Son of Man" spoken of in Daniel 7 and in numerous places in the Jewish apocryphal book of Enoch.

On the basis of many other statements of Jesus about the futurity of the kingdom, and a rather constant allusion to similar thinking about the Kingdom of God in Jewish apocalyptic literature—The Assumption of Moses, The Testament of Daniel, Enoch and IV Ezra—J. Weiss concluded,

> The Kingdom of God as Jesus thought of it is a wholly supernatural entity that stands completely over against this world. It follows from this that in Jesus' thought there cannot have been any place for a development of the Kingdom of God *within the framework of this world*. On the basis of this result it seems to be the case that the dogmatic religio-ethical use of this idea in recent theology, which has divested it completely of its originally eschatological-apocalyptic meaning, is unjustified.[240]

Weiss' conclusion regarding Jesus' understanding of the Kingdom of God was much better established than his father's conclusion, because the son argued not only from a mass of evidence in the synoptic gospels, but also from evidence provided by *Religionsgeschichte*, that is, from similar ideas in Jewish apocalyptic literature, which were pertinent because they stemmed from the same general milieu in which Jesus lived. Faced with such double evidence, it became virtually impossible for a modern man to understand Jesus' statement about the Kingdom of God in terms of cherished contemporary concepts.

This is why J. Weiss' *Jesus' Proclamation of the Kingdom of God* (1892) represents a great turning point in the history of biblical interpretation. It was this book and Wilhelm Wrede's *Messianic Secret in the Gospels* (1901) that provided Albert Schweitzer with the key for showing that nineteenth-century liberalism could no longer find support for its teachings from the Jesus of the synoptic gospels. As Krister Stendahl has said,

> The alleged biblical basis for what has been called 'liberal theology' in the classical form ... was not shattered by conservatives but by the extreme radicals of the *Religionsgeschichtlice Schule* ('history-of-religions school'). [The exponents of this school] could show, on the basis of the comparative material, that such a picture of Jesus or of the OT prophets was totally impossible from the historical point of view

---

[239] *Ibid.*, p. 68.
[240] Quoted by Kümmel, *History of Interpretation of N.T. Problems*, p. 228.

and that it told more about the ideals of bourgeois Christianity in the late nineteenth century than about the carpenter from Nazareth or the little man from Tekoa.[241]

So, the History-of-Religions School presented biblical theology with an exegetical tool which made it virtually impossible for the Bible's message to be molded according to the current philosophy of a given culture. Now the Bible had to speak in terms of the meanings which the biblical writers had intended by the words they used. *Sola scriptura* was now within the reach of all those who would work with the biblical text to grasp its intended meanings and who were not obligated to shape those meanings to conform to some analogy of faith.

But as *Religionsgeschichte* forced us back to the way the Bible thought in its own times and cultures, the relevance of the biblical message seemed, for many, to vanish. As Johannes Weiss expounded the gospels' own view of the kingdom, he observed that "most people will neither be satisfied with this more negative description of the concept [of the Kingdom of God as that which triumphs over Satan], nor want to understand it in this completely supernaturalistic way of looking at things, which is mythological from our standpoint."[242] And Stendahl observed that "the resistance to the *religionsgeschichte Schule* was openly or unconsciously against its disregard for [contemporary] theological meaning and relevance."[243]

Indeed, *Religionsgeschichte* had made it possible for biblical theology to tell "what it meant," but there is little market for exegetical labors which merely describe, with an antiquarian interest, the thoughts of a bygone age. There is, however, a very strong desire (as Stendahl observes) to know "what the Bible means," and this desire has sought fulfillment in two very distinct theological procedures.

Two Alternatives

Karl Barth's procedure for affirming "what the Bible means" begins with the presupposition that though the biblical writers and the present-day interpreters are far removed from each other in terms of their culture, yet they have very much in common in that both have immediate access to the "subject matter" of the Bible. At the beginning of his *Church Dogmatics* Barth affirmed:

Language about God has the proper content, when it conforms to the essence of the Church, i.e., to Jesus Christ ... εἴτε προφητείαν κατὰ τὴν ἀναλογίαν τῆς πίστεως (Romans 12:6). Dogmatics investigates Christian language by raising the question of this conformity. Thus, it has not to discover the measure with which [Dogmatics] measures, still less to invent [that measure]. With the Christian Church [Dogmatics]

---

[241] K. Stendahl, "Contemporary Biblical Theology," *IDB*, 4 vols. (Nashville/New York: Abingdon, 1962) 1. p. 418.

[242] J. Weiss, *op.cit.*, p. 81.

[243] Stendahl, *op. cit.*, p. 419.

regards and acknowledges [that measure] as given (given in its own thoroughly peculiar way, exactly as the man Jesus Christ is given us ...).[244]

Since Christ is given for us today, just as he was for the writers of the New Testament, it is understandable why Barth, at the very outset of his theological career, recommended an interpretational procedure which regarded all exegetical labors with a text's historical and philological data as mere "preliminary work," which was to be followed quickly by a "genuine understanding and interpretation," which means

> ... that creative energy which Luther exercised with intuitive certainty in his exegesis; which underlies the systematic interpretation of Calvin ... [who] having first established what stands in the text, sets himself to re-think the whole material and to wrestle with it, till the walls which separate the sixteenth century from the first become transparent! Paul speaks, and the man of the sixteenth century hears. The conversation between the original record and the reader moves around the *subject matter* [italics added], until a distinction between today and yesterday becomes impossible.[245]

An example of how this all-important "subject matter" (*die Sache*, which in another place in the Church Dogmatics is stated as "revelation remains identical with Jesus Christ"[246]) controlled Barth's interpretation of the text is his handling of passages like 1 Corinthians 15:51f., which affirms that believers "shall all be changed, from mortality into immortality" (vs. 51, 52, 54). But Barth said that in the Christian hope, "there is no question of a continuation into an indefinite future of a somewhat altered life ... [but, rather] an 'eternalizing' of this ending life." His reasoning behind this surprising statement is, it seems, that if believers did actually undergo the inherent change of being resurrected, then something of what is revealed in Jesus Christ would be transposed from Christ over to created beings. But since Barth's *Sache*, or analogy of faith, bars revelation from extending itself beyond Jesus Christ, and since this *Sache* confronted both Barth and Paul, despite great cultural differences between them, therefore, Barth regarded it as proper to restate 1 Corinthians 15:51ff. from his knowledge of it, even though his words communicated a different meaning from Paul's. As Stendahl puts it,

> Orthodoxy never had representation as its program in the periods of its strength. The possibility of translation was given—as it is for Barth—in the reality of the *subject matter* [italics added], apart from the intellectual manifestations in the thought patterns of the original documents. God and Christ were not Semites in such a sense that the biblical pattern of thought was identified with the revelation itself.[247]

---

[244] K. Barth, *Church Dogmatics*, 4 vols. (Edinburgh: T & T Clark, 1936–1968) 1/1. Pp. 11–12.
[245] K. Barth, *The Epistle to the Romans*, 6th ed. (New York/Toronto: Oxford, 1933). This is a statement Barth made in his foreword to the second edition of this book in 1921.
[246] K. Barth, *Church Dogmatics*, 1 / 2, p. 118.
[247] Stendahl, *op. cit.*, p. 427.

The problem with Barth's procedure is that even though Christ might be regarded as given to all believers in Church proclamation, yet this Christ will be preached somewhat differently from church to church, and so each interpreter will read the text in a different light. Hence, this procedure will produce as many interpretations of the text as there are interpreters, and not even as profound and wise a thinker as Barth has any basis for claiming that his interpretation of a biblical text should be taken seriously. Stendahl observes that

> ... Barth speaks as if it were a very simple thing to establish what Paul actually meant in his own terms ... [but] biblical theology along this line is admittedly incapable of enough patience and enthusiasm for keeping alive the tension between what the text meant and what it means. [In Barth] there is no criteria by which they can be kept apart; what is intended as a commentary turns out to be a theological tractate, expanding in contemporary terms what Paul should have said about the subject matter as understood by the commentator.[248]

In contrast, biblical theology, controlled only by philological and historical considerations, regards its first order of business to be to construe an author's intended meaning *in his own terms*. Stendahl argues that biblical exegesis has reached a point where this is now possible for much of the biblical material:

> Once we confine ourselves to the task of descriptive biblical theology as a field in its own right, the material itself gives us the means to check whether our interpretation is correct or not ... From the point of view of method, it is clear that our only concern is to find out what these words meant when uttered or written by the prophet, the priest, the evangelist, or the apostle—and regardless of their meaning in later stages of religious history, our own included.[249]

Barth opposes letting biblical theology have this sovereignty in determining Christian teaching. He regards it as having an equal share of the responsibility along with dogmatic history, systematic theology, and practical theology:

> "Biblical and exegetical theology can become a field of wild chasing and charging when it bows to the idol of a supposedly normative historicism and when therefore, without regard to the positively significant yet also warning ecclesiastical and dogmatic history, or to its co-responsibility in the world of systematic theology (in which it may perhaps make a dilettante incursion), or to the fact that ultimately theology in the form of practical theology must aim to give meaningful directions to the ministry of the community in the world, it claims autonomy as a kind of Vatican within the whole."[250]

---

[248] *Ibid.*, p. 420.
[249] *Ibid.*, p. 422.
[250] Barth, *op. cit.*, 4/3. P. 881.

But in reply we ask: How else can the principle of *sola scriptura* be realized unless we seek to remain silent and let each biblical writer speak for himself, in his own terms? What Barth advocates leads the Church back down the road to scholasticism, just as the early reformers did with their analogy-of-faith hermeneutics.

Stendahl regards Oscar Cullmann's procedure for establishing Christian teaching as representing the alternative to Barth's way. Cullmann is distressed with Barth for not subjecting his theological thinking to the meaning of the text as determined by philological and historical considerations. "Barth is particularly open to this danger, not only because of the richness of his thought, but because systematically he seems to treat philological and historical explanations as too exclusively *preliminary* in character."[251] Cullmann argues that the Holy Spirit who inspired the biblical writings

> … can only speak in human language, and that language must always bear the stamp of the period and of the individuality of the biblical writer. For this reason, … [all philological and historical considerations] help to provide us with a 'transparency' through which, by an effort of theological concentration, we may see *with* the writer the truth which he saw and *with him* may attain to the revelation which came to him. We must thoroughly understand this historic 'transparency;' our vision through it must be so clear that at any moment we may become the actual contemporaries of the writer.[252]

In contrast to Barth, Cullmann wants to find the subject matter of any literary unit in Scripture simply by submitting himself to the pertinent historical and philological data, and by means of these alone to construe an author's intended meaning. Only as interpreters think along "*with* the writer [of the text]" will we have access to the author's subject matter. Cullmann rejects Barth's idea that we interpreters should have prior access to the subject matter through the Church's proclamation of Christ. He says,

> When I approach the text as an exegete, I may not consider it to be certain that my Church's faith in Christ is in its essence really that of the writers of the New Testament … In the same way, my personal self-understanding [*contra* Bultmann], and my personal experience of faith must not only be seen as exegetical aids, but also as possible sources of error.[253]

How then does Cullmann proceed where the Reformation foundered, namely, in the matter of avoiding subjectivity when the time comes to bring all of the teachings of the Bible together? He answers that with the closing of the canon—which imposed itself

---

[251] O. Cullmann, "The Necessity and Function of Higher Criticism," *The Early Church*, J. Higgins, ed. (Philadelphia: Westminster, 1956) p. 16.

[252] *Ibid*. p. 13. Cullman's use of Barth key word, "transparency," supra note 34.

[253] O. Cullmann, *Salvation in History* (New York/Evanston: Harper & Row, 1967) pp. 68–69. A Lutheran, Cullmann nevertheless believes Luther's rule of faith ("What urges Christ") needs to be modified to include the whole of redemptive history (*Salvation in History*, pp. 297–298).

upon the Church rather than being established by some arbitrary bias in the early Church[254]—

> … the thing that is new in this concluding new interpretation is the fact that not just individual excerpts of salvation history are presented, as was the case [prior to the composition of the last book in the canon], but that now, through the *collection together* of various books of the Bible, the whole history of salvation must be taken into account in understanding any one of the books of the Bible. When we wish to interpret some affirmation coming from early Christianity not merely as an isolated phenomenon, but as an actual *biblical text*, as a part belonging to a totality, we must call upon salvation history as a hermeneutical key, for it is the factor binding all the biblical texts together.[255]

Thus, Cullmann affirmed that "a dogmatics or ethics of salvation history ought to be written someday."[256]

In this affirmation we hear the echo of Jonathan Edwards' desire to live long enough to develop his *History of the Work of Redemption*, which was a series of sermons he gave in 1739—his son edited and published these as a treatise after his death. The *History* begins with God's creation of the world (and even his purpose in creating it) and inquires how each successive redemptive event, such as the call of Abraham, the Exodus, and so on, makes its distinctive contribution to the realization of God's one great purpose in history. At the beginning of this work Jonathan Edwards said, "In order to see how a design is carried on, we must first know what the design is … Therefore, that the great works and dispensations of God that belong to this great affair of redemption might not appear like confusion to you, I would set before you briefly the main things designed to be accomplished in this great work, to accomplish which God … will continue working to the end of the world, when the work will appear completely finished."[257] In the editorial introduction to this work his son remarked that his father "had planned a body of divinity, in a *new* method, and in the form of a *history*."[258]

To the objection that making redemptive history the perspective for understanding any given passage of Scripture is just as subjective as any of the other rules, or analogies, of faith, Cullmann answers that salvation history is what called forth certain writings as canonical in the first place, and therefore, only salvation history can provide the perspective from which they are to be interpreted. "I simply do not see any other biblical notion [besides salvation history] which makes a link between all the books of the Bible such as the fixing of the canon sought to express."[259] For Cullmann, salvation history

---

[254] Cullmann, *op. cit.*, pp. 293–304; and his essay "The Tradition," *The Early Church*, pp. 55–99.

[255] Cullman, *Salvation in History*, p. 297.

[256] *Ibid.*, p. 292.

[257] J. Edwards, *The Work of Redemption*. The Works of President Edwards, 4 vols. (New York: Leavitt & Allen, 1858) 1. P. 302.

[258] *Ibid.*, p. 296, italics added.

[259] Cullman, *op. cit.*, p. 298.

never allows the thinking of one writer to be suppressed in favor of another (as various analogies of faith do). He says,

> [The scholar] must … resist the temptation to bring two texts into harmony when their affirmations do not agree, if he is convinced that such a synthesis is incompatible with the critical control exercised by philology and history; this he must do, however painful the biblical antinomy with regard to one point or another, once the synthesis has been rejected.[260]

Cullmann believes that such antinomies exist in Scripture because he sees "distorting influences involved in the interpretation of the historical character and the kerygmatic meaning of the event."[261] He thinks, however, that he can detect which interpretation is a distortion and can correct it by looking more closely at the event which it was trying to interpret. The problem with this is that redemptive events in Scripture are always so inextricably bound up with interpretations that we should despair of ever separating an event from the interpretation given it by the person reporting it. Furthermore, even if we could remove all interpretive features from a reported event, we could not then work back from this bare event to decide which interpretation was most valid. For example, knowing only that a man named Jesus rose from the dead carries with it no implication of its significance.

Cullmann, however, does have statements where he speaks of later events in redemptive history as providing "reinterpretations" of earlier ones. For example, when the Old Testament kerygma passes on into the New Testament, he says, "This *kerygma* passes through new interpretations more radical than all those undertaken within the sphere of the Old Testament, because they are all subsequently oriented toward the Christ event." Furthermore, "the evangelists [Matthew, Mark, Luke and John] still offer their reinterpretation of the form of a life of Jesus at a relatively late stage in the formation of the primitive Christian *kerygma*.[262]

But this "reinterpretation" does not mean that older interpretations of a redemptive event are discarded as no longer useful. The "correction" of the interpretation of a past saving event "… never happens in such a way that an earlier account is disputed. Rather, aspects formerly unnoticed are by virtue of the new revelation now placed in the foreground, creating a correspondingly wider horizon."[263] Elsewhere he uses such words as "completed" and "refined"[264] to define what he means by "reinterpretation," and he also expressly criticizes Von Rad's understanding of later interpretations in redemptive history as invalidating earlier ones.[265] Therefore, older interpretations of a redemptive event continue to make valid contributions to our understanding of that event, even though

---

[260] Cullmann, "The Necessity and Function of Higher Criticism," p. 15.
[261] Cullmann, *Salvation in History*, p. 96.
[262] Cullmann, *Salvation in History*, p. 113.
[263] *Ibid.*, p. 88.
[264] *Ibid.*, p. 112, 136.
[265] *Ibid.*, p. 88.

later revelation adds new information about it so that the perspective by which we view it shifts from that provided merely by the earlier interpretations.

On the basis of such an approach Cullmann argues that we hear what the Bible itself is trying to say, and the very objectivity of this message, arising from the sequence and meaning of the Bible's redemptive events, constitutes the proper object to which faith responds. The very "otherness," or "strangeness," of the biblical message increases, rather than detracts from, the Bible's applicability to life. In that the biblical message is so out of step with human thinking in any age, it calls for a response from us that involves a complete break with the ways we are prone to view things. Cullmann affirms,

> The 'application' of the subject matter to myself [paraphrasing the famous statement of Bengel given in the eighteenth century] presupposes that in complete subjection to the text (*te totum applica ad textum* [Bengel]), silencing my question, I struggle with the '*res*', the subject matter. But that means that I must be ready to hear something perhaps foreign to me. I must be prepared to hear a faith, an address, running completely contrary to the question I raise, and in which I do *not* at first feel myself addressed.[266]

At this point George Ladd criticizes Cullmann for not having taken the "second step in biblical theology—that of interpreting how the theology of salvation history can be acceptable today … Biblical theology must be alert to this problem and expound reasons why the categories of biblical thought, admittedly not those of the modern world, have a claim upon our theological thinking."[267] One reason Ladd gives for why we should welcome the claim made in the Bible's history of salvation is that because "Christ is now reigning as Lord and King," and will continue to reign until he has put all enemies under his feet (1 Corinthians 15:25), therefore, "his reign must [eventually] become public in power and glory and his lordship universally recognized (Philippians 2:10–11)."[268] A salvation history, in which so many promises already have been fulfilled and which now promises that all the enemies that presently bring us such woe will someday be banished, inspires a confidence for the future, which it would seem, all of us would most readily welcome.

---

[266] *Ibid.*, p. 70.
[267] G. Ladd, "The Search for Perspective," *Interpretation* 25, 1 (January, 1971) p. 48. Stendahl ("Biblical Theology, p. 421) voices the same criticism. Cullmann deliberately avoids pointing to any psychological or existential need which the biblical message fulfills, because of the danger that such a need would become an "analogy of faith" by which every biblical line of thought would be interpreted. This is what happened in Bultmann's thinking; and Cullmann wants none of that.
[268] G. Ladd, *A Theology of the New Testament* (Grand Rapids: Eerdmans, 1974) p. 630.

Appendix B: More Helps for ARCing a Passage

1. Working from a sentence diagram, decide how many propositions there are in a given passage. Remember that in general you determine propositions (1) by the *verbs*—finite verbs, adverbial participles, and, rarely, infinitives used in adverbial clauses (but never infinitives used in *noun* clauses), or (2) by a *predicate nominative*. Occasionally a prepositional phrase will also be important enough to construe it as a separate proposition, but you must reword it so that it contains a subject and a verb. You should also reword participial clauses with a subject and a finite verb: "being confident of this" would then read "*because* (or some other appropriate connective) I am confident of this ..."

2. On the lower half of a sheet of paper write out your propositions, each on a separate line and numbered with reference to its place in the text: 22a, 22b, 22c, 23, 24a, 24b, etc. Their order should agree with that of the Greek words in the text, e.g., a subordinate clause that necessarily occurs second in a diagram may actually be first according to the Greek. At this point do not concern yourself with the indentations.

3. About a quarter of the way down the paper, draw a horizontal line for your arcs; then draw an arc for each proposition, and place its number beneath it.

4. Begin with the first arc and try to determine its relationship to the second. Look for hints in the Greek: an οὖν suggests an inference; a γαρ a ground; ἵνα an action-purpose and ὥστα an action-result relationship. These hints, however, are simply that; they do not *always* introduce such a relationship. Logic, or the *reasonableness* of a relationship, has the last word.

5. Place the appropriate symbol for the relationship in its tentative location, beneath the number of the arc, and below that draw the proper level. If the relationship is a restatement or coordinate, the levels will be the same; if it is one of the distinct relationships, one level will be lower. Of the distinct statements, the lower level never varies in ground (__G), inference (__∴), conditional (If/Th), Temporal (__T), Locative (__L), and concessive (__Csv). But for action-purpose (Ac/Pur), action-result (Ac/Res), and situation-response (S/R), you must determine the higher and lower levels by the sense of the passage, i.e., which of the two ideas is more important to the author's purpose? That will be the higher level, and its symbol will be circled to indicate this fact.

6. Follow this procedure for each arc, always trying to determine how an arc is related to that which follows it. The question you are continually asking yourself in this process is: What makes the best sense? Sometimes there will be no direct relationship. E.g., an arc—let's call it 17a—may be followed by a 'ground,' an arc that supports it, 17b. 17c may be a restatement of 17a, so that 17b has no direct relationship to it. But when 17a and 17b are arced together (and this is a basic principle of arcing), then the supporting arc, or lower level, 17b, is forgotten; thereafter only 17a is to be considered, and then it can easily be seen that 17c is a restatement of 17a. Don't, however, be too hasty in joining lower levels to higher ones. First be sure that everything that belongs to that

lower level is arced together. E.g., perhaps 17c is not a restatement of 17a but is instead a 'ground' for 17b, with 18a being the restatement. Then you will want to arc 17c to 17b before arcing 17b to 17a. Your arcs would then look like this:

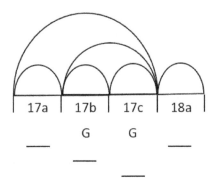

Another possibility would be that 17b and 17c are both 'grounds' for 17a. Then your arcs would look like this:

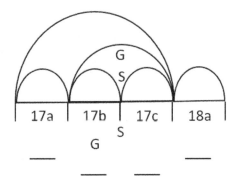

The important thing to remember is that you must be sure that everything that belongs to a lower level is joined to it before you join it to a higher level—otherwise arcs will be left as orphans, with no place to go.

7. When you have determined the relationships of all the arcs in a given passage, then begin to put them together. (Some of the lower levels may already have been joined as you went along, if it was clear, as in the example above, that you are safe in doing this.) Always begin with the lowest levels and work upward. Again, the arc that is a restatement is telling more about its earlier counterpart, this logically is an idea-explanation (Id/Exp); if it sets forth another possibility, which is not negated but stands as a live option, 'alternative' (A) would be the proper relationship. But in putting together the larger arcs, it is important to be sure that everything that belongs to a relationship is included—a 'situation,' for example, has been joined together before it is arced to its 'response.' And of course, you will also want to be sure that all the arcs that go to make up the 'response' have been joined to it before you arc it to the 'situation.' You should finally have one arc—with no symbol in it—over the passage. (Incidentally, this principle holds for all arcing: whenever two arcs are joined, that the larger arc has no symbol

in it; only the two smaller arcs [or one, depending on the relationship] have symbols. Then when that larger arc is eventually joined to another arc, it does receive its proper symbol—but the arc that joins it remains blank until joined to its counterpart.)

8. Finally, adjust (or recopy) your propositions so they are indented to correspond to the levels in your arching: higher levels farther to the left and lower levels to the right. Every proposition (except possibly the first) should have a connective underlined that indicates how the proposition is related to the arc that precedes or follows.

A helpful fact to remember in arcing is that if an imperative appears in a passage, it will always be the highest level, for this is what the author wants to become true.

Three relationships that are often confused because all may use the connective "but" are alternative, negative-positive, and concessive. To differentiate them it is important to remember that in an alternative relationship, while two possibilities are being set forth, both remain live options; no choice has as yet been made as to which is preferable. In negative-positive, on the other hand, one possibility is being denied, while the other is being affirmed. In a concessive relationship, an obstacle is being overcome in order for something to happen, some truth to stand, etc. In trying to decide if you have a concessive, see if the two ideas can be restated using the connectives "although … nevertheless …" (occasionally these will be found in the Greek text, but in general you will have to determine from the sense of the propositions whether or not these would be appropriate.

Examples

Matthew 7:28–29

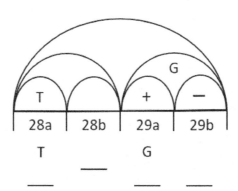

28a	When Jesus finished these sayings,
28b	the crowds were astonished at this teaching,
29a	for he taught them as one who had authority
29b	and [he did] not [teach] as their scribes.

Matthew 5:11–12

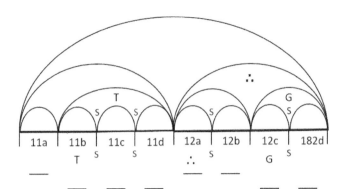

11a You are blessed
11b   when people revile you
11c   and persecute you
11d   and say all kinds of evil against you falsely on my account
12a Therefore rejoice
12b and be glad,
12c   for your reward is great in heaven,
12d   for so people persecuted the prophets before you.

Matthew 6:1–2

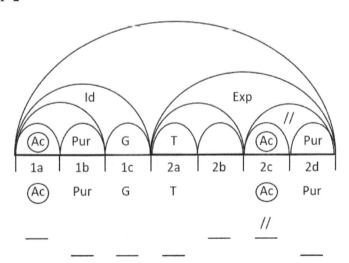

1a Beware of practicing your piety before others
1b   in order to be seen by them,
1c   for then you will have no reward from your heavenly Father.
     (To be specific)
2a   When you give alms,
2b sound no trumpet before you
2c as the hypocrites do in the synagogues and in the streets
2d   that they may be praised by others.

Matthew 6:19–21

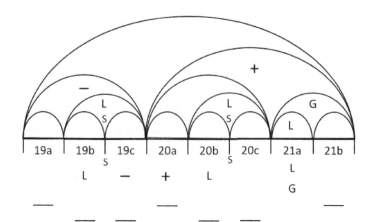

19a	Do <u>not</u> lay up for yourselves treasures on earth
19b	<u>where</u> moth and rust consume
19c	<u>and where</u> thieves break in and steal.
20a	<u>But</u> lay up for yourselves treasures in heaven
20b	<u>where</u> neither moth nor rust consume
20c	<u>and where</u> thieves do not break in and steal.
21a	(<u>for</u>)
	<u>where</u> your heart is
21b	there will your heart be also.

John 15:10

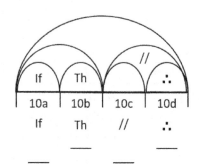

10a	<u>If</u> you keep my commandments,
10b	<u>then</u> you will abide in my love,
	(<u>just as</u>)
10c	<u>because</u> I have kept my Father's commandments,
10d	<u>therefore</u>, I abide in his love.

Matthew 5:38–41

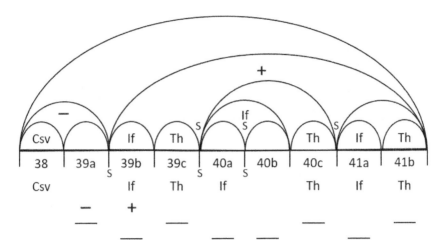

38		Although you have heard it said,
		"an eye for an eye and a tooth for a tooth,"
39a		nevertheless, I say to you, "Do not resist one who is evil,
39b		(but)
39b		if anyone strikes you on the right cheek,
39c		then turn the other one to him also;
40a		and if anyone would sue you,
40b		and take your coat,
40c		then let him have your cloak as well;
41a		and if anyone forces you to go one mile,
41b		then go with him two miles.

Matthew 5:43–45

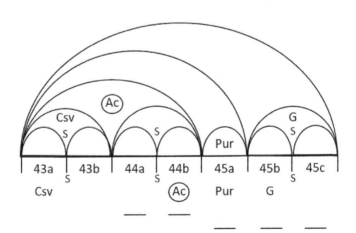

43a		Although you have heard it said that you should love your neighbor
43b		and hate your enemy,
44a	nevertheless, I tell you to love your enemies
44b	and pray for those who persecute you,
45a		in order that you may be sons of your heavenly Father
45b		for he makes his sun rise on the evil and the good,
45c		and he sends rain on the just and the unjust.

Matthew 6:7–8

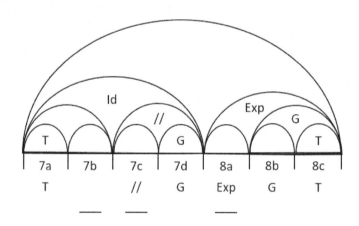

7a		When you pray,
7b	do not heap up empty phrases
7c	as the Gentiles heap up empty phrases,
7d		because they think they will be heard for their many words.
8a	I mean, do not be like them,
8b		for your Father knows what you need
8c			before you ask him.

Appendix C: Suggestions for Completing the ARCing of Philippians 1–2

Actions to Take

1. Since we always start with the lowest level, we should first relate 22a–24 to its counterpart. Does it go better with what follows or what precedes?

2. Since 22–24 logically relates better to what follows, just how much of what follows is Paul's response to it? Where does his own response end, and his purpose for making such a response begin? Only Paul's response should be related to his situation of 22–24.

3. Now we can relate the "action," composed of the "situation" and "response," to the "purpose." This leaves us with only three arcs to relate.

4. Since we always work first with lower levels, we must relate 19b–21b and 22–26 (18d being the *highest* level in the passage). From our levels we know that these are restatements, so which of the restatement relationships would best express the sense? Here it is necessary to think precisely. Logically, 22–26 is a *specific* example of how Paul will magnify Christ, i.e., because the Philippians' faith will increase, and as a result, so will their rejoicing and magnifying of Christ, because Paul will come to be with them again. But arguing for Id–Exp, or even "series," would also be acceptable. But do try to sharpen your thinking on this.

Mistakes to Avoid

1. Avoid trying to join 19–21b to 18d; you need to realize that there is much more involved in this "ground"—all the rest of the passage, in fact.

2. Also, do not join 25a-c to 25d–26 as "action" to "purpose," because this leaves 22–24 with nothing to be related to, unless you see 25d–26 as the lower level; but this makes it impossible to see 25d–26 as restating 19–20. Work hard to see the similarity between the idea in 25d–26 and that in 19–20.

3. The "R" of "response" and the "Pur" of the "purpose" should be circled.

Philippians 1:18d–26

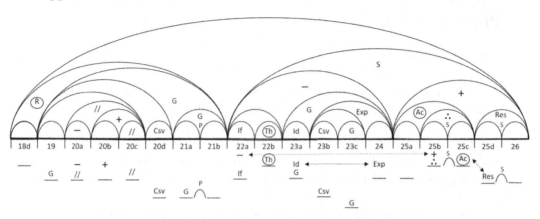

18d	<u>And</u>, <u>furthermore</u>, I will continue to rejoice
19	<u>because</u> I know these events will turn out for my deliverance
20a	<u>just as</u> I expect <u>not</u> to be ashamed in them
20b	<u>but rather</u> that by my courage Christ will be glorified;
20c	<u>just as</u> he always has been glorified,
20d	<u>even though</u> death is at present as possible as life for me
21a	<u>for</u> to me to live is Christ
21b	<u>and</u> to die is to be even closer to him.
22a	<u>If</u> continuing to live means fruitful work,
22b	<u>then</u> I do not make known what I prefer for myself.
23a	<u>For</u>, I am hard pressed between the two;
	(<u>that is</u>)
23b	<u>while</u> (although) my own desire would be to go be with Christ,
23c	<u>for</u> that is more preferable to me,
24	it is more necessary for you that I remain in the body.
25a	(<u>Rather</u>) <u>since</u> I am convinced of this,
25b	<u>therefore</u>, I know I will remain
25c	<u>and</u> I will continue with you,
25d	<u>for in so doing</u>, you will progress in the joy of faith
26	<u>and</u> (because in so doing) your joy in Christ will overflow.

Philippians 2:1–11 (Condensed)

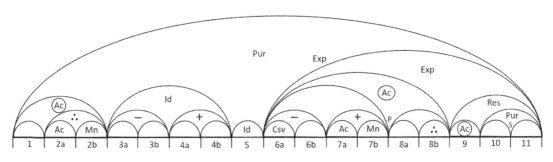

Therefore (resuming 1:27e's command to *unity*, which is repeated four times in 2:2. This is a highest-level statement, on a par with 1:10a, 27a, d, and 28a.)

1   Since there is consolation in Christ, and encouragement from God's love, and fellowship in the Holy Spirit, and Christ's affections can be experienced so deeply (normally four arcs connected in series),

2a   therefore, let me rejoice in hearing that your manner of life aims you all in one direction,

2b   in that you love the same goal [furthering the gospel], and your life force is concentrated on this goal, and the way your lives revolve around this goal.

3a   In order to achieve the above unity, you must do nothing through strife or vainglory,

3b   but you must consider ways that others are better than yourself;

4a   and, do not, each of you, just on his/her own concerns

4b   but each of you focus also on the concerns of others.

5   In other words, let this way of life be among you that was also in Christ Jesus:

       (That is)

6a   Although he was always in the form of God

6b   yet he did not seize the opportunity to manifest himself as such;

7a   but he emptied himself

7b   in that he took on the form of a slave in the likeness of humanity.

       (Furthermore)

8a   because he appeared in this way

8b   he therefore humbly became obedient to a death on the cross

9a   so that God highly exalted him with a name above every other name,

10   in order that at Jesus' name every knee should bow

11   and every tongue confess Jesus as Lord to the Father's glory.

Philippians 2:12–18

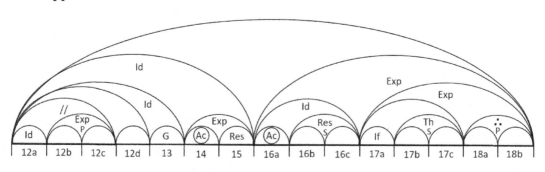

	Therefore (inference from 2:3–11, resuming the level of 2:2, but repeating the command of 1:28a)
12a	just as you have always obeyed,
12b	that is, you have been obedient not only in my presence,
12c	but you have also been obedient in my absence;
12d	so carefully continue working at your own salvation
13	for God is the one producing among you both the desire and the activity necessary to please him.
14	Specifically, do all things without murmuring or disputing (cf. Deuteronomy 32:5)
15	in order that you may be blameless and harmless children of God in the midst of a perverse world among whom you are light bearers.
16a	What I mean is, hold fast the word of life,
16b	in order that in the day of Christ I may not have run in vain
16c	nor toiled in vain.
	(In other words [ἀλλά signifies a break from 16bc]
17a	if I am expended in serving to further your faith,
17b	then I rejoice in my martyrdom;
17c	and I invite you to a "joy-in" with me in it.
	(Now since I have the same attitude toward dying that Jesus had)
18a	Therefore, in the same manner, be glad at the prospect of dying in service of the gospel,
18b	and you should rejoice with me.

Philippians 2:19–30 (Condensed)

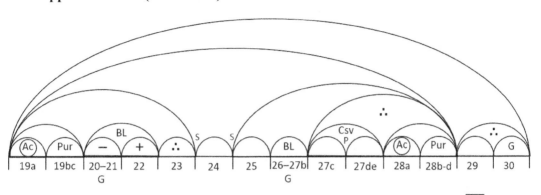

2:19a	I hope, in the Lord, to send Timothy to your soon
19	in order that I may be cheered up by your response to this letter,
20–21	for I have no one like Timothy who cares for you, unlike those who don't have Christ's concerns for his own.
22	But (from the [–] in vs. 20) you know how Timothy has served me in the gospel like a son.
23	Therefore, I hope to send him as soon as I see how things go with me.
24	And (in series with 2:19–23) I am confident that I will also be coming to you soon.
25	Also (in series with 2:24) I have considered it essential to send Epaphroditus to you,
26–27b	for he has been longing to see you all, since God healed him from sickness and depression.
	(Therefore)
27c	although (looking forward to 28a) God not only had mercy on him
27de	but God also had mercy on me so I might not have too much sorrow;
28a	nevertheless, I have sent Epaphroditus back sooner than I would have preferred
28b-d	in order that my response to your joy in seeing him will diminish my sorrow.
29	Therefore, joyfully receive E. in the Lord—holding all of us in honor—
30	because E. almost died for Christ by completing your service to me.

Philippians 1:3–2:30

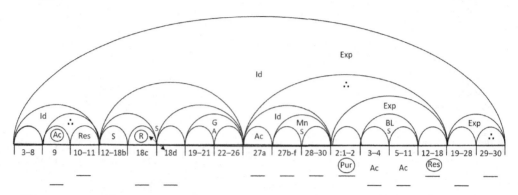

1:3–8   <u>Because</u> I thank my God for you even when I supplicate him about your shortcomings,

:9   <u>therefore</u>
      I pray your love will abound more and more in all wisdom and discernment,

:10–11 <u>so that</u> you may distinguish between the merely good and the best.

12–18b (<u>In other words</u>)
      <u>Since</u> my imprisonment has resulted in the gospel's being advanced in two ways that pertain to your two problems at Philippi,

:18c   my <u>response</u> to this is to rejoice.

18d   <u>And</u>, I shall ever rejoice

:19–21   <u>because</u> I shall magnify Christ <u>either</u> in life or death [how Paul solves his fear problem],

:22–26   <u>or</u> I shall magnify Christ through further ministry in which more people will rejoice in his sufficiency. [Paul's altruism of seeking the benefit of others rather than his own selfish interests should help the schism problem at Philippi.]

:27a   <u>Therefore</u>, live worthily of the gospel

:27ef   <u>in that</u> you stand fast in one spirit,

:28–30 <u>and</u> you don't panic at the threat of unbelievers.
      (<u>Specifically</u>)

2:1–2   1. Have the <u>same</u> manner of life as you aim toward the <u>same</u> goal of furthering the gospel

:3–4   <u>by</u> being humble and altruistic,

:5–11   <u>and</u>, <u>by</u> exhibiting the attitude Jesus manifested in his incarnation and death,

:12–18 2. <u>so that</u> instead of fearing the threats of unbelievers you rejoice as you hold fast the word of life.
      (<u>In other words</u>)

:19–28   <u>because</u> you consider the characteristics of Timothy, myself, and my circumstances in returning Epaphroditus, you will see the deep intentions that work for unity among Christians.

:29–30 <u>Therefore</u>, receive such people and continue to hold them in all honor as representative of living for the very best (cf. 1:10a).

Appendix D: Relational and Comprehension Decision Questions for ARCing Philippians 1:3–2:30

Deciding how to relate the various propositions in a text is neither simple nor easy. The following questions demonstrate the complexity inherent in the process used to understand Paul's arguments and to create the arcs in the above diagrams.

1:3–11

1. In Philippians 1:9–11 Paul gives the gist of how he is supplicating (cf. 1:4 δησις) God to make things right in the Philippian congregation. What is the highest-level, ultimate request that he makes, the <u>purpose</u> for which all other requests in this prayer are <u>actions</u>? (a) We must demonstrate our understanding of this request by restating it "in other words." (b) Locate the seven places in 1:12–2:30 (see the highest levels in the summary arcs of 1:3–2:30) where the idea of this request appears again as a command restating it in other words *either* in general *or* as one of the two commands that are specific parts of this request, which commands allude to one of the two problems the Philippians need to overcome at the time of the writing of these two chapters.

2. The worst enemy of the "best" can often be the merely "good." (Can you illustrate from your own life where you have seen this to be true?) Understand what two aspects of congregational life in Philippi were wrong; explain how, by living for some "good" things, the Philippians were failing to live for the "best."

1:12–26

3. Which of the two discrepancies at Philippi do verses 13–14 help solve, and *how* does Paul expect these verses to help in solving that one problem?

4. Which of the two problems at Philippi do verse 15–18b help solve, and how does Paul expect these verses to help solve this second problem? (Hint: recall the chiasmus in part of 15–18b, and what is significant about the first and fourth elements of it.)

5. What has been true about Paul's goal in life as described in 1:12–18b that leads him to rejoice (1:18c)? *Why* is it that we can rejoice only if we have this as our one and only goal?

6. Which problem at Philippi does 1:19–21 help solve and how was Paul's writing these verses supposed to solve it? In like manner, which problem does 1:22–26 help solve and how?

7. Taking the two general commands that appear within the bounds of 1:27 into account, how does Paul's purpose so to live in 1:19–21 and 22–26 ensure that he, and others who think as he does, will rejoice, no matter what, in the future (1:18d)?

8. What do we need to understand in order to explain how Paul can so confidently assert in 1:25–26 that he will again see the Philippians, when in 1:20 and 27 he speaks in a way that makes his seeing them again problematic? How does Paul's speaking this way help him model one of the two requisites for unity that he set forth in 2:3–4?

1:27–30

9. In "striving for the faith of the gospel" (27e) and "behaving worthily of the gospel" (27a), just what is one constantly seeking to do? (Hint: look ahead to the admonitions not to grumble in 2:14 and to hold fast to the word of life in 2:16.)

10. After commanding the Philippians not to panic at threats their pagan fellow citizens make (1:28a), Paul gives *two* considerations or reasons that he means to help the Philippians (and others, like us) not to be afraid. We must decide which propositions contain each of these reasons, and be able to state each in our own words, and show just how, when these two considerations are understood, they make it much easier to obey 1:28a. (*Warning*: 1:28b & c are two (2!) propositions making up only the *first* of the two arguments for why the Philippians (and we) should not be afraid.)

11. Precisely why is it that along with God's gracious gift (cf. ἐχαρίστη) of giving us the opportunity to believe, he also gives, as an equally gracious opportunity, continued occasions to suffer (1:29)?

12. Identify the verse in 1:12–30 that shows that what Paul has said about his situation at Rome was meant to help the Philippians in their situation. Be able also to explain *how* this verse makes what happened to Paul applicable to the Philippians.

2:1–11

13. How do the four "if" clauses of 2:1 argue for Christian hedonism's affirmation that the incentive for obeying commands is the greater enjoyment of the blessings of having fellowship with God? Explain why Paul prefaced these four clauses with "if" instead of "since."

14. What is the one thing the Philippians are to consider (φρονέω, 2a &d)? What is the one goal which they are to love in the sense of valuing it enough to attain it, around which they are to be united in spirit (σύμψυχος)?

15. What two requisites for the unity enjoined in 2:2 are given in 2:3 and 4?

16. Which of the two problems at Philippi is Paul seeking to overcome in 2:1–4?

17. Cite an element of Jesus' behavior in 2:6–8 which, when emulated, will help solve the schism problem by means of one of the prerequisites of 2:3–4.

18.. What is the function of 2:9–11 in (a) the ethical theory of the interpretation of 2:5–11 in my paraphrasing and arcs, and (b) in the salvific theory of interpreting 2:5–11 held by Dr. Ralph Martin and others?

2:12–18

19. Noting the ὥστε (so then) with which verse 12 begins and the emphasis on obedience in this verse, what relationship does verse 12 have to verses 6–8? To verses 9–11?

20. From a single proposition in either 1:25, 1:27, or 2:16 argue that what should be feared above all else in the command "continue working at your own salvation with fear and trembling" is unbelief. How will living this way produce fearlessness in the face of opposition?

21. Explain how 2:13 supports 2:12 in such a way that a hearer is not lulled into thinking that God will not work mechanically in a person, but that he will sensitize us to obey him as a deliberate, considered (i.e., *free*) act.

22. How do two propositions in 2:16 confirm the interpretation of "with fear and trembling" that was given for 2:12? (cf. Deuteronomy 32:5)

23. Give three evidences (and show how the argument proceeds from them to prove) that the function of 2:12–18 is to overcome the fear problem (cf. 1:28a) at Philippi, and not the disunity problem (as 2:1–4 was intended to do). By the way, what is the function, then, of 2:5–11?

2:19–30

24. In 2:19–23, what does Paul say about Timothy that provides an example that would help solve one of the problems at Philippi? (Hint see 2:4.)

25. How does Paul's statement of the possibility that he might be coming there again (2:24) function to solve both problems at Philippi? (Hint: remember 1:12–18c and 1:19–26.)

26 How does it help Paul's purpose of remedying the needs at Philippi to use in 2:28c the *double-negative*, and the *comparative* (ἀλυπότερος, less anxious)? How does the καὶ found in elision in κἀγὼ help Paul achieve his purpose?

27. Which of the two problems at Philippi is Epaphroditus especially suited to remedy as the Philippians welcome him home in joy, and render all honor to him, given the specific things Paul says about him in 2:30?

28. What changes will have to take place in the hearts of the Philippians before they can receive *such* people (note the plural! —who are they?) with *all* joy and hold them in *honor*?

Appendix E: Review Questions for the Entire Book

Chapter 1

1. One basic thesis in Chapter 1 was that we must have *understanding* of a text before we can expound it. But Gadamer would object by saying, "Understanding is not understanding unless it is expressed in words. In expressing your understanding of a text, you use the words of your own contemporary situation. Therefore, your understanding is determined by your own contemporary situation, and it is impossible for you to understand Paul in his terns, for these terms of his age are no longer the terms in which you speak. Hence, all so-called 'understanding' is just exposition and nothing more, nothing less." What essential step in the sequence leading to exposition has Gadamer overlooked? What would be several real-life situations, common to every one of us, that illustrate the flaw in his argument?

2. Why is it that our way of *understanding* Jonah will not change as our life situations change (unless, of course, grammatical-historical facts about the text come to our attention that change our way of construing it), but that our way of *expounding* it will always change as our target audience changes and as our own life situations change?

Chapters 1, 2

3. Why, when we refuse to let the grammatical-historical data alone determine our understanding of a biblical passage, do we minimize the chance of thinking the thoughts of the prophets and apostles after them?

Chapter 2

4. Why is it permissible for us to leave the immediate context of Philippians 1:27 and go to the remote context of 4:2–3 (which mentions the schism involving Euodia and Syntyche) to help us understand what Paul meant in 1:27e, "that I may hear that you stand fast in one spirit," but we should not construe 1:22, where Paul speaks of his apparently insoluble dilemma, by going ahead to 1:25, where he speaks of how he does resolve it?

Chapters 1, 6

5. What is the "hermeneutical circle"? Why does it tend to be a vicious circle if we affirm that the understanding of a text's parts can be grasped only after we have determined what the basic point of the text is, even though what the basic point is can only be determined after we have grasped each of its parts?

6. Why is it easier to think of breaking the "hermeneutical circle," if instead of speaking of the "whole" and the "parts" of a text, we speak rather of every text's having a small percentage of *unvarying traits* that indicate its *intrinsic genre*?

7. What was the "intrinsic genre" (the purpose that motivates the author) of Philippians 1–2? Of Jonah (it will have much to do with the intention of his life)?

Chapter 6

8. Why is Adler's first, "inspectional" reading, consisting of skimming a book, so dangerous that it should not form a part of what we do when we read a book for the purpose of gaining enlightenment and understanding of the intended meaning which the author wished to transmit?

Chapter 7

9. What is the most elementary way to discover where the paragraph-size literary units occur in the narrative form? Be able to illustrate this principle by the break that occurs between Jonah 1:16 and 17, and also between 4:4 and 5.

10. What is fundamentally different about the way authors impart understanding in a narrative form and the way they impart it in a propositional form?

Chapter 8

11. Does being "presuppositionless," as we determine whether or not the Bible is true, mean that we rule out arguments that begin with assumptions, or arguments that begin with axioms or facts?

12. This chapter asserts that we "should not" (logically *ought* not) be so easily pleased with the use of our powers in overcoming a little finitude. Why does this "should not" make us guilty of inserting an arbitrary assumption?

13. What are three or four ways we hide from their not being able to find "happiness" (i.e., rest, fulfillment, contentment, and peace) by using our powers to manipulate the things at our disposal?

14. Why would it be tantamount to a first step in humbly submitting ourselves to God for us to own up to our failure to find life-satisfying fulfillment in manipulating the powers at our disposal, and not to run away from this fact?

15. What arguments support the assertion that the following religions could not make us happy: polytheism, speculative philosophy, animism, Hinduism, Buddhism, Confucianism, Zoroastrianism, and Islam?

16. What is it that the Old and New Testaments of our Bibles affirm in distinction to the other monotheisms which, if true, would make the Bible the only place where we could feel right about spending our limited time and energy to determine whether what they say is true?

Chapter 9

17a. What would Calvin and E. F. Young reply to this chapter's affirmation that failure to show why the Bible is true on the basis of reason and evidence alone (cf. Adler) renders the greatest insult to the Bible?

17b. Why is it that without presenting compelling evidence that Christianity is true, it is an insult to another human being to expect him or her to accept that it is?

18. Why do Calvin and Kierkegaard affirm that a faith that rests only on empirical evidence is incapable of producing the wholehearted passion that a religious faith should have?

19. What is this chapter's objection (seeking to argue on common ground with Calvin and not from any special assumptions) to Calvin's assertion that "we have received the Bible from God's own mouth ... [and this is] superior to that of any human judgment and equal to that of any intuitive perception of God in it," and that this intuition is "knowledge as is supported by the highest reason"?

20. Arguing on common ground, how should we respond to Calvin's and Kierkegaard's objection that mere high probability cannot produce the wholehearted passion that religious faith should have?

21. Why do we have no historical control for the early chapters of Genesis but do have it for Galatians 1:13–14?

22. How could Paul claim that he had always lived so as to have a good conscience (in pre- as well as post-conversion days—Philippians 3:6; 1 Timothy 1:13; and 2 Timothy 1:3) and also affirm that his life before conversion was lived so as to make him "the chief of sinners" (1 Timothy 1:15)?

23. Why was it impossible for Paul to be consciously deceiving people in telling them of his earlier zeal for the Jewish traditions (e.g., Galatians 1:13–14)?

24. Why could Paul not be deceived when he explained that his willingness to head up the mission to the Gentiles (so distinct from all earlier Gentile missions launched by the Pharisees, cf. Matthew 23:15) was because Jesus appeared to him and commissioned him as his spokesman?

25. On what basis do we claim to have valid knowledge that Paul was verbally inspired whenever he was engaged in making people wise to salvation in his apostolic efforts?

26. How do we know that writings from other apostles besides Paul are also verbally inspired?

27. What are the steps in the argument that Acts, although written by Luke, who was not an apostle, is as inspired as Romans, which was written by the apostle Paul?

28. What was the decisive reason that led the early Church to acknowledge the 27 books of the New Testament as canonical and to reject 1 Clement, even though it was probably written before the book of Revelation?

29. Why is it that everyone who believes the present books of our Bible to be canonical cannot consistently permit more recent claims to revelation to be canonical (e.g., the Book of Mormon)?

30. How do we know that the 39 books of the Old Testament canon are inspired, but not the Old Testament apocrypha?

31. How should we affirm that if a writing (giving Christian teaching) from Apollos, Paul's companion, were found, it should be stapled in with the rest of the text in our Bibles?

32. How can we heartily affirm not only that "faith rests in the evidences" but that it is also "does not walk by sight" (cf. 2 Corinthians 5:7)?

33. Why would we be correct to claim that David Hume, in his way, had to allow for the possibility of miracles in his all-out attempt to deny the possibility of knowing that they happened?

34. Why are historians, who have no theological axe to grind, nevertheless sincerely convinced that any historical knowledge would become impossible to acquire if they admitted that miracles do occur from time to time in history? (Be sure to know why this book argues that miracles' happening in history do not make all historical knowing impossible.)

35. The chief evidence that Paul uses to remind the Thessalonians that the gospel came to them in power (cf. καθώς—1Thessalonians 1:5) is the way he and his associates acted toward them. Why is this gracious behavior the ultimate demonstration of gospel power?

36. What are the "marks of divinity" that the Bible displays that enable us to know—without going through all the historical argumentation of the earlier parts of chapter 9—that the Bible is indeed the word of God?

37. How is it that the "marks of divinity" which commenced the argument of the next to the last section of chapter 9 ("A Historical Faith for non-Historians"), is really the nub of the argument for the truth of the Bible which stemmed from the radical change in Paul's behavior from being a proud Pharisee to one who proffered the blessings of Abraham to non-circumcised, pork-eating Gentiles on the basis of repentance and faith?

Chapter 10

38. I could have used Calvin's words, "being illumined by [the Holy Spirit], we now believe the divine [origin] of Scripture ...", but whereas Calvin, by the word "illumined," meant ___, I would mean ___?

39. What do the words "receive" and "know" mean, in distinction to what they do not mean, in interpreting 1 Corinthians 2:14?

40. In a sentence, what part of the biblical message constitutes a stumbling block (an offense) to people; and why is this offensive to people who are not regenerated by the Holy Spirit?

41. Why is 1 Corinthians 4:7, even though its truth is axiomatic and does not need the Bible's authority to support it, so very offensive to an unregenerate person?

42. What are the very special sort of circumstances under which an unbeliever, such as Edwin Burtt, can nevertheless have accurate cognition of, and even play "devil's advocate" for, the biblical message? (cf. the same with Ernest DeWitt Burton.)

43. What are the two things a committed Christian must do in order to minimize the risk of distorting what the Scripture is trying to say as we make an exposition of what we think its intended meaning is?

44. Whereas Origen said that the Holy Spirit is essential for interpreting the Bible in that he does certain indispensable things in the believer's heart, this book also says that the Holy Spirit is essential for an accurate interpretation of the Bible because he does another indispensable thing. What was the indispensable thing for Origen, and what is it for this book?

45. How can it be true that Francke was right to say that we must be crucified to the world in order to understand the biblical texts, while a dissolute atheist can, under certain circumstances, understand them?

46. How can our Christian experience help us gain a more accurate interpretation of passages in Scripture but also lead us to distort these passages?

47. Why does believing the Bible on the basis of the internal testimony of the Holy Spirit (Calvin, *Institutes* I, 7, 4) provide a considerable encouragement to let the same Spirit figure more in the interpretation of Scripture than the grammatical and historical data?

48. Why was Jesus not in error in speaking of the mustard seed as "smaller than *all*" the seeds, even though botanists know of smaller seeds?

49. Why would Jesus have been in error (note how "error" must be defined) if he had alluded to what is indeed the smallest seed when he illustrated how a little faith moves mountains?

50. Why will the teachings of the biblical texts be distorted if the results of exegesis do not lead us to construct a coherent biblical worldview?

51. Why is the insistence that the Bible's allusions to non-revelatory matters be inerrant (i.e., have a one-to-one correspondence to what is alluded to) tantamount to putting the Bible under, instead of over, the Church?

52. Why was Jesus statement about the mustard seed just as important as any revelatory statement and equally inspired as such?

53. Can ALL or just MOST revelatory statements in Scripture be confirmed by historical and scientific methodology?

54. Why is the method of knowing revelatory truth no different than the method for gaining other non-revelatory knowledge?

55. How do we know when we are facing a non-revelatory affirmation in Scripture? How do we know when we face a revelatory affirmation?

Made in the USA
Las Vegas, NV
22 December 2023

83456510R00125